Praise for the first edition

'An easy to use text, particularly helpful for postgraduate students wishing to find out more about specific areas of the curriculum. The focus on creative approaches makes this a particularly topical resource.'

Kate Allott, Education, York St John University

'This is a helpful book for students on placement (and existing practitioners) as it provides details on non-core National Curriculum subjects – unlike a lot of other texts out there. Really useful.'

Sharron Galley, Centre for Childhood Studies, University Centre, Stockport College

'A very good overview of primary curriculum subjects. Each chapter has similar structure which is clear and logical. Good, up-to-date references.'

Dr Richard Greenwood, Primary Education, Stranmillis University College

'This is a book that does what it claims to do. It offers a clear, concise and creative introduction to the primary curriculum. It is written in a most accessible style by well-known and well-established teacher educators who have vast experience of supporting the professional, academic and personal development of student teachers and teachers. It is an excellent resource for students and beginner teachers. I expect it will become the core text on teacher education courses.'

Professor Kathy Hall, University College Cork

'I have used this text extensively across a number of modules this year and found it a really useful text.'

Zenna Kingdon, Education, University of St Mark & St John

'A helpful guide showing how creativity can be fostered and included as part of everyday classroom practice.'

Michelle Lowe, Staffordshire University

'This is an engaging text placing the child at the core of the primary curriculum. The range of curriculum areas discussed from a specialist perspective is informed and supports reflections on learning and content. The development of subject knowledge is expanded by the themes of the creative teacher and cross-curricular links and promotes critical and sensitive teaching and learning.'

Dr Estelle Martin, University of East London

'A good general introduction to the issues in learning to teach in primary schools.'

Sue Temple, Education, University of Cumbria

Second Edition

The Primary Curriculum

A Creative Approach

SAGE was founded in 1965 by Sara Miller McCune to support the dissemination of usable knowledge by publishing innovative and high-quality research and teaching content. Today, we publish more than 750 journals, including those of more than 300 learned societies, more than 800 new books per year, and a growing range of library products including archives, data, case studies, reports, conference highlights, and video. SAGE remains majority-owned by our founder, and after Sara's lifetime will become owned by a charitable trust that secures our continued independence.

Los Angeles | London | Washington DC | New Delhi | Singapore

Edited by

Patricia Driscoll, Andrew Lambirth *and* Judith Roden

Second Edition

The Primary Curriculum

A Creative Approach

Los Angeles | London | New Delhi
Singapore | Washington DC

Los Angeles | London | New Delhi
Singapore | Washington DC

SAGE Publications Ltd
1 Oliver's Yard
55 City Road
London EC1Y 1SP

SAGE Publications Inc.
2455 Teller Road
Thousand Oaks, California 91320

SAGE Publications India Pvt Ltd
B 1/I 1 Mohan Cooperative Industrial Area
Mathura Road
New Delhi 110 044

SAGE Publications Asia-Pacific Pte Ltd
3 Church Street
#10-04 Samsung Hub
Singapore 049483

Editor: James Clark
Assistant editor: Rachael Plant
Production editor: Nicola Marshall
Copyeditor: Elaine Leek
Proofreader: Sharon Cawood
Indexer: Silvia Benvenuto
Marketing manager: Lorna Patkai
Cover design: Naomi Robinson
Typeset by: C&M Digitals (P) Ltd, Chennai, India
Printed and bound by CPI Group (UK) Ltd,
Croydon, CR0 4YY

First edition published 2012, reprinted 2013

This edition first published 2015

Library of Congress Control Number: 2014947256

British Library Cataloguing in Publication data

A catalogue record for this book is available from the British Library

ISBN 978-1-47390-364-7
ISBN 978-1-47390-387-6 (pbk)

At SAGE we take sustainability seriously. Most of our products are printed in the UK using FSC papers and boards. When we print overseas we ensure sustainable papers are used as measured by the Egmont grading system. We undertake an annual audit to monitor our sustainability.

This book is dedicated to the memory of Frances Templeman. She was much loved and her work lives on in the colleagues and teachers she inspired.

CONTENTS

ABOUT THE EDITORS

Patricia Driscoll is a Reader in Education at Canterbury Christ Church University. She has worked in the field of languages for over 25 years in primary, secondary and tertiary education. Patricia teaches on undergraduate and postgraduate programmes and has led a bilateral exchange programme for student teachers from England and mainland Europe. She has also conducted both small- and large-scale studies in language learning and teaching in schools. Patricia's recent publications include: 'The sustainable impact of a short comparative teaching placement abroad on primary school language teachers' professional, linguistic and cultural skills', *The Language Learning Journal* (Special Edition for Teacher Education), 2014; 'The role and nature of the cultural dimension in primary modern languages', *Language, Culture and Curriculum*, 2013, 26 (2), pp. 146–60; *A New Era for Languages in Debates in Modern Languages Education* (eds Driscoll, Macaro and Swarbrick) (Routledge, 2014); *The Final Report of Language Learning at Key Stage 2: The Longitudinal Study* (2006–2009), London, DCSF.

Andrew Lambirth is Professor of Education in the Faculty of Education and Health at the University of Greenwich. Before joining higher education, he was a primary school teacher in Peckham and Bermondsey in South-East London. Andrew has published widely in the field of the teaching of Literacy and English, including: *Primary English* (2005, Learning Matters); *Creativity and Writing: Developing Voice and Verve* *in the Classroom* (2005, Routledge), with Grainger and Goouch; *Understanding Reading and the Teaching of Phonics: Critical Perspectives* (2007, Open University), with Goouch; *Teaching Early Reading and Phonics: Creative Approaches to Early Literacy* (2011, Sage), with Goouch; *Literacy on the Left: Reform and Revolution* (2007, Bloomsbury); *Making Poetry Matter* (Bloomsbury, 2013), with Dymoke and Wilson. Andrew is currently President Elect of the United Kingdom Literacy Association.

Judith Roden has over 35 years of experience teaching science in schools and in teacher education. She is currently a Principal Lecturer at Canterbury Christ Church University where she is a well-known and highly respected member of the primary science community. She holds Chartered Science Status (CSciTeach) and has directed a number of school-based primary science projects sponsored by the AstraZeneca Science Teaching Trust (now called the Primary Science Teaching Trust – PSTT). Judith has published a number of books and articles, including *Primary Science Reflective Reader* (Learning Matters/Sage, 2005); *Extending Knowledge in Practice* (Learning Matters, 2007); *Teaching Science in the Primary Classroom: A Practical Guide* (Sage, 2008); and *Primary Science for Trainee Teachers* (Learning Matters/Sage, 2014). Currently she is very interested and involved in school-based routes into teaching. She is currently the lead tutor for Primary Science on the Teach First Primary and Early Years programmes and in 2013/14 has worked with Teach First colleagues and participants on a Primary Science Teach First project sponsored by the Primary Science Teaching Trust (PSTT). Although Judith enjoys teaching science to Teacher Education students in the university, she has maintained close links with schools in the university's school partnership. Her personal research interests are varied within the field of science education and she encourages her students to research their own practice within both PGCE and undergraduate programmes in which she teaches. In recognition of her outstanding work with students across programmes of Initial Teacher Education she was awarded the prestigious Teaching Fellowship Award by Canterbury Christ Church University in 2014.

ABOUT THE CONTRIBUTORS

James Archer is a Lecturer in Primary Education at Bradford College. He has a strong interest in both science and design and technology, especially in how these disciplines can be combined and taught effectively in the primary phase. After graduation, he taught in South Africa. After returning to the UK, he taught in East Sussex, both in primary and secondary schools. While working in a secondary school, he was involved in providing CPD for a cluster of primary schools. He has also been a Senior Lecturer in Primary Education at Canterbury Christ Church University. James enjoys working with trainee and qualified teachers and to this end had been a member and director of a multi-primary academy and has supported a host of schools to develop creative and innovative approaches to the teaching of science and design and technology.

Jonathan Barnes is Senior Lecturer in Education at Canterbury Christ Church University. He has lifelong interests in music, geography, history, religion and art. These cross-curricular leanings led him first to teach history and geography and the history of art in two Kent secondary schools in the 1970s, then to become a primary class teacher for most of the 1980s. His passion for relevance and engagement in learning led him to devise a ground-breaking interdisciplinary curriculum based wholly on the school locality in the Kent school of which he was head throughout the 1990s. Since 2000 as a teacher educator, Jonathan has researched links between the 'science of learning', cross-curricular and creative approaches and the well-being of teachers and children. Extending his deep interest in curriculum, he now researches links between the arts in schools and the well-being of children aged 3–11.

Karl Bentley lectures in Computing and Education and Academic Studies as well as link-tutoring students in school. Following a career in industrial instrumentation, measurement and control he entered primary education via the GTP route to eventually become a school-based ICT Advanced Skills Teacher before entering higher education at Canterbury Christ Church University. His main interests are the implementation of the new Computing curriculum and the use of technologies to deliver university course content as well as continuing with his own doctoral research into teacher CPD.

Gina Donaldson was a primary school teacher for 11 years before moving into higher education. She is a senior lecturer and the Curriculum Team Leader for Primary Mathematics at Canterbury Christ Church University. She has a degree and MA in Mathematics and Education, and a Doctorate in Education. She is particularly interested in children's mathematical thinking and the mathematical knowledge of primary teachers. Her doctoral research considered the deep subject knowledge of mathematics.

Justine Earl is a senior lecturer in Education at Canterbury Christ Church University, where she is the Programme Director for the Primary PGCE part time route into teaching. On this Programme, she has the privelege to work with and support dedicated, mature students. She has worked in primary education for over 20 years, including time as a class teacher and a local authority advisor. Her areas of specialism include English, primary languages, professional studies and music. She is also interested in developing effective partnerships with schools.

Aidan Gillespie is a senior lecturer at Canterbury Christ Church University and is the subject lead for Primary Religious Education at under- and postgraduate level. His research interests are teachers' understandings and expressions of spirituality. He has published on areas such as Christian identities in education and using visual literacy to help develop children's understanding of religion.

Claire Hewlett has many years' teaching experience, both in local primary schools in Kent and as a senior lecturer at Canterbury Christ Church University. In school, Claire spent time as both an Art and a Science subject leader, as well as a headteacher. An interest in developing meaningful links in learning between these two subjects has helped to fuel an ongoing interest in developing creative approaches to teaching. Work with the AstraZeneca Science Teaching Trust (now called the Primary Science Teaching Trust – PSTT) on a personalised learning project with schools in Kent and Medway enabled Claire to continue to explore how art can be used as a tool to support learning in science, alongside other curriculum subjects. Claire has worked on projects with teacher training institutions both in India and Malaysia, where opportunities to experience and explore cultural diversity in education have further influenced her own approach to teaching and learning.

Simon Hoult is Director of Initial Teacher Education (11–19) at Canterbury Christ Church University and teaches on the 7–14 and 11–18 PGCE courses in geography education. Prior to this, he taught geography in comprehensive schools in the southeast of England. He has published student teacher texts on professional studies and teaching and learning at Masters level, and his current research is looking at the effects of international study visits on student teachers and their practice.

Kristy Howells is the Faculty Director of Physical Education at Canterbury Christ Church University. She has a passion for physical education (PE) and physical activity, health and well-being and wishes to inspire all teachers, children and student teachers alike to enjoy, to be engaged in and to be motivated by PE and physical activity as lifelong activities. She has recently completed a PhD in Sport and Exercise Sciences at Canterbury Christ Church University which explores children's physical activity levels within the primary school day, with a particular focus on the contribution PE lessons potentially make to children's physical activity. She wishes to acknowledge Joe Pellett from Hamstreet Primary Academy, Emily Leggat and Sarah Spencer for discussions that helped contribute to her chapter and the children from Egerton Church of England Primary School for their help with photographs.

Claire March has been a senior lecturer in Primary Education Science and Art at Canterbury Christ Church University since 2006. She joined the university after having taught in the primary setting for nine years. During this time she managed subject development as well as professional development in both science and art.

Lynn Revell is a Reader in Education at Canterbury Christ Church University, specialising in Religious and Citizenship Education. She has published in the area of religion and morality in education and on children's understanding of Islam and ethnicity. She is currently researching the politicisation of RE and the way in which religions are represented within the curriculum.

Rosemary Walters read History at the University of East Anglia, which she followed with a PGCE at the University of Liverpool. She has taught History and RE in a comprehensive school in the Midlands, and following a Diploma in Religious Education from Westhill College, Birmingham, became the RE Support Teacher for Walsall Metropolitan Borough. From 1993 to 2003 she was the Schools Officer at Canterbury Cathedral and studied for an MA in Theology and Hermeneutics at Canterbury Christ Church University, where she lectures in History and RE and also specialises in PHSE, SMSC and Collective Worship.

Vanessa Young has been involved in teacher education for much of her career. Prior to taking up her post at Canterbury Christ Church University, she spent many years teaching in primary schools in London and Kent. Her principal interest is in primary music. She has been involved in a range of consultancy work within the field of education, including membership of a number of national working parties for music education. Currently, she is involved in a 'Babysong Project', a professional development and research project intended to engender mindful interactions with babies through singing. She is the Chair of the Regional Network Coordinators for the Cambridge Primary Review Trust (CPRT) and Coordinator for the South East Region.

ACKNOWLEDGEMENTS

We would like to acknowledge and thank the following for their help in the writing of this book:

Jess Harley and other colleagues from the Teach First Primary and Early Years programmes

The headteacher, staff and pupils of:

Ashford, St Mary's Primary School, Kent

Egerton Church of England Primary School, Kent

Folkestone Primary Academy, Kent

Hamstreet Primary Academy, Kent

Hythe Bay CE Primary School, Hythe, Kent

Newington Community Primary School, Ramsgate, Kent

Pluckley Primary School, Ashford, Kent

St Peter's Methodist Church, Canterbury, Kent

We would also like to acknowledge and thank the following teachers for generously allowing us access to their practice:

Miss Victoria Blake

Ms Kerry Donati

Ms Hannah Green

Ms Emily Leggat

Ms Shalley Lewis

Miss Morven MacDonald

Mr Joe Pellett

Ms Sarah Spencer

In addition, we would like to acknowledge:

Diagram of Thinking Fork on p. 94 from *How to Create and Develop a Thinking Classroom* by M. Fleetham (2004) Cambridge: LDA. Further free resources can be found at:

www.thinkingclassroom.co.uk

www.LDAlearning.com

Publisher Acknowledgements

SAGE would like to thank the following reviewers whose comments have helped shape this second edition:

Kate Allott – York St John University

Elizabeth Broad –University of Roehampton

Anita Chamberlain – University of Cumbria

Linda Cooper –University of Chichester

Justin Gray – Newman University

INTRODUCTION

This is a book that aims to introduce readers to the primary curriculum and the best ways to teach it; but it is not only about that. Primary education is unique in that the activity of teaching young children requires practitioners to also be dedicated carers. This demands a special kind of attention from teachers in the classroom. The education of the very young has been called an 'act of love' (Freire 1993). This view is central to the belief that teachers need to enjoy the company of young children and recognise that their charges are people in their own right, who want to be looked after carefully as well as taught effectively. Good teachers care for the children in ways that are unique to all other jobs and professions. A teacher's job is not *only* about transmitting culturally valued knowledge, to raise standards of achievement in tests and examinations and prepare them for the world of work. The best teachers are those who recognise 'intersecting axes' (Alexander 2010: 409) in which the heart and the head – the child and the subject – are both part of the education matrix. Children want teachers who possess 'equity, empathy and expertise' (Alexander 2010: 408). So, along with a good knowledge of the subjects to be taught, teachers are also fair and empathetic, and know about the demands of teaching a single national curriculum to children in a culturally rich and diverse community. To teach the curriculum well teachers will need to know their children and the families from which they come, and the knowledge and experience the children already possess and bring with them to school.

This book offers an introduction to teaching and learning the primary curriculum in this context and with the knowledge that one can only be a successful teacher of primary-age children if a good and equitable dialogue is formed with the children in the class and the community. Readers will find that the writers discussing the subjects of the curriculum in this book do so with all this in mind.

The writers of this book want their readers to be excited about their future professional career. They want their readers to be determined to be the best teachers they can be and to gain the confidence they need to succeed. Ovid, the Roman poet, said 'People are slow to claim confidence in undertakings of magnitude' and this is true of the experiences of those in the teaching profession. Teaching is an extraordinary job and can make differences to people and their lives – both positive and negative. It is little wonder that teachers are slow to claim confidence in what they do. In this book we offer forms of professional knowledge that will assist readers in gaining more confidence.

Teaching the knowledge found in the primary curriculum is based upon the idea that 'knowledge is personal as well as public, dynamic rather than static, and to an extent recreated in every learning encounter' (Alexander 2010: 413). It is with this perspective that this book wishes to engage its readers and begin the process of developing them into professional and knowledgeable practitioners.

Curriculum

Universal education is still a relatively new idea and practice in the UK. Newer still is the notion of a National Curriculum. It was the 1988 Education Reform Act that introduced a National Curriculum for England and Wales. The 1944 Education Act had introduced universal state education, but 'what' was taught and 'how' the curriculum was delivered tended to reflect earlier content and practice. Legally, schools could teach what they liked, except for Religious Education which was a required element of post-Second World War education in the UK. Sometimes the content of the curriculum was guided and influenced by Local Education Authority priorities.

In 2009, the Cambridge Review found strong support for the notion of a National Curriculum amongst the profession. They concluded that 'having a national curriculum is now generally accepted as beneficial, particularly if it succeeds in establishing a clear, basis entitlement for children's learning across the country's ... primary schools' (Alexander and Flutter 2009: 16). Despite this, the nature and role of a National Curriculum continues to be contested. There are pertinent questions that need to be raised over issues of power. Who selects the curriculum content? Does it represent and affirm particular ideologies of specific social groups of people? Does it disempower the values and attitudes of those it does not represent (Bourdieu and Passeron 1977; Hill 2001)? A curriculum can never be politically neutral and this should not be forgotten as readers digest the chapters in this book. There are references to the political nature of the curriculum in many of the chapters. We would like to think that readers, as new teachers, will question and approach all the work in this book in a critical fashion. Education at its best is based on enquiry and is not just about turning learners into 'little living libraries' (Bruner 1963: 66). New teachers' own learning and development can be no different. A critical and questioning perspective needs to run through all the work of a teacher and we hope this book will enrich this approach.

In this latest edition of our book, the authors are writing at another time of curriculum change in England. The Conservative-led Coalition government introduced a new National Curriculum in 2014. This curriculum too has many critics, some of whom are writing in this book. These criticisms have included its over-prescription, leaving little room for teacher and school flexibility. There have been questions about the relevance of some aspects of the curriculum, e.g. not enough notice has been taken of what is known about how children learn or allow sufficiently for individual differences. Some of the programmes of study are said not to be age-appropriate, risking a sense of failure and disengagement amongst some pupils (Primary Umbrella Group 2012). However, the task of the authors of this book is to introduce new teachers to working with the National Curriculum in a practical but critical way. We are updating our book in the light of the new changes. All the authors have amended their chapters to take into account the needs of our readers who must thoroughly acquaint themselves with the curriculum.

Structures

For convenience, the subject chapters in this book have been organised in a uniform manner. All the writers conceptualise the subject and area of the curriculum they discuss in a clear introduction at the start of each chapter.

Each author then introduces what we have called 'the state of the art' for teaching of each subject. This will enable readers to know what they can expect to find in the schools.

The authors then present what they consider to be innovation in the teaching of their subject. The rationale for this section is to offer teachers and student teachers an understanding of what is considered as innovative practice. This is then complemented by a section on what creativity may look like in the teaching of their subject.

Lastly, all the authors provide an introduction to the crucial area of assessment.

References

Alexander, R. (ed.) (2010) *Children, Their World, Their Education: Final Report and Recommendations of the Cambridge Primary Review*. Abingdon: Routledge.

Alexander, R.J. and Flutter, J. (2009) *Towards a New Primary Curriculum: A Report from the Cambridge Primary Review. Part 1: Past and Present.* Cambridge: University of Cambridge, Faculty of Education.

Bourdieu, R. and Passeron, J. (1977) *Reproduction in Education, Society and Culture.* London: SAGE.

Bruner, J. (1963) *The Process of Education.* New York: Random House.

Freire, P. (1993) *Education for Critical Consciousness.* New York: Seabury.

Hill, D. (2001) 'The National Curriculum, the hidden curriculum and equality', in D. Hill and M. Cole (eds), *Schooling and Equality: Fact, Concept and Policy.* London: Kogan Page.

Primary Umbrella Group (2012) A Joint Statement in Response to the Department for Education's Consultation on Primary National Curriculum Draft Programmes of Study. At www.teachers.org.uk/files/PUG-Joint-statement-FINAL.doc (accessed 07/11/2014).

CHAPTER 1

AN INTRODUCTION TO ENGLISH

Andrew Lambirth

Chapter Aims

This chapter will:

- introduce the ways literacy in the English curriculum has been conceptualised by different theoretical traditions and how these perspectives influence the ways literacy has been taught

- describe and critique the state of the art for the teaching of reading, writing and speaking

- discuss innovation through the widening of the conceptualisation of literacy in response to the rise in digital technology

- present ideas for how teachers' creativity may be nurtured

- offer an introduction to assessment of English

Introduction

Teaching is a job for professionals. A professional teacher is passionate about education, and is determined to ensure the educational well-being of the children in their class. The professional teacher's practice is honed from an understanding of rigorously researched theoretical knowledge, generated in schools, universities and other research institutions or associations (Carr and Kemmis 1997). Teaching is not a job for amateurs, or for those who just want to be told how to do it. Teaching professionals are *educational activists* (Sachs 2003) and enthusiastic about knowing more from their reading, discussions and debates with children, colleagues and academics on how they can enrich the learning experience for their students. They take a critical approach to everything they hear about teaching and make well-informed choices about how they will teach. This chapter is aimed at those who aspire to this level of professionalism in the teaching of English. To this end, I will be providing a starting point by introducing the issues, perspectives and concepts that I feel new teachers of English must know at the start of their professional careers. Readers will also need to be critical of my approach too. All educational positions have an ideological source. Teaching is never just 'common sense' – it always has a theoretical foundation and it is not politically neutral.

The National Curriculum 2014 states: 'The overarching aim for English in the National Curriculum is to promote high standards of literacy by equipping pupils with a strong command of the written and spoken word, and develop a love of literature through widespread reading for enjoyment' (DfE 2013: 1). Literacy is central to the National Curriculum for English in primary schools. Literacy is complex and its teaching continues to be contested between teachers, academics and policy-makers. To help you become familiar with the arguments, I begin by offering a number of important perspectives on definitions of literacy and how it should be taught within the National Curriculum for English. These different definitions and teaching approaches will act as the foundation to an understanding of the perspectives on teaching reading, writing and speaking that you will encounter in the schools you visit.

The Traditional View of Literacy – Cognitive–Psychological Perspectives

Literacy education has often been conceived as learning that must have a steady and linear trajectory of development. Based on cognitive–psychological theory (Ehri 1987, 1995), this perspective contends that children need to be introduced to certain skills and knowledge in literacy at specific ages as it is assumed that all children should be taught to progress in similar ways. This is thought to be true for the teaching of reading, writing and speaking. Governments in the UK and in the advanced Western industrial nations are heavily promoting the general approach and the National Curriculum for English 2014 reflects this perspective. The curriculum conceives literacy as a set of discrete skills that can be learned and taught in a number of different contexts. This is contested: for example, Street (1984) described this model of literacy as *autonomous*. This means that for cognitive–psychologically influenced perspectives, literacy is a neutral 'package' of skills (Street and Street 1991) that can be simply transferred from one person to another. It is a value-free literacy applied to all, despite the different needs and experiences of those who are expected to learn it. Street and Street (1991) argue that with this way of perceiving literacy, language is treated:

> as if it were a 'thing', distanced from both teacher and learner and imposing on them external rules and requirements as though they were passive recipients. (Street and Street 1991: 144)

It is argued (Goodman 1996) instead that language is a natural phenomenon, learned in home environments very early, and is linked closely to identity and culture (Gee 2004); therefore children already possess linguistic skills before they begin school. However, cognitive–psychological approaches often appear to treat the teaching of literacy as if it were an entirely new set of skills that children come to school lacking.

It is important to understand why government policy-makers favour this cognitive–psychological approach. During the 1980s there was increasing anxiety over perceived rising levels of illiteracy in the United States and the United Kingdom. There was widespread belief that post-industrial society had led to fundamental changes in working practices and a change to the structure of the labour market. Concerns were voiced that workers may no longer have the capacity to contribute effectively to the demands of a growing service sector that was replacing manufacturing industries (Lankshear and Knobel 2003). In addition, English Ofsted (1996a, 1996b) inspection reports of schools claimed to show a decline in standards of reading and writing. According to these reports, far-reaching educational reform had to be implemented to improve functional literacy levels in primary schools. Children's development in these basic literacy skills needed to be tracked very carefully along a defined trajectory and initially in England and Wales; Statutory Assessment Tasks (SATs) were introduced as the measure of children's literacy success. Rigid efficiency in education like this is, of course, also less costly than more progressive measures that tend to need more time and resources. In addition, some argue that contemporary 'efficient' measures label those children who are unable to learn at the rate required as 'inadequate in some way' (Larson and Marsh 2005: 5) and who are often from homes in deprived circumstances (Larson and Marsh 2005). Yet, it is this approach that one will currently witness in many primary schools in England today. Many advisors and school senior managers, driven by policy from current governments, encourage and indeed demand a cognitive–psychological model to teach reading, writing and speaking. However, in my view, professional teachers need to take a more critical approach and be aware of alternative arguments about literacy in the English curriculum and decide how best to teach their children in the contexts within which they practise. Cognitive–psychological influenced methods are now enshrined in law; however, teachers must be professional and know what educationalists, teachers and researchers, who should be mainly independent of governments, are finding out about how children learn.

Literacy as Social Practice – 'Progressive' Measures

Barton and Hamilton (1998) have shown that literacy is not the same in all contexts. How people use words and utilise print varies depending upon the social environment where it is used. Literacy is not just the one promoted in schools. Literacy is a social practice and it is sculpted by the social, cultural, economic and political contexts within which it is found.

> Literacy does not just reside in people's heads as a set of skills to be learned … Like all human activity, literacy is essentially social, and it is located in the interaction between people. (Barton and Hamilton 1998: 3)

According to this model, literacy is situated only within social contexts and is formed and shaped through interaction between people. Literacy is not then merely an autonomous, discrete set of skills; it is 'alive', changing and dynamic. There is not one *literacy*, as portrayed in curricula, but many *literacies*, each intrinsically forming part of a specific social context and culture.

Culture is about how groups of people make meaning. Our culture is made through our histories and our experiences (Hall 2003). It was Bruner (1996) who wrote that our minds could not have been created without a culture. Our thoughts and the meanings we make derive from the culture within which we reside. Learning and thinking are always situated and are dependent upon the tools available within that specific social environment. The most important intellectual tool is language. Language is the symbol system that allows us to make meaning and to create our own identities within a culture.

It follows from this socio-cultural perspective that school literacy learning uses language in ways that are not neutral or autonomous, but have an ideological and cultural source. The literacy of school and curricula, according to this socio-cultural perspective, is based on a reductionist definition of literacy. It purports to offer a neutral set of skills and knowledge that are free from cultural domains. In doing so, it arguably marginalises and penalises those from different literacy cultures and normalises the middle-class literacy experiences that are privileged through school assessment (Larson and Marsh 2005). From this perspective, it may help us understand the consistent patterns of underachievement found in certain socio-cultural groups, as we begin to recognise that education and literacy learning are part of a culturally based process. It would follow from this that school literacy practices advantage those children who use school forms of literacy at home and disadvantage those who use words differently. As teachers we need to be aware of these arguments, and if we agree, we need to begin to plan our teaching in a way that attempts to intervene to disrupt these social reproductive processes which seem to lead to consistent patterns of underachievement.

Language Learning as Natural – Psycholinguist Perspectives

Psycholinguist perspectives, like socio-cultural positions, contend that literacy learning does not begin in school. Kenneth Goodman (1996) argues that children already possess a wealth of literacy experiences and have developed an implicit knowledge of language before they come to school. Goodman (1996) states that what makes language necessary and possible for human beings is our ability to think symbolically. We are a symbolic species (Deacon 1997) and for this reason our engagement and use of language is natural. In other words, we use things to represent other things and language is one of the most powerful ways of doing this. Language enables us to construct complex systems that can represent experiences, feelings, concepts and ideas.

The psycholinguist perspective follows the work of the linguist Noam Chomsky (1965) who stated that humans have an innate predisposition to learn a language. We all learn to speak and construct complex grammatical utterances without any form of tuition. This might suggest that our ability to do so comes from within rather than from any external source of pedagogy. Chomsky stated that humans have evolved to make language development a part of the brain's function. Learning and using language is natural and the psycholinguists take this further than the learning of oral language. Goodman suggests that learning written language is no less natural. He argues that oral and written language both develop from the need for humans to think and communicate through symbols. Written language is developed when needed, when oral communication through face-to-face and here-and-now language is no longer sufficient (Goodman 1996). This is not to suggest that, like oral language, we draw on evolved inner mechanisms to learn to read and write. The use of the written word is a relatively new phenomenon in humankind's development and there has not been sufficient time for such inner mechanisms to have formed. Language development, both oral and written, is natural because humans are a symbolic species with an innate propensity to represent the world through symbols, through language. It is in our nature to want to use language, both oral and written, and to exploit these language tools for a deeper understanding of our surroundings.

Both socio-cultural and psycholinguistic perspectives on literacy teaching reject the idea that all children come to school without a literacy. They honour young children with a belief that from a very young age they bring a wealth of literacy experiences based around their own cultural backgrounds and want to build on these forms of experiences. For these reasons, the pedagogy they propose is very different from more so-called traditional, cognitive–psychological positions on teaching literacy. They would deny that a linear and staged curriculum is appropriate for all children and reject the need for creating conditions in classrooms that enable direct staged instruction to be the main way of teaching. Socio-cultural and psycholinguistic teachers propose creating conditions that favour more independent learning, honouring children's own interests in the forms of texts and language they encounter at home as well as those texts associated with the school curriculum. They argue that learning a literacy is a cultural process (Lave and Wenger 1991; Rogoff 1990) where a community of learners is developed that share multiple perspectives on how language is learned, needed and used (Rogoff et al. 2001).

There are many modern primary school classrooms that use some of the practices that derive from psycholinguist and socio-cultural perspectives. Yet the contemporary pressures of standardised tests that measure children's learning of one form of literacy at selected stages of children's schooling arguably inhibit the freedom of many teachers to work in this way. However, professional teachers need to decide with their colleagues which theoretical position, or positions, they want to take and then work towards creating the conditions, both politically and educationally, to enable them to work the way colleagues know is best for the children in their classes. The National Curriculum is enshrined in law and teachers are bound to teach to it in all state schools, with exceptions among academies and free schools, yet within these constraints teachers can still create learning environments that are right for the children in their classes to succeed and begin to love reading and writing.

The State of the Art in Pedagogy

Reading

Cognitive–psychological models of teaching reading are the current dominant perspectives that drive educational policy across the Western industrialised world. These methods are commonly found in state primary schools in England and the UK. The extent to which this theoretical position is applied will vary from school to school.

The *Independent Review of the Teaching of Early Reading* (Rose 2006), often called the Rose Review, commissioned by the New Labour UK government (1996–2010), emphasised the need to teach children to learn to read through a method called synthetic phonics. The review argues that the teaching of synthetic phonics is the most important strategy to teach young children to read. This approach is likely to be continued in broadly the same ways by successive governments for the foreseeable future and is enshrined in the National Curriculum for English 2014. Yet, teachers need to know that this perspective on teaching reading continues to be contested (for example, Davies 2013).

The psycholinguist Goodman (1967) maintained that children need to draw on three of what he called cueing strategies: grapho-phonic, semantic and syntactic. Grapho-phonic is similar to what the Rose Review advocates that children should be taught first when learning to read – decoding graphemes (letters) into phonemes (sounds) and blending them to sound out the word. The National Curriculum for English 2014 demands that this cueing strategy is taught first and in isolation to others.

Syntactic cueing strategies, Goodman (1973) argued, are how readers are able to predict the next word by drawing on their implicit knowledge of language structures and the order of words in sentences and utterances. If a child comes across a word that she cannot read, instead of using grapho-phonic strategies to sound out the word, the teacher asks the child to read to the end of the sentence and then go back and read the sentence again. By doing so, the child can hear the sentence drawing out pattern-markers and inflectional suffixes and cues and predict the word. In other words, the child draws on her own knowledge of language and language structures to read the words.

The third cue that Goodman describes is semantic. Using this cue, like the syntactic cues, asks the child to draw on her own knowledge, but this time, knowledge of the world and the contexts within which the book she is reading takes place. Children know about the world, for example, that grass can be green, the sky can be blue and knowing about these things and the language that conceptualises and describes them enables children to predict the words that are coming up in a text. With the help of more experienced readers, children learn to orchestrate their knowledge (Chittenden et al. 2001) about language and the world by using all the cues together.

However, since the Rose Review and the National Curriculum for English 2014, this way of articulating the strategies needed for children to read is no longer favoured. The teaching of grapho-phonic skills is now the preferred first teaching approach for young children, emphasising a more cognitive–psychological approach.

Synthetic Phonics

Using synthetic phonics, the individual phonemes associated with particular graphemes are each isolated, pronounced and blended together (synthesised) to read and write a word. For example, h/a/t has three phonemes and three graphemes. Children are taught to *segment* words into their individual phonemes. For instance, the word b/r/u/sh is made from four phonemes. Segmentation assists children to spell. A child needs to segment a word they want to spell into its component phonemes, providing a grapheme (letter) or combination of graphemes to represent each phoneme.

Teaching synthetic phonics will also entail instructing the children how to *blend* a word. This means merging the phonemes together to pronounce a word. When reading and confronted with an unknown word, the children are taught to attribute a phoneme to each letter or letter combination and then merge them to sound out the word. Psycholinguists believe that this is not enough and that children need to learn all the cueing strategies from the moment they begin to learn to read. They argue that experienced readers use all three and so children must learn to do this from the beginning. However, present governments insist that using synthetic phonics must be the first strategy that children learn.

Whole-Language Learning

These cognitive–psychological methods are roundly rejected by psycholinguists and socio-cultural teachers of reading. Instead, they broadly use what has been called a 'whole-language approach' to the teaching of reading. This includes teachers introducing the three cueing strategies to children together from an early age within the context of good books. This approach concentrates far more upon teaching the processes as well as the skills, as many argue that children will not wish to read unless they understand the processes that make the activity so enjoyable and worthwhile. Concentrating on discrete skills, as cognitive–psychological models favour, has the danger of making reading appear as a form of labour devoid of any pleasure. While many cognitive–psychological models of reading teach skills in isolation, whole-language approaches emphasise the importance of reading rich literature (Holdaway 1979; Meek 1988), sometimes called 'real books', to allow children to experience the pleasures of reading. Texts are chosen to which children can relate: multi-cultural stories, tales that involve children from different religions, races and social classes. Teachers will also draw on popular culture – the television and film industry – enticing children into reading by demonstrating the pleasure it can give to everyone. Whole-language approaches aim to create stimulating experiences for children to learn to read. They combine direct teaching in different group sizes with opportunities for children to experience the 'untaught lessons' that books can offer; again, this happens from an early age to demonstrate from the start that reading is more than a dry act of labour.

In addition to the three cueing strategies that are taught both formally and informally, teachers from a whole-language perspective teach the processes (Grainger and Tod 2000). These are the processes with which accomplished readers engage and which children need to learn:

- **Predicting** – anticipating what will happen next in the story from what has occurred earlier and how other similar stories often operate.
- **Picturing** – being aware of how reading a fictional text can create pictures in one's mind's eye. These pictures are given to the reader both by the writer's work and by the experiences that children have had in their real world.
- **Connecting** – from an early age children will make connections with events and characters in a text with their own lives and other stories they have read in books or seen in films or on television.
- **Questioning** – good readers tend to generate questions about the texts they read (Benton and Fox 1985). We constantly ask questions of the narrative, the characters and events, demonstrating that reading is not a passive activity.
- **Engaging** – how many of us have cried at the end of a novel or been terrified and had to shut a book? Children also need to discuss how they engage with a text and understand and experience the effects of good writing.

- **Evaluating** – having what is sometimes called 'critical literacy' broadly means that readers feel confident to make judgements about the texts they read. Children must be encouraged to evaluate texts from different perspectives – political and aesthetic.

Children are taught to engage in these processes and understand their pleasures while at the same time learning the cueing strategies that are essential for reading too. Both skills and processes are vital in becoming a reader. The pedagogy for whole-language learning is a combination of direct and independent teaching and learning. While cognitive–psychological models of reading are much more a 'drilling and skilling' of children using synthetic phonics, whole-language teachers are enthusing children to read by offering authentic experiences with great books.

 Case Study 1.1

Robert is a teacher who defines reading as a search for meaning in texts. He teaches reading using synthetic phonics for those children in his Year 1 class who need it, but is also acutely aware of the need to help children to read using other cueing strategies too. Robert believes that a large proportion of the children in his class have yet to learn the pleasure that can be found in reading books alone and with others. In preparing his class for September when he met the children for the first time, he decided that books and the pleasure of reading would define the layout in his classroom. He set up a well-organised and attractive reading area in his class. He set aside a large corner of the room for his classroom books. He ensured he had a good range of literature and included comics, children's magazines and catalogues in the collection. He divided the books by genre and put them into their own labelled baskets so children knew where to go to find their favourite texts and those that were unknown to them. He provided comfortable seating and brought in colourful posters that promoted reading for pleasure. Every day he set aside 30 minutes for quiet reading and read to the children at least three times a day (sometimes reading three books in one sitting). The reading corner became the centre of the developing culture of reading in his class. The children enjoyed Robert's passion for books and he became known in the school as the 'reading teacher who loves books'.

Writing

Vygotsky (1978) believed that reading and writing are two halves of the same process: mastering written language (Barrs and Cork 2001). What writers must do is to find themselves 'shuttling between spoken resources and an increasing store of forms inter-nalised from their reading' (Britton 1982, cited in Barrs and Cork 2001: 42). So, from this perspective, reading experiences are integral to being able to write, as well as the belief that one's spoken language resources can also be utilised in written composition. I suspect no one would disagree with these ideas, yet it is how to provide children with these skills and knowledge that continues to be where disagreement lies. Following on from what has been said previously in this chapter, cognitive–psychological theorists would advocate that children need to be directly taught the skills required. This would involve practice through exercises. However, if we wish to avoid teaching a generation of clerks, many will argue, particularly psycholinguists and socio-cultural theorists, that children must be shown how writing will open up opportunities for them to increase communicative repertoires. Children can recognise these benefits of writing if we encourage them to make choices about their writing – form, content and purpose – and allow them to find their personal voice (Clarke 2000).

The National Curriculum for English 2014 emphasises the importance of teaching the structure and language features of writing, arguably at the expense of emphasising the meanings that children can produce for their own personal, aesthetic or practical satisfaction. As you now know, this corresponds with cognitive–psychological per-spectives on the teaching of literacy and this will be a consistent feature of current educational policy. You should expect to be asked to teach writing skills directly to the children in a de-contextualised way, often as exercises to teach specific skills. However, there are some ideas about the teaching of writing that are often generally agreed upon and should be taken very seriously when planning how to teach writing in the primary classroom. I intend to discuss them here.

Writing begins with other forms of symbolising (drawing, modelling, play, drama). If humans are symbolic species, they are attracted to finding ways to express them-selves through the use of symbols. Right from being very young children, we have always attempted to communicate symbolically – for example, 'the gesture is the initial visual sign that contains the child's future writing as an acorn contains a future oak' (Vygotsky 1978: 107). Teachers have the responsibility of introducing children to con-ventional written ways of making meaning through signs. Psycholinguists would argue that teachers can do this best by building on children's natural interest in symbols and celebrating the ways they are using symbols before they come to school. In other words, treat children as meaning makers from the beginning, encourage the early marks they make on paper and treat them as serious forms of writing that convey meaning. The literacy we teach in schools is not entirely new to children: they have used signs before.

The writing process can be divided into two parts and this is how it is presented in the National Curriculum for English 2014. The first of these is *composition* – this is the capturing of ideas, authoring, construction of the narrative, choosing genre and gram-mar. To compose one needs no means of written transcription. It happens all the time: for example, children compose narratives in their games and adults compose to a dictaphone or when they meet and talk to people on an everyday basis. We know that 'writing and speaking are different but writing, without an understanding of its roots in speech, is nothing' (Graves 1983: 162). Composition, one might argue, is the heart of writing; it is where meanings are generated and arguably it should be the part of writing that needs to be nurtured the most.

Transcription is the second part. This consists of the handwriting, spelling and punctuation that are also crucial to successful communication through writing. It is children's early mark-making, but it is also what secretaries need to be good at as they transcribe what has been composed on the dictaphone. Strangely enough, this is often the part of writing that is given the most importance in many schools, and the National Curriculum 2014 has been accused of continuing this trend (PUG 2012). It is very important of course, but it is a part of the writing process and not all of it. Both parts need to be nurtured, nourished and taught together and, I would argue, in meaningful contexts.

For writers to be motivated and to write successfully they need to know the:

Purpose: This seems obvious, but children become far more motivated when the teacher has found authentic purposes for their writing. This may be as simple as knowing that it will be read by a real audience – it will be displayed on a wall or will be part of a book or a website. Too often writing is destined for exercise books and put away in drawers, read by no one but the teacher.

Form: Writers need to know what type of writing will be most appropriate to their purpose and in what type of writing they can organise their ideas. What types of writing are available? What sort of vocabulary and grammatical constructions best serve their intentions? From an early age teachers expose children to a wide range of texts that are used for various purposes: by doing so through talk and discussion about the texts' success, children recognise the affordances of these text types.

Audience: Who will read the children's writing? What effect do the children intend their writing to have on their audience? What assumptions can they make about their readership?

Teaching the Writing Process

It has been said that:

The best way to understand and encourage interaction between the child's growing linguistic system and her emerging ability to write is to see the latter as a developmental process, which first emphasises fluency, then clarity, and finally correctness. (D'Arcy, 1999: 97)

What is being stressed here again is the importance of teachers encouraging children to draw on the language resources they bring to school and showing them how to use this knowledge and experience to develop their writing abilities. The fluency is encouraged right from the beginning, celebrating children's early mark-making and compositions; recognising these attempts as being genuine forms of writing; raising confidence and then developing clarity and then correctness. For this educationalist, too often children are taught to write from the other way round. Clarity and correctness is privileged over fluency. Children are told early on that their efforts on paper have little worth as they have not yet grasped the conventions of written language. Many argue that cognitive–psychological models often emphasise correctness and teach skills too early, providing a message to the children that their early mark-making and compositions are not valued. This model assumes children come to school ignorant of the ability to compose and transcribe.

Many teachers emphasise the writing process and, within a real context that requires composition and transcription, teach each stage of the process thoroughly. The process broadly looks like this:

- re-reading
- revising for meaning
- editing
- proofreading.

Professional writers often complain that they rarely confine their creativity to this form of writing process. Indeed, teachers may wish to be aware that real writers, like themselves, sometimes never get to the end of the process, as writing is not always for an audience and so children do not need to always go through the whole process for all writing. However, it is a good guide to what needs to be taught and experienced by the children.

 Case Study 1.2

Helen teaches in an inner-city primary school in a deprived catchment area. She became aware that because of pressures from a test-driven curriculum the children in her Year 5 class were not being given the opportunity to write independently, choosing subjects and forms with which to express themselves. Helen decided to introduce writing journals. She gave all the children an exercise book and asked them to customise it using pictures from magazines, and protect it with some clear plastic covering. The children claimed ownership over the books by covering them in images that were meaningful to them. Helen fitted in a journal-writing session three times a week that lasted up to 30 minutes each.

She gave the journals a big introduction. The children were told that the journals were to be used to write anything in them they wanted. Importantly, Helen told them that she would never mark them in any way and she would only read what they had written with their permission. Helen made some suggestions about what they could write (reports of football matches, stories, poems, lists and so on) and during the first session asked children to tell the others (with their permission) what they were doing. The impact was dramatic. The children loved writing in the journals. Even reluctant writers felt liberated by them. Helen kept her own journal and wrote alongside the children.

Speaking

As I have already tried to stress in this chapter, language is a distinctly human characteristic and learning to talk and to listen is where it begins. We learn to talk without any direct instruction. Our brains have evolved to learn spoken language and we use language both to communicate to others and to think. We learn to use spoken language from our cultural environments and we go to school already talking and thinking. Language is a tool of the mind (Olson 2001) and brings coherence and meaning to our world. Language forms our very consciousness. It is fundamental to our identity – language makes us who we are. Through our use of language we make the knowledge we have (Vygotsky 1978) of the world. Talk, therefore, becomes an essential component to any successful learning experience and is fundamental to a healthy classroom learning environment.

It is because language is a part of our identity and derives from our cultural background that many teachers and educationalists argue for sensitivity when teaching children 'how' to speak and listen. After all, children can do this already. However, as we have seen, literacy is not a neutral entity; some forms of literacy and language use are imbued with more power in society than others and so teachers are required to teach children to use spoken language in particular ways that may bring this power. I have discussed the resulting inequality and the tensions of this phenomenon earlier on and teaching children to speak and listen 'properly' is contested too. For example, Fairclough (1992) argues that in teaching children to speak in particular ways that may be very different to how they are accustomed may undermine their own speech from local communities. Fairclough (1992) contends that if we teach that one form of talk is better within prestigious and powerful contexts like schools, it makes children's own habitual ways of talking marginal and irrelevant.

Teaching spoken language skills must respect the language backgrounds of the children in the class. All kinds of dialects can be found in schools. A dialect is distinguished by its vocabulary, grammar and pronunciation. Where a distinction can be made only in terms of pronunciation, then the term to use is *accent*. So, for example, one can speak using a Standard English dialect with a Scottish accent.

Standard English is another dialect with its own set of grammatical rules and it is this which teachers are required to teach. Children will need to learn to distinguish between dialects and recognise how some are more powerful than others. However, one needs to be aware of the dangers of implicitly creating negative messages about children's home use of language and consequently their own identity. If instead teachers celebrate all forms of spoken language, compare differences and discuss their use in different contexts then it may be possible to avoid alienation of children who often come from other cultures and classes.

The removal of speaking and listening as a separate attainment target in the National Curriculum for English 2014 is seen as a flaw by many (for example, NPTEC 2013), despite its inclusion in the general NC framing. It is argued that its absence undermines the crucial importance of pupils' development as speakers and listeners and of oracy as a tool for learning and thinking across the curriculum.

Children can be encouraged to reflect on the use of language:

- their own talk – building confidence to speak in a range of contexts; examining their own oral histories
- others' use of language – how people talk differently; the use of standard English
- construction of talk – what creates differences in the use of language; the structure of utterances.

Innovation

Innovation in literacy teaching can come in many forms. The use of new technology and the advent of screen texts, gaming, chat rooms and social networking sites has prompted a large number of teachers and academics to advocate the use of the term 'digital literacies' and to suggest that the current literacy curriculum must reflect the changing nature of literacy much more than it does in the face of growing accessibility to these forms of communicative repertoires (Kress 2003; Marsh and Millard 2000). Sadly, there is scant mention of digital literacies in the National Curriculum for English 2014. Yet, there is enormous potential for teachers to innovate by exploiting children's growing awareness of how new technology enables meaning to be made through a combination of words, images and sound. This is called multi-modality because different modes of meaning-making are combined to enrich communication. Many teachers are encouraging children to make blogs to complement and enrich the work undertaken in the classroom; to communicate through email and webcams with children in other schools both nationally and internationally, all of which requires children to use language in different ways, adapting to the audiences with which they communicate. Twitter is also being used in primary classrooms (Waller 2010).

Lankshear and Knobel suggest that we need to recognise the four roles that characterise the practices of people who engage in multi-modal text production as they learn to produce, distribute and exchange texts. These people are 'digitally at home' with new technology (Lankshear and Knobel 2003):

- **Text designer** – the word design is used here deliberately rather than authorship for multi-model digital texts require the utilisation of the written word, the image and sound. Teachers need to decide how these design processes can be supported and extended.
- **Text bricoleur** – this term comes from the concept of bricolage – 'the artisan of inventiveness' – where people draw on what is to hand to make meaning. Lankshear and Knobel (2003) draw on the ways web users create texts within on-line communities. They raid various sources to produce their texts. Teachers can facilitate the use of the web to make a text bricoleur.
- **Text broker** – skills are taught that are associated with those who manage discussion boards or those who give online web materials like blogs and articles a rating.
- **Text jammer** – this involves skills needed for the process of changing and adapting electronic texts in order to subvert the messages given – online critical literacy practices.

Teachers can innovate their literacy practice by becoming the trail blazers for teaching, enriching and reflecting upon the skills required to effectively operate as multimodal meaning-makers. These new literate behaviours associated with new technology require new skill sets, many of which children already utilise at home. Schools can enrich these skills for those who already use them, provide the hardware and software for those who do not and introduce the skills and facilitate learners' reflection upon the issue of power which is associated with all forms of communicative media. In addition, children are also extremely motivated to work with new technology and can open up possibilities to create synergy between digital literacies and more traditional forms.

Creativity

English creativity makes teaching exciting. Teachers can offer literacy education that both adheres to national statutory requirements and is influenced by, but also challenges, the rich cultures and intellectual traditions of the community within which the school is placed. In my view, teaching professionals take risks and often push at the boundaries of expectation, challenging pre-conceived ideas of national governments and agencies, but also those of the community in which they work. English teachers and teachers in general encourage critical engagement with the world; they want their students to ask questions, interrogating what can often come to be common knowledge and sense. Teaching and learning can be exciting, disturbing and challenging.

As Bernard Shaw remarked, learning something initially always feels like losing something (Eagleton 2007).

Teachers can also ensure that they too stay in touch with their own creativity, their passions and interests. I have met many teachers who, although often feeling exhausted by the end of the week, take steps to feed their own creative imaginations and intellect. They do this by attending events and activities that they know they find intellectually or physically challenging. Those who like the theatre or sports make sure they still go to watch or participate, while others maintain active involvement with areas of interest that provide stimulus – whatever that may be.

The best teachers I know read. They read material that interests them as well as taking an interest in genres with which they may be less familiar. All the good literacy teachers I know read children's literature. They often have their own collections and cannot help diving into a bookshop to find all the latest books that they can read to their class.

A love of children's literature will be passed to the children one teaches, but so will one's own interest in one's own writing. Work I have undertaken with teachers (Grainger et al. 2005), to improve the teaching of writing in primary schools always involves teachers recognising and re-connecting with their own talents as writers and building upon them. Teachers become writers: they keep 'writing note books', they write poems and stories and sometimes share them with their class, their family or their friends and colleagues. Teachers I know now write alongside the children on writing projects with which the class is involved. They feel confident enough to do the same writing that the children have been asked to do – often modelling the struggle that writing can be. They do this not once a term, but as often as they possibly can, building a community of writers that includes the adults too. It is a simple idea that children seem to enjoy and from which they learn.

Assessment of Children's Literacy and English

Statutory Assessment Tasks (SATs) and tests remain the way governments expect teachers to assess their children's progress at the end of each Key Stage in England. Yet, teachers also need to make formative assessments of their children's progress in order to plan the teaching that will see them continue to progress in their literacy learning. I offer an introduction to the processes that teachers use to assess their children.

Teachers need to know about the processes and skills children are learning. They need to know about:

- the knowledge and understanding children have about reading, writing and speaking and listening
- children's confidence and independence to read, write and talk

- the reading, writing and oral language experience children have already
- the strategies children are using to read and write
- children's reflectiveness about reading, writing and speaking.

(Adapted from Barrs and Thomas 1991)

Running Records for Reading

Running records are an important way of learning about the children's use of cueing strategies mentioned earlier in this chapter – grapho-phonic, syntactic and semantic. It is a simplified version of miscue analysis (Goodman 1973), which can be used for older children and was developed by Marie Clay (1985). Running records work well with children in Key Stages 1 and 2 (see Goouch and Lambirth 2011).

Miscue for Writing

Eve Bearne (1997) devised a miscue analysis specifically for writing. It seeks to analyse a piece of writing for the meaning the writer wishes to make. Bearne recommends that the teacher observes the child while they write and then engages the child in a form of writing conference (see below). The two discuss the writing process; the alterations the child has made to the text; how the child sought assistance from various strategies; the success of writing for a particular audience; the spelling; the punctuation (depending upon which part of the writing process they were currently working on).

Reading and Writing Conferences

One-to-one conversations are a perfect opportunity to learn more about individual children in the class. It can become a forum for children to talk about their likes and dislikes with reading and writing and facilitates teachers finding out about children's attitudes and their ability to reflect on their own development. These conferences are just chats, but teachers may wish to do as Barrs and Thomas (1991) recommend for reading and create two occasions a year when individual children and the teacher sit down for a longer and more focused talk. Some teachers make a record of the children's comments to provide a focus for the next discussion a while later to note changes. Children who have English as an additional language will be able to discuss the reading and writing they have been undertaking in their mother tongue or indeed any other languages they know.

Informal Observations

We know from research (Medwell et al. 1998) that effective teachers include 'continuous monitoring of children's progress through the tasks provided and the use of informal assessment to give the basis for teaching and reporting on this progress' (p. 5). This entails:

- initiating ideas – drafting
- making notes of children's enjoyment of books
- discussing children's reading diaries
- working with small groups of children, 'probing, questioning and supporting' (p. 41)
- making observations and note-taking in informal ways.

Guided Reading and Writing

Guided reading and writing sessions are a very good time for observation of the children. Guided reading and writing was formally introduced to primary classrooms with the National Literacy Strategy in 1998 (DfEE 1998). It consists of a small group (maximum five) of children chosen to work with a teacher in order to target specific aspects of their learning to read or write. These may not be static groups and the teacher will choose the groups for various reasons and children may find themselves working with different children. The sessions have a specific content carefully chosen and a lesson planned with precision. It is during these sessions that teachers can record aspects of the children's development in order to assist in future planning.

Assessing Speaking

Children's ability to speak and listen in the classroom can be monitored and discussed with the children in many of the assessment opportunities I have provided. However, it is very important that teachers regularly sample children's oral ability in different situations, both formal and informal in nature. As has been found (National Oracy Project 1991), because of the variables that affect talk, it is not possible to make absolute judgements about children's oral ability. Teachers can note children's successes in:

- explaining
- supporting others
- listening and responding
- using questions
- summarising a group discussion
- seeking consensus.

It is important to support one's statements about the child's development with quotes from the events one has watched. We are looking for:

- the part children play in discussion
- how children give and follow instructions
- how children use talk to work through problems and to clarify situations
- how children adjust their talk to different situations and audiences
- the quality of the content of children's talk.

Conclusion

As you will now be aware, the teaching of literacy is like no other job. It does not require teachers to be simply technicians, but instead needs teachers to be sensitive, creative, intelligent, passionate and committed. Teachers need to be activists, as I mentioned at the beginning of this chapter. Teaching English is unique and wonderful. It is political too and, in my mind, it is crucial that teachers are aware of this so as to judge what successive governments are expecting of them and the political motivations that lie behind what they ask. As a teacher, it is no good ignoring this fact. Language development is intrinsically linked to consciousness and identity; it defines the way we all think. For that reason alone it will always be the concern of politicians. Being a professional and being proud of this status will help ensure that teachers mediate the practice in schools. Teachers have enormous social power that comes partly from their ability to encourage their children to question and to make education as a 'form of inquiry' at the forefront of all they do.

 Reflection Points

1. How did you learn to read? Can you remember the strategies and processes you were taught when you were at school? Do you remember reading at home with parents and other members of the family? How did this help you to become a reader?
2. Do you know the latest and best children's literature available? Go to the Books for Keeps website at http://booksforkeeps.co.uk/ to make a start on finding out about children's literature.
3. You will be teaching children to write a range of different texts. Do you ever write the kinds of work you will be asking the children to write? Do you think it matters?

Further Reading 📖

Barrs, M. and Cork, V. (2001) *The Reader in the Writer: The Links between the Study of Literature and Writing Development at Key Stage 2.* London: The Centre for Literacy in Primary Education.

Barrs, M. and Thomas, A. (1991) *The Reading Book.* London: The Centre for Literacy in Primary Education.

Bearne, E. (1997a) 'Mis Cue Analysis: Part 1', *Primary English Magazine* 3 (1): 17–20.

Bearne, E. (1997b) 'Mis Cue Analysis: Part 2', *Primary English Magazine* 3 (2): 18–22.

Larson, J. and Marsh, J. (2014) *Making Literacy Real: Theories and Practices for Learning and Teaching*, 2nd edn. London: SAGE.

References

Barrs, M. and Cork, V. (2001) *The Reader in the Writer: The Links between the Study of Literature and Writing Development at Key Stage 2.* London: The Centre for Literacy in Primary Education.

Barrs, M. and Thomas, A. (1991) *The Reading Book.* London: The Centre for Literacy in Primary Education.

Barton, D. and Hamilton, M. (1998) *Local Literacies: Reading and Writing in One Community.* London: Routledge.

Bearne, E. (1997) Miscue for Writing. *The Primary English Magazine.* Sheffield: National Association for the Teachers of English.

Benton, M. and Fox, G. (1985) *Teaching Literature: Nine to Fourteen.* Oxford: Oxford University Press.

Britton, J. (1982) 'Prospect and retrospect', in G.M. Pradl (ed.), *Selected Essays of James Britton.* London: Heinemann Educational.

Bruner, J. (1996) *The Culture of Education.* Cambridge, MA: Harvard University Press.

Carr, W. and Kemmis, S. (1997) *Becoming Critical: Education, Knowledge and Action Research.* London: Falmer Press.

Chittenden, E. and Salinger, T. with Bussis, A.M. (2001) *Inquiry into Meaning: An Investigation of Learning to Read*, rev. edn. New York: Teachers College Press.

Chomsky, N. (1965) *Aspects of the Theory of Syntax.* Cambridge, MA: MIT Press.

Clarke, L. (2000) 'Lessons from nursery: children as writers in early years education', *Reading* 34 (2): 68–73.

Clay, M. (1985) *The Early Detection of Reading Difficulties*, 3rd edn. Auckland: Heinemann.

Davies, A. (2013) 'To read or not to read: decoding synthetic phonics', *Impact: Philosophical Perspectives in Education Policy* Special Issue No. 20. http://onlinelibrary.wiley.com/journal/10.1111/(ISSN)2048-416X (accessed September 2014).

D'Arcy, P. (1999) *Two Contrasting Paradigms for the Teaching and the Assessment of Writing: A Critique of Current Approaches in the National Curriculum.* Loughborough: NATE.

Deacon, T. (1997) *The Symbolic Species: The Co-Evolution of Language and the Human Brain*. London: Penguin Books.

DfE (Department for Education) (2013) *English Programmes of Study: Key Stages 1 and 2. National Curriculum in England*. London: DfE.

DfEE (Department for Education and Employment) (1998) *The National Literacy Strategy: Framework for Teaching*. London: DfEE.

Eagleton, T. (2007) *How to Read a Poem*. Oxford: Blackwell.

Ehri, L.C. (1987) 'Learning to read and spell words', *Journal of Reading Behaviour* 19: 5–31.

Ehri, L.C. (1995) 'Phases of development in learning to read words by sight', *Journal of Research in Reading* 18 (2): 116–25.

Fairclough, N. (1992) *Critical Language Awareness*. Harlow: Addison, Wesley, Longman.

Gee, J.P. (2004) *Situated Language Learning: A Critique of Traditional Schooling*. Abingdon: Routledge.

Goodman, K.S. (1967) 'Reading: a psycholinguistic guessing game', *Journal of the Reading Specialist* 4: 126–35.

Goodman, K.S. (1973) 'Psycholinguistic universals in the reading process', in F. Smith (ed.), *Psycholinguistics and Reading*. New York, NY: Holt, Rinehart and Winston.

Goodman, K.S. (1996) *On Reading*. Portsmouth, NH: Heinemann.

Goouch, K. and Lambirth, A. (2011) *Teaching Early Reading and Phonics: Creative Approaches to Early Literacy*. London: SAGE.

Grainger, T. and Tod, J. (2000) *Inclusive Educational Practice: Literacy*. London: David Fulton.

Grainger, T., Goouch, K. and Lambirth, A. (2005) *Creativity and Writing: Developing Voice and Verve in the Classroom*. London: Routledge.

Graves, D. (1983) *Writing: Teachers and Children at Work*. London: Heinemann Press.

Hall, K. (2003) *Listening to Stephen Read: Multiple Perspectives on Literacy*. Buckingham: Open University Press.

Holdaway, D. (1979) *The Foundations of Literacy*. London: Ashton, Scholastic.

Kress, G. (2003) *Literacy in the New Media Age*. London: Routledge.

Lankshear, C. and Knobel, M. (2003) *New Literacies: Changing Knowledge and Classroom Learning*. Buckingham: Open University Press.

Larson, J. and Marsh, J. (2005) *Making Literacy Real: Theories and Practice for Learning and Teaching*. London: SAGE.

Lave, J. and Wenger, E. (1991) *Situated Learning: Legitimate Peripheral Participation*. Cambridge: Cambridge University Press.

Marsh, J. and Millard, E. (2000) *Literacy and Popular Culture: Using Children's Culture in the Classroom*. London: Paul Chapman.

Medwell, J., Wray, D., Poulson, L. and Fox, R. (1998) *Effective Teachers of Literacy*. Exeter: Exeter University.

Meek, M. (1988) *How Texts Teach What Readers Learn*. Stroud: Thimble Press.

National Oracy Project (1991) *Teaching, Talking and Learning in Key Stage 2*. York: National Curriculum Council.

Ofsted (Office for Standards in Education) (1996a) *The Teaching of Reading in 45 Inner London Schools.* London: Ofsted Publications.

Ofsted (Office for Standards in Education) (1996b) *Subjects and Standards: 1994/5.* London: Ofsted Publications.

Olson, D. (2001) 'Education: the bridge from culture to mind', in D. Bakhurst and S.G. Shanker (eds), *Jerome Bruner: Language, Culture, Self.* London: SAGE.

Primary Umbrella Group (PUG) (2012) A Joint Statement in Response to the Department for Education's Consultation on Primary National Curriculum Draft Programmes of Study. www.teachers.org.uk/files/PUG-Joint-statement-FINAL.doc (accessed 07/11/2014).

Rogoff, B. (1990) *Apprenticeship in Thinking: Cognitive Development in a Social Context.* New York: Oxford University Press.

Rogoff, B., Goodman-Turkanis, C. and Bartlett, L. (2001) *Learning Together: Children and Adults in a School Community.* Oxford: Oxford University Press.

Rose, J. (2006) *Independent Review of the Teaching of Early Reading.* Nottingham: Department for Education and Schools (DfES) Publications.

Sachs, J. (2003) *The Activist Teaching Profession.* Buckingham: Open University Press.

Street, B. (1984) *Literacy in Theory and Practice.* New York: Cambridge University Press.

Street, B.V. and Street, J. (1991) 'The schooling of literacy', in D. Barton and R. Ivanic (eds), *Writing in the Community.* Thousand Oaks, CA: SAGE.

Vygotsky, L.S. (1978) *Mind in Society: The Development of Higher Psychological Processes.* Cambridge, MA: MIT Press.

Waller, M. (2010) 'It's very very fun and exciting using Twitter in the primary classroom', *English 4–7,* http://changinghorizons.net/2010/08/using-twitter-in-the-primary- classroom/.

CHAPTER 2

AN INTRODUCTION TO MATHEMATICS

Gina Donaldson

Chapter Aims

This chapter will:

- reflect critically on the place of mathematics in the curriculum and the content of the mathematics curriculum taught in primary schools

- consider what it means to understand mathematics

- analyse current and innovative practices in mathematics education as to the way they support children in understanding mathematics

Introduction

This chapter is aimed at providing new teachers with a framework to understand and critically evaluate experiences of primary mathematics in the classroom. It is designed to challenge you to formulate your own principles of what is good practice, based on an understanding of theoretical ideas and research findings.

Mathematics has a high status. It has been labelled a 'core' subject within the primary curriculum for Key Stages 1 and 2 (DfE 2013), and is a specific area of learning and development across the early years (DfE 2012). In school it is generally taught every day and in the morning, when children often appear to be more likely to learn. The first section of this chapter will explore why it is such an important area of learning and consider what sort of mathematics should make up the primary curriculum. A range of views and theories will be explored and considered in terms of their impact on the classroom.

The chapter will go on to challenge the reader in considering what it is to understand mathematics. State of the art practices in pedagogy and new innovative practices will then be explored and analysed as to the extent to which they promote children's mathematical understanding. The reader will be asked to critically analyse the contribution of mathematics to creativity and consider procedures for assessment. By the end of the chapter, it is hoped that you will be able to analyse your experiences in the classroom in an informed and professional manner, and articulate your own principles for teaching mathematics creatively to promote children's fascination for, enjoyment and understanding of mathematics.

Why Mathematics?

Why should children learn mathematics? As in all areas of education, the way that teachers understand mathematics themselves and their beliefs about its place in the curriculum influence the way they present it to children. There are different ideas that might underpin the rationale for the place of mathematics in the curriculum. This section will explore aspects of two of these and consider their impact on the experiences of children in the classroom.

Mathematics Underpinning Other Learning

First, it can be argued that mathematics is important because it provides the basis of our everyday life, enabling us to function and thrive. We might find tasks such as shopping, cooking and using public transport difficult without key mathematical skills. The National Curriculum (DfE 2013) argues that mathematics 'is essential to everyday life, critical to science, technology and engineering, and necessary for financial literacy and most forms of employment' (p. 3). Mathematics is important because it enables us to understand the world, and therefore have some power to change it. We use mathematics, for example, in public decision-making and in understanding our control on the impact we have on the environment. Mathematics can be seen as key to serving the maintenance and progress of society (ACME 2008). A curriculum based on this view would be set firmly in real-life, relevant contexts and develop a fluency in basic skills and mental calculations. An understanding of statistics, and how data can be represented in potentially misleading ways, would also be important.

There is also a view, expressed, for example, by Ofsted (2008) and Williams (2008), that mathematics is important in its contribution to our understanding of culture. Certainly, knowledge of mathematics can help us to identify patterns and motifs in historical artefacts and places of worship, and to engage with culturally defined practices, say of recording number and calculating. Exploration of, for example, the development of our number system or the Roman number system can be an enriching part of a history topic and a study of these is part of the Mathematics National Curriculum requirements.

Mathematics is often described as a language (Smith 2004; Williams 2008). Certainly, there is a collection of mathematical terms that children will need to understand and use in their learning. These terms are in some cases purely mathematical and in others have differing mathematical and everyday meanings. The subject is sometimes justified as underpinning learning in other areas by providing a universal language that is precise and powerful in its ability to represent abstract thinking. Smith (2004) argues for the role of mathematics in underpinning work in science and technology. Using algebra, mathematical symbols represent ideas in an abbreviated way that can be manipulated to explore arguments. A curriculum based on this view would focus on language and draw links between mathematics and other areas of the curriculum.

Mathematics for Its Own Sake

An alternative view of the rationale of mathematics is that rather than supporting learning in other areas, it is important in its own right as a fascinating and valuable subject (for example, ACME 2008; Smith 2004). Not only should children experience mathematics in real-life contexts but they should also undertake investigation of mathematics itself. Mathematics provides a unique set of ideas, properties and ways of thinking which children should experience and recognise. These are valuable activities in themselves. For example, children might explore which totals can be made when adding three consecutive numbers. This activity might have limited direct relevance to their everyday lives but can lead them to appreciate the pattern within numbers and develop their understanding of our number system, sometimes called 'number sense' (Anghileri 2006).

The mathematics curriculum can be designed to promote mathematical perseverance, curiosity, logical thinking skills and positive attitudes (ACME 2008). Williams (2008) argued that it is still socially acceptable for adults to state their dislike of and lack of success in mathematics. If the primary curriculum is to promote mathematical thinking and positive attitudes, then it should focus on problem solving and investigating, introduce children to fascinating ideas and include a certain amount of success. A further argument is that mathematics provides a unique aspect of children's spiritual development (Winter 2001). As children explore number, they appreciate the beauty of its pattern and the elegance of mathematical arguments. For example, they might come to an understanding of why the total of two even numbers is always even. Young children can identify powerful ideas such as infinity. There can be a sense of satisfaction and self-esteem (ACME 2008) when a problem has been solved. Key mathematical reasoning processes such as spotting patterns, applying logic, making predictions and general statements can empower children to think creatively and originally. The National Curriculum (DfE 2013) states: 'A high-quality mathematics education therefore provides a foundation for understanding the world, the ability to reason mathematically, an appreciation of the beauty and power of mathematics, and a sense of enjoyment and curiosity about the subject' (p. 3).

In the light of these arguments for the central place of mathematics in the curriculum, it is worth considering the focus of mathematics you have experienced in your own schooling. It may be possible to identify whether mathematics was presented as a valuable subject with fascinating ideas to explore or as a powerful basis to learning in other subjects and in everyday life. Most versions of the curriculum quite rightly include both and present mathematics as a subject itself and as part of purposeful cross-curricular work. As a new teacher, you will need to consider the importance of both aspects of mathematics in the curriculum.

The Content of the Mathematics Curriculum

Given then that mathematics has a valuable place in the early years and primary curriculum, what should be the content of the mathematics curriculum? The curriculum content requirements are listed within age-related Key Stages in, for example, the Statutory Framework for the Early Years Foundation Stage (DfE 2012) and the National Curriculum (DfE 2013). Both provide outlines of the stages of learning expected for each year group from the early years, and then Year 1 to Year 6. The staging of the content is based on the view that mathematics is a set of knowledge and skills, which is generally hierarchical. It is possible to draw expected lines of progression in children's learning. For example, children might be expected to learn about numbers up to 10 before larger numbers. They generally develop strategies to add smaller numbers and build on these strategies to help them to add larger numbers. However, mathematical learning might not always develop in a linear fashion. Children often develop a fascination for large numbers before they develop a secure understanding of smaller ones. They might learn to read the time on a digital clock if this is what they are used to at home, rather than an analogue clock. Learning is not easy to anticipate and the stages in any curriculum can only act as guidance.

There are two main ways of considering the key mathematics that all children should learn before they leave primary school and therefore what should make up the content of the mathematics curriculum. First, mathematics can be seen as a set of particular ideas or concepts, calculation skills and facts to be introduced to children, which can be listed specifically. For example, children learn about number, place value, addition, subtraction, multiplication and division. They learn to identify shapes and their properties and use the language of position. They are introduced to the measures of time, turn, length, area, capacity, volume and mass. They learn about the language, units, equipment and skills of measurement. They learn to collect data, represent it clearly and interrogate it to answer questions. Although the detail and expectation for children at each stage of the primary phase might be contested, these are clearly important mathematical ideas. They will both underpin children's adult life and enable them to appreciate mathematics itself. This listing of key ideas in a staged way can be seen, for example, in the programmes of study in the National Curriculum (DfE 2013).

An alternative way of considering the content of the mathematics curriculum is in terms of the skills of problem solving and mathematical thinking, often called mathematical reasoning. Here the curriculum is defined not only in terms of the calculation strategies, say of addition, but also the skills needed to know when it is necessary to add to solve a problem. These skills involve children in learning how to solve problems by thinking carefully about what is being asked, choosing operations, performing them accurately and then finding solutions. For example, they might consider problems involved with working out percentages in a shop sale. They also investigate open-ended activities, exploring examples systematically, looking for patterns, making predictions and reaching their own generalisations. Some children might state general statements using algebra, others more simply in everyday language. They then reflect on why the general statement is true. For example, they might explore how many matches would take place in a football league involving four teams. They then might consider a league with five or six teams, spot a pattern and a general rule that would enable them to work out the number of matches for a league with any number of teams. Children are therefore asked to be mathematicians (Alexander 2009), in that they are required to explore ideas, reach their own generalisations and communicate their arguments as they solve problems. They develop the distinct skills of mathematical reasoning. The problems and investigations might be both set in the real world and within mathematics itself. This view of the curriculum relates to the idea of Freudenthal (1991) that mathematics is a human activity. When we learn it we are actively reinventing the subject for ourselves.

The National Curriculum (DfE 2013) rests on three aims. The first states that children should be taught to be fluent with the main mathematical ideas contained in the curriculum. The other two aims relate to the importance of children being taught to reason mathematically and solve problems.

The National Curriculum for mathematics aims to ensure that all pupils:

become **fluent** in the fundamentals of mathematics, including through varied and frequent practice with increasingly complex problems over time, so that pupils develop conceptual understanding and the ability to recall and apply knowledge rapidly and accurately

reason mathematically by following a line of enquiry, conjecturing relationships and generalisations, and developing an argument, justification or proof using mathematical language

can **solve problems** by applying their mathematics to a variety of routine and non-routine problems with increasing sophistication, including breaking down problems into a series of simpler steps and persevering in seeking solutions.

(DfE 2013 p. 3)

 Case Study 2.1

Consider the following case study:
A class of 6- and 7-year-olds are learning how to add and subtract 9 and 11 from two-digit numbers. The lesson begins with the class counting in 10s from any number such as 7, 17, 27, 37 … forwards and backwards. Then they practise adding 10 to any two-digit number, writing their responses on individual whiteboards and talking in pairs about the fact that the unit digit stays the same. Then the teacher shows them how to add 9 by adding 10 to a two-digit number and then subtracting one. They then try some examples where they add or subtract 9. Some children use a number line to help them. They go on to explore how to add and subtract 11 from any two-digit number. They become increasingly fluent in this calculation strategy, increasing in their accuracy, speed and confidence. In the next lesson, their teacher asks the children to apply this strategy. She provides them with a selection of word problems, which require the children to either add or subtract 9 or 11 to find the solution, such as:

Jenny has 28 conkers. She collects 9 more. How many does she have altogether?
There are 30 children in a class. 11 of them are boys. How many are girls?

The class talk together, discussing how they will know whether each problem requires them to add or subtract. Then they work in pairs to solve the problems, using the calculation strategy they have learnt previously. In these lessons, the teacher provides a balance between directly teaching calculation strategies and challenging the children to apply these strategies to solve problems by reasoning about the context of each problem. In this way the children address the three aims of the National Curriculum.

Recent key documents (such as Ofsted 2012) have recognised that problem solving does not have significant status in the classroom. What should be the place of problem solving and reasoning in the curriculum? In some cases this is a separate area of mathematics. Some schools choose to have a specific day in the week or week in the term devoted to solving problems and engaging in investigative work to develop children's mathematical reasoning. In this case, the lessons' learning intentions would relate to problem solving and reasoning. Other teachers present all the mathematics in their lessons as an opportunity to solve problems and to engage with mathematical reasoning, therefore although the lesson's learning intention might, for example, relate to learning to add, the lesson would include opportunities to solve problems that include addition. Problem solving and reasoning might be seen as a 'bolt-on' or a 'built-in' approach. Clearly both approaches have advantages. The 'bolt-on' approach allows a direct focus on the specific skills of reasoning and problem solving: spotting of patterns, choice of method, exploration of general statements, proof or disproof of mathematical statements, making predictions, explaining thinking. The 'built-in' approach presents mathematics as a dynamic process where every area of mathematics is open to investigation. It does not lend itself easily to tight objectives and may be more time-consuming and more difficult to manage. However, it does offer children opportunities to experience mathematics as a mathematician.

Research by Nunes et al. (2009) suggests that children's ability to reason mathematically is at least as important as their knowledge of arithmetic, or the more closed content areas of mathematics, in terms of their success in Key Stages 2 and 3.

A curriculum based on reasoning and problem solving would include, for example, solving real-life and mathematical problems, presented conventionally in words or unconventionally as a picture or a statement to explore, and which are complex and have more than one solution, and undertaking puzzles and investigations that are open-ended and allow children to choose their own methods and direction. This sort of curriculum requires children to engage with mathematical reasoning, to provide mathematical arguments to convince others and to seek answers to problems with curiosity and perseverance.

Understanding Mathematics

Finally, this section will discuss ideas about what it means to understand mathematics. This is designed to enable you to critically evaluate the curriculum in the classroom and to clarify your aim for the children you teach. Ofsted (2012) called for a focus on teaching mathematics to promote understanding, in contrast to teaching to promote performance in tests:

> While the best teaching developed pupils' conceptual understanding alongside their fluent recall of knowledge, and confidence in problem solving, too much teaching concentrated on the acquisition of disparate skills that enabled pupils to pass tests and examinations but did not equip them for the next stage of education, work and life. (Ofsted 2012: 9)

What does it mean to understand mathematics? Skemp (1989) provided a useful model to consider what it means to understand mathematics. He used an analogy of walking around a city to define what he termed instrumental understanding and relational understanding. In an unfamiliar city, a walker might learn one route between two places. This might be an effective route but if the walker takes a wrong turn or meets with an obstruction, they have no alternative way. The route only works with exactly the same starting point and destination. Skemp described this sort of understanding as instrumental. Children with instrumental understanding in mathematics might be able to recall facts such as number bonds or carry out a particular mathematical process such as the standard method of addition, but their understanding is limited to a specific type of question. Conversely, in a familiar city, a walker can take any of a number of routes. They have a mental map of interconnecting pathways. Given an obstruction, they can find an alternative route and can travel between any starting point or destination. Skemp called this a relational understanding. In mathematics children with a relational understanding, say of division, can recognise when they need to divide and choose a method that suits the particular problem. They can provide a justification for their choice of method. They can use the method flexibly and work backwards and forwards along this method. Skemp explains that in some cases children need to develop an instrumental understanding of ideas but that relational understanding is what teachers themselves should have and should promote in children.

The National Curriculum uses terms similar to Skemp's (1989) instrumental and relational understanding. The first aim of the curriculum states that all children:

> become fluent in the fundamentals of mathematics, including through varied and frequent practice with increasingly complex problems over time, so that pupils develop conceptual understanding and the ability to recall and apply knowledge rapidly and accurately. (DfE 2013: 3)

The curriculum values procedural fluency. This means that it is designed to encourage children to be confident in their use of number. It promotes rapid and accurate recall of number bonds. For example, the curriculum aims for children to memorise accurately pairs of numbers that add up to 10, and use these to remember pairs of numbers that add up to 100 or 10,000 or 1. Children can use mental and written calculation procedures that are quick, accurate and efficient. They also learn other mathematical procedures such as how to construct shapes, measure and draw graphs. The programmes of study set out the procedures and facts to be learnt in each year group and the aim of the National Curriculum emphasises the importance of practice in these procedures.

Procedural fluency is linked to conceptual understanding, which is similar to Skemp's relational understanding. Conceptual understanding includes comprehension of mathematical ideas such as even and odd, multiply, average and prime. It enables children to work flexibly, solving non-routine problems and to work backwards through a problem, when they are given the answer and must find the corresponding question. Children can explain their thinking and their understanding of mathematical principles that underpin the procedures they use. This enables them to solve problems that are presented unconventionally.

 Case Study 2.2

Consider the following case study:
Two 8-year-old children are calculating:

$$
\begin{array}{r}
7\ 5^4{}^12 \\
-1\ 2\ 6 \\
\hline
6\ 2\ 6
\end{array}
$$

Each child works through the calculation quickly and accurately, using the decomposition method. Their teacher asks them to explain their method. The first child, Joe, explains the procedure. He was not able to subtract 6 from 2, so crossed out the 5 to make it a 4 and then subtracted 6 from 12. He wrote down a 6 in the column on the left. He then subtracted 2 from 4 in the next column and wrote down a 2. Finally, he subtracted 1 from 7, writing a 6 in the last column on the left. He was not able to explain why he crossed off the 5 to make it a 4. He explained that this was the method his previous teacher had taught him to use. His teacher judged him to have procedural fluency, but little conceptual understanding. In the next few lessons Joe made some errors with the calculation method, as he was relying on his memory. The second boy, Dean, explained his method using different language for each column, for example referring to the 5 as 50. He explained that as he was unable to subtract 6 from 2, he had changed one of his tens into ten units. He demonstrated this using hundreds, tens and units resources. This had left him with four tens or 40 in the tens column and 12 in the units column. He was then able to complete the calculation, subtracting 6 from 12, 20 from 40 and 100 from 700. The teacher assessed him as having conceptual understanding of the place value behind the method and procedural fluency of the method itself. Dean was able to progress quickly to subtracting larger numbers using the same method.

In summary, it is important for new teachers to consider what they think are the most important areas of mathematics which they would like to ensure children learn in the primary years, and the nature of mathematical understanding they hope to promote. Not only will this help you to interpret observations and experiences you have in the classroom, it will also enable you to articulate your own principles of effective teaching and learning in mathematics. However, this involves you in considering your own beliefs and understanding with some honesty.

Although dated, Skemp's ideas about understanding in mathematics are still influential today and can be seen as relating to the National Curriculum's focus on both procedural fluency and conceptual understanding. Both of these are important for children's learning. A child with strong fluency will remember facts and calculate confidently. A child with conceptual understanding will recognise when to use these facts and calculation procedures, and will have a deep understanding and appreciation of the subject. Try to identify opportunities in the classroom for both procedural fluency and conceptual understanding.

The State of the Art in Pedagogy

This section will describe and analyse some of the contemporary approaches to mathematics. There will be a consideration of the use of mathematical connections and of approaches to presenting the curriculum to children through teaching inputs and the use of mathematical play and activities.

Making Connections

The National Curriculum states that mathematics is a highly connected subject. Mathematical ideas are indeed characterised by connections (Askew et al. 1997; Haylock 2014; Skemp 1989). They are often connected to each other. Addition and subtraction are connected as they are inverse operations. Multiplication links to addition as it can be represented as repeated addition. One idea can be represented in a number of ways. For example, fractions, decimals and percentages allow the same number fact to be expressed in different ways. We can think about the number sentence 5 – 3 as connecting, for example, the problems: What is the difference between 5 and 3? How much more than 3 is 5? How many is 5 take away 3? A further feature of mathematics is that it involves compressing information (Gray 2008) into shorthand and often abstract representations. 5 – 3 can represent many situations: 5 children are in a group, 3 of them go out to play, how many are left? What is the difference in height between a tower made of 5 bricks and one made of 3 bricks?

Although it might be possible to list the requirements for children's learning in stages in the curriculum, children do not necessarily learn a mathematical idea once, in one form, before moving on to something more complex. They need to experience ideas in different forms and contexts in order to have conceptual understanding. For example, ¾ could be experienced as part of a 2D shape, ¾ of a set of objects, a number on a number line, or 3 pizzas shared between 4 hungry people. All of these are important in order to gain a full conceptual understanding of ¾ itself. Children need to explore connections between ¾ in each context.

Research by Askew et al. (1997) explored the characteristics of effective teachers of numeracy, grouping teachers by their beliefs or orientations and measuring the learning of children in their classes to identify those who were most effective. They found that the most effective teachers typically demonstrated what they called a connectionist orientation. They tended to use teaching approaches that reinforced connections between areas of mathematics, and encouraged children to express their own reasoning and ways of mental calculation. They used the mathematics lesson to explore the mathematical area with children and to assess the children's understanding, making connections to previous learning.

The Teaching Input

In most classrooms, a daily mathematics lesson includes teaching input from the teacher. In an early years setting such as a Nursery or Reception classroom, this might be a very short session with the children grouped on the carpet and the teacher sitting on a chair. This session might include singing number rhymes, action songs and counting on large number tracks. With older classes, the teacher will often stand at a whiteboard or an interactive whiteboard (IWB), sometimes for a longer period of time. Often this is towards the beginning of the lesson, and then followed by short mini plenaries during the lesson and a longer plenary at the end. This practice often dates from the National Numeracy Strategy (NNS) (DfEE 1999) guidance to provide direct and interactive teaching, usually to the whole class. Sometimes there might also be direct teaching of a group of children.

There is a sense that children will not discover mathematics themselves or if they do, that this will not be time-efficient. The teacher takes responsibility for identifying the mathematics to be learnt in the lesson, expressing this in terms of a learning objective and sometimes success criteria, and directly teaching it, generally to the whole class. The teaching input provides the sort of scaffolding that children require when working beyond the areas where they are able to be independent. The practice contrasts with earlier experiences of children before the NNS, where they might have worked through a textbook individually at their own pace with little guidance from the teacher unless they encountered difficulties.

The picture of the teacher at the board explaining ideas to children might suggest a 'chalk and talk', behaviourist or transmission approach. In this scenario, the teacher understands the mathematics themselves and transmits it to the children. The children's role is quite passive during the teaching input. However, such a practice is not seen as direct and interactive teaching. Following the NNS guidance (DfEE 1999), teachers have been encouraged to use the teaching input to increase children's understanding of mathematics. The session is required to be lively and move the children's learning on, with suitable pace. Sometimes the children have their own whiteboards and pens and engage with tasks during the session. Teachers use visual and mental images to explain ideas to children. For example, they might have a 100 square on the IWB or a digital photograph of 2D shapes taken from around the school. They model the mathematical tasks that might be included in the children's work later in the lesson. They think aloud as they engage with the tasks, modelling mathematical reasoning. Children are asked to explain their ideas and strategies. They will often move to the front of the class and demonstrate their methods. The input is interactive. This might involve teachers in using questions to enable children to engage in high-quality talk. Often teachers will ask children to discuss their responses to open questions in pairs before having a group discussion. This should not be a passive time for the children.

An effective teaching input would demonstrate the features of a connectionist orientation identified by Askew et al. (1997). Ideas are represented in different ways and contexts to encourage exploration of connections and conceptual understanding as well as procedural fluency. Teaching is connected to the children's previous learning and to their interests and contexts. However, new teachers might consider the challenge of purposefully engaging the whole class, with a wide range of abilities, for a lengthy period of time.

Children's Activities and Play

The building of procedural fluency and conceptual understanding is not only addressed in the teaching input of the mathematics lesson. Children are usually asked to complete activities or given opportunities for play, in groups, pairs or as individuals, as part of the mathematics lesson. The nature of learning in this part of the lesson will now be considered.

In an early years setting, a Nursery or Reception class, and sometimes with older children, much time is set aside for children's play. The teaching input is relatively short and the children are given opportunity for child-initiated or adult-initiated activities. For example, children might be offered time to play in a role-play area set up as a cafe, hospital or building site. A number of related resources are provided and the children are given time to explore them. It is not possible to predict the sort of learning that might occur in, for example, a cafe role-play area. The children might act out setting the table, giving orders, arranging food on a plate or paying the bill. Many of these will include mathematical learning, but there will also be learning in other areas (of course, the children might choose to use the cafe area in a completely unrelated and unexpected way). The teacher uses observation and discussion to assess learning as it happens and to correct misconceptions. These observations can then feed back to inform the teacher's planning of future whole-class carpet sessions or play activities. Play activities are rich in learning but can be difficult to predict (Gifford 2005).

Teachers also use adult-directed play activities where children are invited to work with a teacher using play resources but for a specific objective. For example, the teacher might ask a small group of children to order some birthday cards showing numerals from 1 to 10 or to set the table for a tea party for a given number of toys. Here the teacher is specifically teaching and assessing an area of mathematics. The learning may be playful, but it is directed. Again, the teacher assesses the children's learning, challenging misconceptions and supporting progression, and uses this information to inform future planning.

In Key Stage 1 and 2 classrooms, more structured activities are provided for children during the mathematics lesson, although some teachers of older children use mathematical play. Activities set for older children often present mathematical ideas to children through resources or manipulatives and visual images. These will be discussed in the next section. Children engage with tasks related to the learning intention. These tasks might be differentiated and provided for children sitting in ability groupings. Or they might be open-ended tasks provided for all children, perhaps sitting in mixed-ability groups, where they proceed through the task at different rates. Some tasks are labelled low-threshold, high-ceiling tasks, which allow children to progress through to different levels of complexity. The teacher then supports groups and individual children, and uses mini plenaries and the final plenary to provide more direct teaching and to address any misconceptions.

Innovation

This section will analyse how the teaching of mathematics might be further developed to ensure children's full understanding of what is such a fascinating subject. There will be a consideration of the use of manipulatives and visual images, and the role of mathematical dialogue in mathematical learning.

Use of Manipulatives and Visual Images

This chapter has discussed an argument for the rationale for mathematics as an abstract method of reasoning and communicating ideas. However, the abstract nature of mathematics can make it seem a difficult subject to learn, and several writers have argued for the need to base early mathematics learning in real and meaningful contexts for children (Atkinson 1992; Austin 2007; Hughes 1986: Worthington and Carruthers 2003). Therefore, mathematical ideas are often presented to children through concrete resources or manipulatives, visual and mental images to help children to talk and think mathematically. For example, in a primary classroom it might be possible to observe children playing with sand and capacity containers, adding the score of two dice when playing a board game, making 3D shapes, counting multi-link cubes and using coins (Rowland et al. 2009). They might engage with visual images such as hundred squares, number lines and place value cards, which are designed to embody specific mathematical ideas. The children manipulate these physically in order to help them to create mental images (Drew and Hansen 2007).

The argument for using such resources or manipulatives to support children's learning can be traced, for example, back to Bruner (1996). He suggested that resources can scaffold children's learning, providing support that can be withdrawn when it is no longer needed. He identified three phases for children's learning: the enactive, which involves physical action; the iconic, which involves pictorial images; and the symbolic, which involves mental manipulation. For example, a child might throw a dice and move a counter along a number track as part of a board game, then use an empty number line to perform an addition by counting on, and then add numbers by counting on in their head. The phases overlap but they do present a useful model for children's activities.

In particular, resources can be used to ensure conceptual understanding as well as procedural fluency in key ideas of place value. Our number system is based on ideas of grouping and equivalency. For example, 10 units is equivalent to one ten, 10 tens is equivalent to one hundred. Exploring straws in bundles of 10 and place-value resources designed to show units, tens and hundreds can enable children to explore these ideas. The teacher can also use visual images to explain, for example, equivalent fractions or to help children to make sense of word problems, a technique often used in Singapore (Oftsed 2011).

Haylock (2014) identified the need to present mathematical ideas to children through language, symbols, pictures and concrete situations. Of course, the inclusion of a range of resources and images does not in itself ensure that children understand mathematical ideas, but each representation allows children to explore a mathematical idea in a different context and so can help them to develop procedural fluency and conceptual understanding.

Mathematical Dialogue

Williams (2008) identified a growing concern (Alexander 2009; Ofsted 2008) about the missed opportunities in some classrooms to use mathematical dialogue to support and challenge children's learning. The role of mathematics as a language has long been acknowledged (Smith 2004, for example) and there has been a focus on mathematical vocabulary and the need for teachers to teach this directly and model its use accurately (Ofsted 2012). Williams called for the need for teachers to reflect on the role of effective teacher–child dialogue that goes beyond the initiate, respond, feedback approach, to a model of the sort of dialogue mathematicians might themselves participate in. This might involve lengthier contributions from children, explaining their thinking, being asked to provide convincing arguments, choosing their own examples and commenting constructively on the ideas of others (Williams 2008).

Ryan and Williams (2007) provide a useful model of this sort of dialogue in the mathematics classroom. They discuss examples of talk which begin with the consideration of an error or difficult step in mathematics with a group of children. The children are asked to give their views offering a justification. The teacher facilitates the discussion, allowing children to articulate, consider, challenge and reformulate their views. The discussion might be uncomfortable when children disagree, but this should mirror the work of mathematicians and be undertaken in a sensitive and safe ethos.

In each part of the lesson there should be opportunities to model mathematical arguments and to encourage children to convince others and explain their reasoning. For example, children might be asked to consider general statements, such as all prime numbers are odd, or the total of an odd number and an even number is always even, and discuss why they think they might be true or false. In this way they engage with simple ideas of mathematical proof, exploring arguments to justify their thinking. This type of mathematical dialogue promotes teachers' and children's accurate use of vocabulary and language, and discussion of strategies and methods to solve mathematical problems.

Mathematics lessons and activities should offer opportunities in the classroom for high-quality mathematical dialogue. There may be barriers to such dialogue. Timetabling, tight learning intentions, teachers' subject knowledge and confidence can all have an impact. Look out for opportunities in the classroom for paired talk between children, group work and opportunities to talk to adults about mathematics. Consider how this supports the children's mathematical reasoning, their procedural fluency and conceptual understanding.

Creativity

How does the primary mathematics curriculum contribute to children's creativity? We have seen that the mathematics curriculum promotes both fluency with mathematical concepts and facts, and the essential skills of problem solving and reasoning. Both of these contribute to creativity, but especially the latter. Children are introduced to specific skills of working systematically, spotting patterns, predicting, identifying general rules and providing arguments to convince others of their reasoning. Children should be supported in solving a range of problems and recording ideas innovatively. The mathematics curriculum can challenge them to refine their thinking by offering them different contexts and problems to consider, and opportunities to explain their reasoning. Children should make connections between ideas, looking for links that might not be immediately obvious. These skills lend themselves to creativity.

The rationale for mathematics draws heavily on its use in problem solving, and this chapter has suggested that mathematics should include both problems set in purposeful cross-curricular contexts and problems set within mathematics itself. Solving intriguing problems and puzzles, often presented in non-routine forms, challenges children to be creative. This is particularly true when the mathematical challenges have more than one solution, or perhaps no solution at all, and where there is an ethos in the classroom where the method of solving the problem is at least as valuable as the solution itself.

Consider how conceptual understanding, with its building of connections and experiences of mathematical reasoning, contributes to children's creativity.

Assessment

This section will consider key issues relating to how teachers assess children's learning in mathematics in order to ensure progression. If teachers aim to support and challenge children to understand mathematics in a conceptual and procedural way, then assessment procedures need to address both these sorts of understanding.

We have seen that mathematical learning can be viewed as a process of making connections. These connections can be between ideas or between representations of the same idea. The most crucial connection that teachers make is between something new and something that is already understood by the children (Ausubel 1968). The process of 'assessment for learning' where teachers monitor current learning is therefore essential in planning the following lesson.

However, assessment for learning in mathematics is often about identifying misunderstanding as well as understanding. Mathematics is a subject where misconceptions and errors limit understanding and are often deep-rooted. Consider, for example, the following rules which children might be taught:

- Multiply by ten by adding a zero
- When we multiply, the number always gets larger

These rules lead to misunderstanding: for example, 3.6×10 is not 3.60. A child who multiplies by ten by adding a zero does not necessarily understand the relative value of the columns in our place-value system, which underpins their later learning of decimal fractions. In a further example, $6 \times \frac{1}{2} = 3$. When we multiply by a fraction, the answer is smaller.

The importance of teachers' identification and challenge of children's misconceptions has been acknowledged for some time as a key feature of assessment for learning (for example, Ofsted 2012). Teachers' ability to do this effectively depends, of course, on their subject knowledge and on their own procedural fluency and conceptual understanding. It seems that teachers need to know each area of mathematics in many ways and also consider what it is to know it incorrectly in many ways.

Therefore, the requirements of teachers are, first, to be aware of common errors and misconceptions and to teach in such a way as to avoid these or directly challenge them. Second, teachers are asked continually to assess their class in order to identify misconceptions as soon as they occur (Ofsted 2008). Assessment strategies usually involve teachers in observing children at play or working practically, entering into discussion with the children and marking written work. The use of the plenary or mini plenary is then key in addressing the misconception and supporting progression in learning. A classroom ethos of willingness to try new ideas and to see errors as constructive is vital, with a focus on talk and children's explanations for their methods and reasoning. As we have seen, Ryan and Williams (2007) use errors as a basis for high-quality talk where children articulate their thinking and provide reasons and examples. These can then be challenged or supported by other children or their teacher.

As a core subject, there is a requirement to assess children's learning against the Early Learning Goals for the Early Years Foundation Stage (DfE 2012) and the National Curriculum (DfE 2013) for older children. A range of assessment strategies is required for this. Procedural fluency might be assessed through normal written classroom activities. However, teachers may need to spend more time asking questions and listening to children to assess their conceptual understanding. Problem solving and mathematical reasoning are typically lengthy, unpredictable and messy. Children need time to explore ideas and may not record these suitably for an audience until towards the end of their thinking. Conclusions might not be reached until an hour after the lesson has finished, or a day or a week later. Reasoning mathematically requires children to communicate their thinking and reasoning, and to convince others. This can be difficult in speech and even harder in writing. We have also discussed the need for mathematics to be set some of the time in purposeful cross-curricular contexts. Nationally set test papers cannot recreate the meaningful experience children might have on a school trip, in their school grounds or when investigating a particular topic or theme. Therefore, it is important to use a range of assessment strategies, observing, discussing and marking written responses to mathematics in different contexts and tasks to assess children's learning. These assessments can then be mapped on to the Early Learning Goals and the National Curriculum.

Conclusion

This chapter has discussed the unique place of mathematics in the curriculum, as a fascinating and powerful subject in its own right and as a way of thinking and communicating that underpins learning in other areas. Mathematics provides skills necessary to thrive and flourish in an adult life and contributes to creativity. It is a subject that values elegance in its arguments and the beauty of pattern in number and shape. This chapter has argued that the mathematics curriculum should include both the specific content areas of mathematics and the essential, creative processes of problem solving and reasoning mathematically.

Williams (2008) found that mathematics is still a subject that adults dislike and are prepared to admit to failing in. This attitude is easily passed on to children. It is a subject where a focus on a right or wrong answer can promote anxiety. Mathematics does not have to be presented in this way.

Freudenthal (1991) warned against teachers presenting a ready-made mathematics, where children are introduced to procedures and algorithms in a set way, and by which they are judged. For example, a teacher might demonstrate a ready-made method for long division which the children then practise several times, dividing different sets of numbers. Success in the lesson will depend on the number of correct answers. Where their experiences are not based on understanding, the children rely on memory. This chapter has aimed to challenge the idea that mathematics is only to do with memorising procedures, although these are valuable in their own right. Children have a right to both procedural fluency and conceptual understanding of mathematics.

Mathematical understanding has been the key idea of this chapter. It provides a way of analysing current and innovative approaches in the classroom, and ideas about creativity and assessment procedures. This chapter has aimed to challenge readers to reflect on their practice in terms of the extent to which they promote procedural fluency and conceptual understanding in the children they teach, and to begin to articulate their own principles of mathematics education. Use these questions to explore your thinking.

Reflection Points

1. What are your beliefs about the rationale for the place of mathematics in the curriculum and the sort of content to be covered within mathematics?
2. What sort of understanding in mathematics will you develop in the children you teach? Do you have both procedural fluency and conceptual understanding of the mathematics in the primary curriculum?
3. What are the features of teaching mathematics for understanding? How can your organisation of mathematical learning, your teaching of creative mathematical thinking and your assessment of mathematics promote and support children's understanding of mathematical reasoning and problem solving, as well as the procedures and facts listed in the curriculum?

Further Reading

Barmby, P., Harries, T., Higgins, S. and Suggate, J. (2009) *Primary Mathematics: Teaching for Understanding*. Maidenhead: McGraw-Hill.

Haylock, D. (2014) *Mathematics Explained for Primary Teachers*, 5th edn. London: SAGE.

Rickard, C. (2013) *Essential Primary Mathematics*. Maidenhead: McGraw-Hill.

Ryan, J. and Williams, J. (2007) *Children's Mathematics 4–15*. Maidenhead: McGraw-Hill.

Taylor, H. and Harris, A. (eds) (2013) *Learning and Teaching Mathematics 0–8*. London: SAGE.

Thompson, I. (ed.) (2010) *Issues in Teaching Numeracy in Primary Schools*, 2nd edn. Buckingham: OUP.

References

ACME (Advisory Committee on Mathematics Education) (2008) *Mathematics in Primary Years*. London: ACME.

Alexander, R. (2009) *Towards a New Primary Curriculum*. Cambridge: Cambridge University Press.

Anghileri, J. (2006) *Teaching Number Sense*, 2nd edn. London: Continuum.

Askew, M., Brown, M., Johnson, D., Rhodes, V. and William, D. (1997) *Effective Teaching of Numeracy*. London: King's College London.

Atkinson, S. (ed.) (1992) *Mathematics with Reason*. London: Hodder and Stoughton.

Austin, R. (ed.) (2007) *Letting the Outside In*. Stoke-on-Trent: Trentham Books.

Ausubel, D. (1968) *Educational Psychology: A Cognitive View*. New York: Holt, Rinehart and Winston.

Bruner, J. (1996) *The Culture of Education*. Cambridge, MA: Belknap Press.

DfE (Department for Education) (2012) *Statutory Framework for the Early Years Foundation Stage*. London: DfE.

DfE (Department for Education) (2013) *Mathematics Programmes of Study: Key Stages 1 and 2. National Curriculum in England*. London: DfE.

DfEE (Department for Education and Employment) (1999) *The National Numeracy Strategy: Framework for Teaching Mathematics from Reception to Year 6*. London: DfEE.

Drew, D. and Hansen, A. (2007) *Using Resources to Support Mathematical Thinking*. Exeter: Learning Matters.

Freudenthal, H. (1991) *Revisiting Mathematics Education*. Dordrecht: Kluwer Academic.

Gifford, S. (2005) *Teaching Mathematics 3–5*. London: Continuum.

Gray, E. (2008) 'Compressing the counting process', in I. Thompson (ed.), *Teaching and Learning Early Number*, 2nd edn. Buckingham: OUP.

Haylock, D. (2014) *Mathematics Explained for Primary Teachers*, 5th edn. London: SAGE.

Hughes, M. (1986) *Children and Number*. Oxford: Blackwell.

Nunes, T., Bryant, P., Sylva, K. and Barros, R. (2009) *Development of Maths Capabilities and Confidence in Primary School*. London: DCSF.

Ofsted (Office for Standards in Education) (2008) *Understanding the Score*. London: Ofsted.

Ofsted (Office for Standards in Education) (2011) *Good Practice in Primary Education: Evidence from Twenty Successful Schools*. London: Ofsted.

Ofsted (Office for Standards in Education) (2012) *Mathematics: Made to Measure*. London: Ofsted.

Rowland, T., Turner, F., Thwaites, A. and Huckstep, P. (2009) *Developing Primary Mathematics Teaching*. London: SAGE.

Ryan, J. and Williams, J. (2007) *Children's Mathematics 4–15*. Maidenhead: McGraw-Hill.

Skemp, R. (1989) *Mathematics in the Primary School*. London: Routledge.

Smith, A. (2004) *Making Mathematics Count*. London: HMSO.

Williams, P. (2008) *Independent Review of Mathematics Teaching in Early Years Settings and Primary Schools*. London: DCSF.

Winter, J. (2001) 'Personal, spiritual, moral and cultural issues in teaching mathematics', in P. Gates (ed.), *Issues in Mathematics Teaching*. London: RoutledgeFalmer.

Worthington, M. and Carruthers, E. (2003) *Children's Mathematics: Making Marks, Making Meaning*. London: PCP.

CHAPTER 3

AN INTRODUCTION TO SCIENCE

Judith Roden

Chapter Aims

This chapter will:

- consider the contribution that science can make to children's learning
- examine the relationship between science and other subjects in the primary curriculum
- highlight current and potential practice for teaching and learning in science
- examine the approach of science within the 2014 science national curriculum

---

Introduction to Science

Science is an important part of the primary curriculum, laying the foundations for the development of a scientifically literate society. Science provides opportunities for children to work in groups, exploring, explaining and challenging ideas, reasoning and developing logical thought, planning practical investigations together and drawing conclusions based on evidence, thereby exploring the world in a systematic way. Depending on the way it is taught, science can provide opportunities for children to be creative and can be interesting, exciting and motivating for young learners. Science can arouse curiosity, thereby going further than merely giving them a 'fun' experience. Concerns for individual safety can be addressed through science. Children can benefit from engaging with potentially risky activities, such as when using tea lights or candles indoors or exploring the natural and man-made world around them within controlled, safe outdoor environments. Crucially, this involves having first discussed potential hazards and dangers with each other and with adults, thereby providing an insight into how to keep themselves and others safe in their lives outside school.

In recent years, science has competed for status, time and space in an overcrowded curriculum where significant emphasis has been on numeracy and literacy (Alexander 2010). This situation continues today, but the 2014 Science National Curriculum (DfE 2013) offers hope for change.

What is Science?

Essentially, science consists of two aspects – 'working scientifically' and the wide-ranging, ever-changing body of scientific knowledge. These are reflected both in the 2014 Science National Curriculum at Key Stages 1 and 2 (DfE 2013) and in the Early Years Foundation Stage (DfE 2012) as part of 'Understanding the World'. Working scientifically involves working as a scientist. Traditionally, the skills involved in being scientific are termed science process skills, such as observation, raising questions, planning and carrying out investigations, interpreting data and drawing conclusions. These are fundamental to scientific enquiry. Developing children's understanding of science is also important. Indeed, the recognition that the development of both strands as interdependent aspects of learning is crucial in the development of the young scientist.

The purpose of science, as set out in the 2014 Science National Curriculum (DfE, 2013), clearly justifies its place as an important aspect of primary education and reinforces the importance of pupils developing the skills of a scientist:

> A high quality science education provides the foundations for understanding the world through the specific disciplines of biology, chemistry and physics. Science has changed our lives and is vital to the world's future prosperity, and all pupils should be taught essential aspects of knowledge and methods, processes and uses of science. Through building up a body of key foundational knowledge and concepts, pupils should be encouraged to recognise the power of rational explanation and develop a sense of excitement and curiosity about natural phenomena. They should be encouraged to understand how science can be used to explain what is occurring, predicting how things will behave, and analyse causes. (DfE 2013: 3)

Science is part of 'Understanding the World' in the EYFS curriculum (DfE 2012) where children regularly explore the world as young scientists. Here children look for similarities and differences in places, objects, materials and living things. They talk about the features of their own immediate environment, how environments might vary from one another and they make observations about animals and plants and explain why some things occur, and talk about changes.

The above view of the purpose of science reflects the importance of science for all. Coupled with this is the economic well-being of the country that requires well-qualified scientists to take up science-related occupations when pupils leave full-time education. A further strand evident here relates to the importance of developing pupils' interest and enthusiasm for science. *How* science is taught is important if pupils are to develop a life-long passion for things scientific, even if they do not later take up a science-related occupation.

The new science curriculum orders (DfE 2013) present explicitly the need for pupils to 'work scientifically' as they develop their understanding of science. Specifying explicit content in this way holds both advantages and disadvantages. Advantages relate to teachers knowing what content to teach. This has not always been the case. In recent years, less confident and less informed teachers have often adopted and relied upon prescriptive and monotonous schemes that lacked depth and provided a plethora of worksheets involving a limited range of facts to be learned at the expense of more open-ended exploration and investigation where pupils had much more ownership and involvement in the direction of their learning in science (Ofsted 2008, 2011, 2013). Disadvantages, however, relate to the real danger that schools will teach the minimum requirement for each year group and go no further. It is important to recognise that the programmes of study are intended to provide a minimum expectation. Schools can choose to extend pupil learning further if they wish to do so.

Science has a major role in developing essential 'thinking skills', especially reasoning and logical thought, that are central to children's learning. Immersion in science involves critique and argumentation (Osborne 2010). Scientific knowledge moves forward as scientists present their ideas for external scrutiny and challenge. Science in primary school should reflect the way scientists work in real life.

Crucially, study of science is important for developing a scientifically literate population. This should be one of the long-term aims of education and must start from the beginning of formal education (Harlen 2008: 13; Webb 2007). This means that individuals have a grasp of scientific ideas and principles and can take part in intelligent discussions about issues related to science as part of their role as a scientifically literate citizen (Harlen and Qualter 2009).

Creativity

Science is a creative subject, but often it is not seen as such because of a perception that science is about facts: a body of unchanging knowledge to be learned. However, this view:

does not acknowledge the tentative nature of scientific theories and the creativity of sci-entific discoveries, which broaden our understanding of the universe, changing the way we think and the way we view the world ... the reason for this seeming anomaly is that creativity is not only difficult to define and is used synonymously with words such as originality, but also has different meanings in science and technology than when used in the context of the arts. (Johnson 2009: 77)

In science, ideas are created through rational but imaginative thought that leads to improved understanding of the world. Scientists are creative when they construct theories, analogies, models and when they articulate them to view the world in new ways and in testing them (Newton and Newton 2009: 46). Reflecting the way scientists work and engaging children-as-scientists has the potential to foster creativity by involving them in 'hands-on' and 'minds-on' activities that involve exploration and problem solving. Such activities help learners to understand the connections between things in their world. Children's explanations are often not in line with accepted sci-entific thinking, but are often intuitive, amazing and undeniably creative. Asking children to give an explanation for an event or scientific phenomenon may lead to the creation of a new idea or misconception. Research suggests that misconceptions are evident across the whole spectrum of science that is studied in the primary school (see, for example, Allen 2010).

Imagination can add to a child's self-reliance and autonomy but the teacher's role is important here. Children need opportunities in science contexts that foster empow-ering, imaginative thought. Although teachers might support the making of mental connections towards understanding, the connecting is something the children must do for themselves (Newton and Newton 2009: 47). However, although many misconcep-tions can be strongly held, they can be challenged through discussion and through appropriate practical activity.

The Relationship Between Science and Other Subjects of the Primary Curriculum

Linking science with other subjects might reduce overcrowding where subjects com-pete for status. Science is especially well placed for this. The idea 'learning through science' has a long history.

English

Practical science has long been recognised as a vehicle for speaking and listening where children can 'think together' (Mercer et al. 2004; Ofsted 2013; Osborne 2010; Webb 2007), as well as for facilitating key group skills such as cooperation and com-munication with others. Providing children with the opportunity to engage in dialogue with peers and adults is important in developing children's ideas about science, 'starting where the children are'. It is very important for children to discuss things scientific to explore, share and explain the ideas they have about the world around them to expose and offer the opportunity to challenge firmly held unscientific ideas about science.

Writing is also important in science and so has a role in developing children's ability to write in different ways. Science also offers opportunity to make use of non-fiction texts in a relevant scientific context.

Mathematics

Application of mathematics is fundamental to many aspects of science, including, for example, using scales and measuring accurately when using balances to measure mass and weight, taking measurements of temperature using a thermometer or measuring forces with a newton meter, or capacity and volume in litres. Computational skills are necessary when pupils are involved in manipulating any data, especially in scientific enquiry that involves taking a number of measurements and then finding an average to increase the reliability and validity of findings.

History and Geography

The relationship between science and geography is reflected in the 2014 National Curriculum in relation to observation of weather and changes of the seasons. Science and history too have a reciprocal relationship, not only because of the potential study of scientists from the past such as Isaac Newton but also because of the fact that many science process skills are important in history, such as collecting and using evidence.

Physical Education

Awareness of the parts of the body, both internal and external, is important in both physical education (PE) and science. Linking science and PE in relation to exercise and healthy eating is a logical development for future practice.

Art

Observational drawings of naturally occurring and man-made things help children to develop observational skills and simultaneously develop drawing skills. In science, recording through a series of drawings of similar things such as seashells or, for example, flowers, leaves, twigs or winged seeds from different trees, can help children not only to see detail that might otherwise have gone unnoticed, but also help them to appreciate the variety of life or develop understanding of how man-made things work.

Design and Technology

Science and technology are important for the UK economy in the competitive global market. The role of science in the 'design' process is important. It is almost impossible to separate some aspects of science from design and technology and vice versa. Early man knew about the properties of the materials around him. Through systematic observation over time he knew that animal hides had specific properties that made them good materials for cutting, shaping and stitching together to make simple clothing. He knew that pieces of bone could be shaped to make simple needles and that the properties of flint made it easy to shape into simple tools and, importantly, that it could be used to light fires. Similarly, artisans solving problems before, during and after the Industrial Revolution knew about their craft through observation, exploration and familiarity with the materials with which they worked. Basic but important scientific process skills were used to develop understanding of simple materials that then led to the design and production of artefacts to solve everyday problems, such as keeping warm. Like very young children, the early technologists may not have been able to *explain*, in exact scientific terms, why known materials had particular properties, but nevertheless the 'craft knowledge' and understanding had been built up and passed down through generations through the use of scientific processes.

In the modern world the testing of streamlined shapes in scientific laboratories enhanced and continues to enhance the quality and performance of motor cars today. Similarly, the development of child car seats, car seatbelts or air-bag technology could not have happened without the rigorous testing of those materials and designs in controlled scientific tests. Here, the interdependence of the two aspects is undeniable. They are like the two sides of a coin. As far as we know, Stone Age man did not 'design' and 'plan' in the way modern technologists would, but neither do very young children today. Young children are not able to write down their ideas; learning largely by trial and error, they 'construct' ideas and plan through practical exploration of their world. Exploration of materials teaches much without instruction and allows children to be creative in their explorations. Design and technology can provide realistic contexts for scientific learning that enable science understanding to be scaffolded (Davies and Howe 2003: 6), thereby helping children to better understand the science, for example air resistance related to parachute or kite making, or flotation and loading of boats.

Practical Work in Science

Science is essentially a practical subject where individuals work together collaboratively to test ideas and develop understanding. Practical work involves a range of activities such as carrying out observational tasks, sorting things into groups, as well as illustrative and investigative activities. Illustrative activities are teacher-directed 'recipe'-type activities characterised by lack of choice by pupils, whilst investigative activities are more child-centred, involving both choice and autonomy. Both are important. Illustrative activities are often used to teach a particular skill, for example developing observational skills or how to use a thermometer or a force meter, or to illustrate a concept such as which metals are attracted to a magnet. They often lead to identical outcomes and are important because the learned and practised skills can be applied later to more open, child-led activities where there is more opportunity for choice. More choice provides ownership, often improves motivation and helps develop autonomy.

The emphasis on children raising their own questions in science and then planning and carrying out their own investigation is fundamental to working scientifically, and making investigative science accessible to all supports provision for diversity and inclusion. More open-ended investigations in science do not have a predetermined, known outcome. Open starting points lead to a variety of solutions with different degrees of complexity and demand.

The 'fair test' investigation which has characterised much practical work is included in the new curriculum as part of working scientifically. However, now there is much more emphasis on other aspects of working scientifically such as observing, sorting and classifying, pattern-finding, surveys, change over time and problem solving which all require to be included, systematically in science teaching at Key Stages 1 and 2.

Children can undertake 'whole' investigations where they make all the decisions, possibly being set the same global question as a starting point for an investigation from which they decide the question to be investigated and how the investigation shall proceed. Groups will respond to the challenges of the task depending on ability and prior experience. Some younger or less able learners may need help from practitioners but nevertheless investigative work allows children to plan their investigation, decide which equipment to use and how results will be collated; they interpret their data and reach conclusions based on the evidence they have collected. Finally, they evaluate their approach, looking to see to what extent their results are reliable and valid, and suggesting ways in which the work might have been improved. Importantly, working scientifically places emphasis on *process* where children explore and manipulate materials and work cooperatively, making decisions together and working towards a common end point.

Undertaking practical work, even in groups, in itself is not enough for the development of understanding of science concepts. Rather than leading to clearer understanding, sometimes carrying out practical work can lead to the development of misconceptions or the reinforcement of wrong ideas (Roden, 2005) and can cause confusion. Care must be taken, therefore, to regularly assess what children know and have learned and to use this information to inform planning to ensure progression and not regression in learning.

State of the Art in the Teaching of Science

Science in English schools has often focused on didactic teaching of scientific principles and content presented out of a recognisable context. This reflects the effect of testing on pedagogy, which has also been noted in other countries (Pearson et al. 2010). Content has often been taught in isolation in a belief that performance in Science National Tests could be enhanced through rote learning and recall rather than based on more active 'hands-on' and 'minds-on' activities. Alexander (2010) calls this 'the test induced regression to a valuing of memorisation and recall over understanding and enquiry' and to a 'pedagogy which rates transmission more important than the pursuit of knowledge in its widest sense' (p. 251). The adoption of a limited range of teaching strategies, lacking in relevance and practical application, reinforced the idea that science is a hard subject. Talking of science in primary schools, Newton (2010: xiii) reported that 'teachers tend to teach scientific vocabulary and facts, and avoid causal explanations and teaching for understanding'. Together this has led to a lack of understanding of scientific concepts and possibly, for some, to unwelcome side-effects in terms of pupils' attitudes towards science.

Every child has a fundamental right to explore, investigate and gain scientific skills and knowledge learning about the big ideas in science (Harlen 2012) and how the world works through practical activity. It is generally believed, however, that some children and teachers have been turned off science in the past because of the perception that there was little room to foster curiosity or for children to develop investigative, questioning and thinking skills because of the emphasis on content and the acquisition of scientific vocabulary. However, this situation was never the intention and this position owes more to the interpretation in practice rather than to the national curriculum itself.

Harlen argues that science should be part of the curriculum for all young people from 5 to 16, but points out, 'it all depends, though, on what and how it is taught' (Harlen 2008: 13). Clearly, teacher attitude towards teaching science is significant here. Although there is some evidence of a recent slight improvement (Tymms et al. 2008: 27), generally primary teachers have lacked confidence in their knowledge and competence to teach science. Although recent initiatives have emphasised the need for creativity in delivery, creative science is thought to pose problems in terms of time, coverage, control, safety and the achievement of learning objectives (Johnson 2009).

Elucidating the strengths and weaknesses of primary school, Ofsted (2013) reported that standards and achievement in science in primary schools were good or better in around three-quarters of the relatively small number of schools visited. The best teachers, they said, put scientific enquiry at the heart of science teaching and set out to sustain pupils' natural curiosity so that they were eager to learn the subject content as well as investigative skills. Best teaching was also characterised by assessment of understanding and skills including analysis and interpretation (Ofsted 2013: 5). Invariably, achievement was highest where pupils were involved in planning, carrying out and evaluating investigations that, in some part, they had suggested themselves. They learned best when they could see how the science they were studying linked to real-world experiences, revealed more about the 'big ideas' in science and connected with and supported learning in other subjects, including English and mathematics. Learning in this fashion was said to engage and enthuse pupils, developing their natural curiosity and motivating them to find out more (Ofsted 2013: 9–10).

Best practice schools made sure that pupils mastered investigative and practical skills that underpin the development of scientific knowledge and could discover for themselves the relevance and usefulness of those ideas. Science achievement was highest when individuals were involved in fully planning, carrying out and evaluating investigations that they had, in some part, suggested themselves. Teachers who coupled good literacy teaching with interesting science contexts helped pupils make good progress in both subjects (Ofsted 2013: 6–7). Explicit connections between science and literacy 'showed clear evidence of better science and literacy outcomes for all pupils. Imaginative teaching allowed pupils to use their science work as a purpose for their reading and writing … there were some exceptions where some pupils and teachers saw science as a "relief" from English and as a subject where pupils did not need to write much' (Ofsted 2013: 10). However, even the best school lessons often lacked sufficient differentiation to allow pupils, especially the more able, to build on their prior learning and make good progress.

Ofsted also found that the best teaching focused on giving each child the time and resources she or he needed to explore and investigate the physical world. Children became engrossed in whatever activity they were doing; teachers capitalised on their interest as they steered activities towards developing children's basic skills (Ofsted 2013: 12). Ofsted recommend that this approach, typical of the approach in the Early Years Foundation Stage, should be extended into Key Stage 1 and beyond.

Choice and Autonomy in Science

Children need some autonomy if they are to act as scientists. Group work is important here. Science for primary children should include practical work with opportunities for children to ask their own questions, and plan and carry out their own investigations to answer those questions. Children should choose equipment, decide what data to collect and how to record as well as interpret data, drawing conclusions whilst providing explanations of their findings.

Evidence suggests though that pupil choice and independence may not feature at all in many primary classrooms. In a small, somewhat limited study, Bullock and Muschamp (2006) investigated the extent to which pupils are involved in decisions that affect their learning and the extent to which they had opportunities to make their own choices. Pupils believed they had no choice or control of activities within core subjects and only a limited choice in the methods that they used in their work. Children frequently described how the activities were given to them by their teacher. Not one child made reference to any negotiation of topics or of having opportunities to select or choose their activities. Indeed, approximately a quarter of the admittedly relatively small groups under study expressed a level of dissatisfaction with the situation (pp. 52–3).

Undoubtedly many teachers find adopting an approach based on children's choice and independence problematic. Johnson (2009) sheds light on this apparent reluctance to give children freedom in the classroom. Imparting knowledge, she explains, takes less time than exploration, discovery or investigation; she also talks of the 'understandable fear' of a whole class practically exploring and investigating. This often leads to whole-class demonstrations that impart knowledge to children en masse. Teachers may well lack confidence in science, but they may also be inexperienced in teaching with a more open, 'opportunist' approach. They may find more didactic teaching attractive in managing the curriculum, maintaining behaviour, controlling children's learning and ensuring safety, but adoption of such an approach can lead to poor quality learning. Surprisingly perhaps, effective science learning arises out of a practical approach that motivates and interests children where they have ownership of their learning and where skills are developed alongside understanding. Children need to try out their own ideas, sometimes making mistakes along the way. Teachers need to adopt a different teaching stance that involves taking risks rather than 'playing safe' in planning. However, the rewards involved in terms of learning, enjoyment and sheer satisfaction for both the teacher and children are potentially enormous. Sadly, too much teacher control and didactic teaching in science not only limits opportunities for creativity in teaching and for pupils to demonstrate creativity in their learning, but also stifles the development of the budding scientist.

Conversely, some research has found a strong commitment to fostering independent learning in the early years classroom where children's autonomy, freedom and ownership of learning are valued and fostered (Whitbread et al. 2005: 40–1). It is no surprise then that Ofsted (2013) judged 89% of science observed in EYFS classrooms to be outstanding. Excellent early years practice is characterised by exploration and play. Undoubtedly the organisation of the early years facilitates autonomy and choice. This includes the way space, time and resources, including outside facilities, are organised.

Early years classrooms often have a wealth of practical equipment readily available for children to use as and when it is required. This may well be significant in terms of confidence in adopting a more open-ended, child-initiated approach. Indeed, Ofsted (2013) reported that early years teachers focused on giving each child the time and resources she or he needed to explore and investigate the physical world. Children became engrossed in whatever activity they were doing; teachers capitalised on their interest as they steered activities towards developing children's basic skills (Ofsted 2013: 12).

Teachers of older children often have to rely on pre-judging what children *might* need in the way of equipment for more open-ended, child-centred work. Nothing undermines the confidence of students and teachers more than children asking for items not provided or not easily accessible on demand. It is much more difficult to organise more open-ended work when required resources are housed in different parts of the school, including in locked cupboards, when 'best guess' supplied resources may not prove adequate. Providing illustrative activities allows the teacher to 'plan' more effectively to pre-determined objectives. Truly open-ended work, at any level, requires far more and better organised resources than recipe-type activities ever will.

Science should involve children in working together in groups, providing opportunities to develop group skills such as communication and other 'key skills'. Working in groups offers opportunities for children to work collaboratively and cooperatively together, putting forward and challenging ideas, and real opportunities for speaking and listening. In doing so, children will develop the ability to reason and to explain their ideas, like scientists justifying their theories. Incorporation of such opportunities is an important consideration in planning. However:

> the use of collaborative peer groups is relatively rare in primary classrooms, although brief episodes of paired talk are now quite common. However, such groups do provide settings and opportunities for effective learning provided that the talk is of a high quality or 'productive' ... [social] gains depend on children engaging in 'exploratory' as opposed to 'disputational' or purely 'narrative' talk. Children trained to work in groups have also learned, for example, to listen to each other, to invite everyone to express their opinions and differing viewpoints, and to reach agreement in the end – all these are highly desirable social and interpersonal skills. (Alexander 2010: 102)

Authentic group work may be unpopular with some teachers, but the lack of genuine group work potentially hampers learning and limits the development of scientific literacy (Webb 2007). Genuine group work *can* be off-putting to teachers because children may become over-excited if they are not used to working in this way, but there are other problems that teachers might face. First, teachers might feel that their own subject knowledge and their own capability is weak, or they might be put off by the high demand in terms of planning preparation and organisation of sometimes limited materials for use in practical sessions. There is certainly a high risk of 'noise and mess', but children should be involved in discussion about this and should be expected to take responsibility for minimising this and clearing away equipment at the end of a practical session. Lastly, it could be argued that it is more difficult to assess children when they are working in groups and engaged in collaborative practical activity, but again, much can be learned from how this is successfully undertaken in early years settings. Together these factors can be off-putting to beginning or unconfident teachers, but with support they are not insurmountable.

Children's Perspectives

Consideration of the future of science would not be complete without some exploration of 'pupil voice'. Children value subjects that spark their curiosity and encourage them to explore (Alexander 2010: 213). Encouragingly, children view science as one of the keys to their understanding of the world around them and find science enjoyable because they are active and involved in their learning (p. 224). The most enthusiastic learning occurs when teachers encourage pupils to come up with ideas and suggestions and, in consultation with their teacher, plan, conduct, record and evaluate their own investigations (Ofsted 2008, 2013).

Ofsted (2013) found that pupils' behaviour was good or outstanding in almost all the primary science lessons seen. In general, the more responsibility pupils were given, the better they learnt, the more they enjoyed their discoveries and the better they behaved. When teachers talked for too long, or limited the challenge, pupils tended to be passive, although even then most remained patient (Ofsted 2013: 12).

Children's attitudes towards science are significant in making them scientifically literate, enabling them to become responsible citizens capable of making a positive contribution to the economic well-being of society. However, some research into attitudes towards school subjects confirmed that science was not the most popular primary school subject and that older primary pupils were significantly less positive about science than younger Key Stage 2 children (Tymms et al. 2008: 24).

Considering attitudes towards science, engineering and technology (SET), Year 5 children were asked to draw 'what scientists/engineers do' (Silver and Rushton 2008: 56). Children held definite discreet images of SET, seeing science as investigative, engineering as repairing, and design and technology as creative, involving designing and making. Eighty per cent of the children drew an engineer as a mechanic. Children associated technology with D&T at school and did not connect enjoyable school SET activities with the actual work of scientists and engineers. This was particularly evident in the almost total lack of recognition of 'designing and making' in their images of engineers (p. 62). Generally, children enjoyed science and design and technology at school, appreciating the benefits of science and engineering to society, but did not wish to become scientists or engineers. Children's stereotypical images of scientists and engineers, rather than dislike of science and design and technology, were said to dissuade them from becoming scientists and engineers. More positive, inspiring images of the work of scientists and engineers are needed if children are to be encouraged to consider these career options (p. 66). However, whilst these findings may well be valid and reliable, anecdotally, primary children often hold unrealistic ideas about future careers, wanting to become pop stars or highly paid sports personalities.

Recent evidence suggests that many children enjoy science in primary schools but there is a real problem in that many do not see themselves taking up science-related occupations upon leaving school (Archer et al. 2013). There is a real need for primary children to understand that there is a wide range of careers open to them in the field of science, technology and engineering, and it might be that an expansion of 'science ambassador' initiatives where real scientists work alongside children in school will encourage better understanding of scientists and technologists. Here, children can learn from experts and enthusiasts, go on science-related visits, learn about scientists from the past and about science from other cultures and times.

Developing Scientific Literacy

Drawing extensively on the work of others, and supported by research subsequently, Webb said:

> Scientific literacy requires that learners are proficient in science language, thinking and the fundamental sense of science as well as understanding the big ideas of science and the relevance and interactions between science technology, society and the environment. (2007: 1)

He provides a simple, innovative framework for an approach to teaching and learning science for developing scientific literacy. His model uses aspects of literacy with a scientific focus, i.e. reading, writing and discussion, to promote effective understanding of scientific ideas and principles alongside a 'hands-on' practical approach where children are encouraged to raise their own questions and carry out investigations from a simple starting point. The approach is systematic and ensures that planning goes beyond 'one-off' activities whilst promoting curiosity and interest in the learner. The nature of science features highly in this model. Webb's (2007) view is that children need to be taught how to discuss and make decisions together without too much adult intervention, thereby promoting authentic learning and autonomy.

The view that children need to be introduced to the nature of science and scientists is also advocated by Loxley et al. (2014) in order to promote enjoyment and understanding. Emphasising the need for children to be engaged in authentic talk and discussion, they also highlight the importance of children understanding how real scientists work and how their work has influenced thinking over time. This view is now reflected in the Science National Curriculum (DfE 2013). A novel suggestion is that teachers should give children a number of talking points to stimulate discussion. Children then have to talk through, in groups and with a scientific topic, a number of statements. They have to decide which ideas are true and which false and why they think so, or if their group is unsure (Loxley et al. 2014: 18). The rationale for this is that this process provides a vehicle for the consideration of a range of points of view; children share their thinking, establish ideas and uncertainty for further work and generally develop their vocabulary and ideas (2010: 43).

Both the above approaches provide opportunities for learners to demonstrate their own creativity alongside developing understanding of scientific concepts and working scientifically. The teacher's role here is crucial, but does not entail a teacher-directed diet of science based on rote learning of scientific facts and vocabulary. Opportunities for children to demonstrate their creativity arise from exploring what they know or think they know, and reasoning and arguing with others to develop their thoughts and planning investigations together where pupil choice features at every point in the process. This includes asking them to explain their thinking, the ideas they have and the conclusions they come to as a result of carrying out investigations. Research suggests that increased performance is evident when learners are asked to discuss, argue and debate ideas (Osborne 2010). This approach is an approach for all children, not just for those of higher ability, which makes it inclusive. It allows an individualised, personalised approach to learning that does not mean children working in isolation on individual learning pathways. Observation of children engaged in authentic discussion reveals that children, working effectively in groups, challenge each others' ideas and move thinking on together. Asking children to decide how to record their observations allows children to be creative whilst providing an insight into their thoughts that can inform planning.

 Case Study 3.1

A Teach First participant working with her Year 1 class (5–6 years)

Vicky, a Teach First participant in her Newly Qualified Teacher (NQT) year, was involved in a Teach First project sponsored by the Primary Science Teaching Trust (PSTT). She had been asked to take part in a sequence of short films working with her Year 1 class which would be used nationally as a training resource with Teach First participants in their first year. Like all Teach First participants in their first two years of teaching, Vicky was working in a school with many children drawn from troubled backgrounds and challenging circumstances.

Although Vicky was familiar with teaching science during her training year, she had not taught science extensively and her work had tended to be teacher-directed rather than child-led. The opportunity to take part in the filming required Vicky to adopt an approach that, whilst not unfamiliar to her, was not typical of her existing practice. Consequently, she approached the project with a little anxiety. Vicky's view was that the project was important and she was keen to ensure that major points from discussion about good practice were included in her work with the children. She was given a sequence of teaching foci and a topic around which to plan her lesson.

The sequence started with a stimulus for observation: minibeasts. Vicky wanted her children to have some ownership of the direction of their learning. The filming took place in early December, and although she would have liked to have taken her children outdoors, the weather was very poor and the minibeasts were not very accessible for collection at that time of year. She did, however, want them to experience collecting minibeasts for themselves, so she created a simple replication of a woodland floor using a large plastic tray where the minibeasts could be found amongst the leaves and soil.

On the carpet the children were introduced to the equipment they would be using that morning: a viewer, spoons and paint brushes. Vicky stressed the need for gentle handling of the minibeasts and the need for respect for the living things, a concept that was very important in their school. The children had not used much scientific equipment before so she instructed them on where to place the minibeast in the viewer before she set the class off to find one.

Figure 3.1   *Using a viewer to observe a minibeast* (photo used with the permission of Revnow Productions Ltd)

(Continued)

(Continued)

The children were highly interested and motivated. They each spent some time observing their creature independently before returning to the carpet as a group to talk about what they had found. After talking together about what they had noticed, Vicky sent them off to find someone who had a different minibeast so that they could share what they each had noticed and communicate this information to another child to extend their learning. Here there was a fantastic opportunity for listening and speaking. The children were extremely interested in the minibeasts. This meant that they actually listened and shared important information about their observations rather than talking at each other.

Tables around the room had been set up for recording observations. Children were given a choice of using either paints, pastels or crayons to record their observations. Vicky had anticipated that the children's drawings might be influenced by the portrayal of minibeasts in children's fiction and cartoons, for example with human-like features, rather than by what was actually observed. Before she set them off to work, they talked about what she wanted them to do, to make their drawing like a photograph, stressing that they should use minibeast colours and not the primary colours they might use in other drawings and paintings.

Vicky was delighted by the responses of the children. It was clear that they had really looked closely and tried hard to represent the minibeasts accurately. Vicky was amazed at the quality of their work.

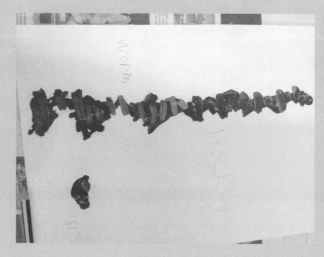

Figure 3.2   Observational painting/drawing of a worm

The painting shown in Figure 3.2 indicates that the child had observed the segments of the worm and had taken note of the changing colours at various points on the worm.

Figure 3.3   Observational drawing of a woodlouse

The observational drawing in Figure 3.3 demonstrates how much care the children took to capture the details and colours of their minibeasts. Rather than just looking at the woodlouse once, this child kept referring back to his minibeast, discussing how its body looked like armour and even asking if the different segments were to allow the woodlouse to curl into a ball.

Figure 3.4   Painting of a snail

(Continued)

(Continued)

The painting in Figure 3.4 is very interesting, showing the underneath of a snail attached to the glass of the viewer. The child has even captured some of the snail's shell which they could just see behind the body of the snail. The child was very interested in how the snail was able to stick to the viewer upside down, which led to inquisitive questions about how snails move.

The next stage in planning for her children to work scientifically involved raising questions that could lead to further observation or investigation. On the carpet, Vicky took on the role of a minibeast, inviting the children to ask her questions. Vicky's teaching assistant, Sharon, recorded their questions on a working wall (Figure 3.5):

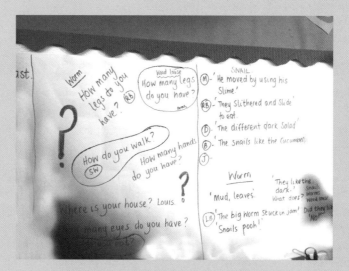

Figure 3.5   The working wall

Questions raised included:

'How many legs does the minibeast have?'
'Where does the minibeast live?'
'What does the minibeast eat?'

Vicky found that she had to listen carefully to what the children said, refine their question and repeat each back to them. Next, the children were asked which question they would like to investigate, how they might investigate it and what equipment they might need.

During the planning stage, Vicky had thought about the possible questions the children might ask and had collected some equipment in anticipation. Reflecting on this Vicky said that this was the most worrying aspect of planning for working in this way. She was very afraid that they might want to investigate questions she had not thought about. In the event, most children wanted to find out what the minibeast liked to eat.

Together, on the carpet, they talked about how they might find out. They talked to their talk partners to decide which question they wanted to investigate. Children suggested ideas and then the investigation started. Children put a range of foods on a tray and introduced snails to the tray. They watched to see what would happen. Later on the carpet they talked about what they had seen and what they had concluded. Children were given a choice of how to record their work.

Vicky had a number of devices that children could use to record their work, such as cameras, speak-easy microphones and a digi-viewer, but her children had not used these before and she did not want their use to detract from the main focus of learning. Quite a number of children chose, independently, to write about their investigation. Vicky was delighted that one of her most reluctant writers was eager to write about her investigation (Figure 3.6).

Figure 3.6   Writing of a reluctant writer

(Continued)

(Continued)

Although numerous errors of spelling and grammar are evident, the writing suggests the most important aspect is that the child felt empowered by her investigation and was excited to share what she had discovered about her minibeasts. Not only had she discovered what her minibeasts liked to eat, but she also found that some minibeasts liked to hide in the dark and did not like being in the light. The child had made some excellent observations of her minibeasts. Noticeable also, though, is a face drawn on one of the minibeasts, which suggests that subliminal messages transmitted by popular culture are difficult to challenge in the classroom.

Vicky was delighted with the response of the children where they had some responsibility for their own learning. The children took their learning beyond what she had anticipated as through close observation the children were beginning to identify the seven processes of life. Throughout the investigation they became scientists – wondering, discovering and theorising. Furthermore, there were opportunities to develop other areas of learning, such as speaking and listening, art, creativity, literacy and numerical skills. Children eagerly looked through a number of secondary resources in order to find answers to their questions and share what they had discovered with their peers. They were also able to extend their learning, generating new questions and continuing their learning at home and in the playground.

Subsequently, Vicky no longer feels anxious about allowing the children to lead their own scientific investigations. She recognises that teacher-led investigations can actually limit pupils' opportunity to truly understand the world around them. The incredible journey her children's learning took from a well-chosen stimulus truly changed her understanding of teaching science and she now aims to begin every science topic with a child-led investigation. In turn, she hopes the children's enthusiasm, curiosity and independence will flourish so that they continue to feel empowered by their discoveries.

 Case Study 3.2

A Teach First participant working with a Year 6 class (10–11 years)

Morven, also a Teach First participant in her Newly Qualified Teacher (NQT) year and also involved in the Teach First project sponsored by the Primary Science Teaching Trust (PSTT), was, like Vicky, working in a school with many children drawn from troubled backgrounds and challenging circumstances.

Morven had been quite experimental in her science teaching during her first year as a Teach First participant, but she had focused mainly on developing her children's knowledge and understanding of science rather than on developing them as scientists 'working scientifically'. The project therefore gave her the opportunity to focus her teaching on developing the children's process skills, particularly observation, raising questions and planning practical investigations to answer their own questions. This involved developing practice into relatively unknown territory. Morven was confident, though, that her class would rise to the challenge. They had been learning about higher order questions in English and she felt sure that her class would be able to apply this to science. Morven planned a sequence of activities for her lesson on the topic of light.

The plan for the lesson, which would be carried out during an extended morning, started with observation, the stimulus being a tea light. The identified learning intention was:

To plan a scientific enquiry to answer a question using scientific equipment to take measurements.

The class was used to being introduced to the learning intention and then involved in the identification of success criteria for the lesson. On the day, through talking to their talk partner and further discussion led by Morven, children identified that they would be involved in 'noticing' and that 'collaboration would be important' and 'perseverance ... because it might be difficult to find an answer to the question'. Tea lights were used as the stimulus. The class created a list of success criteria:

- Work together in partners
- Keep focused
- Use scientific equipment appropriately
- Plan carefully

They could also have added up to answer the question!

Initial observation of the tea lights involved children noting down their observations on Post-it notes. Children were very engaged and many made excellent observations without prompting. Some needed to look again. Morven provided the opportunity to do this, which was a good investment of time as the children were able to move beyond more obvious observations such as the colour of the flame to more sophisticated notes about shadows and movement. The class then shared their observations with others, which extended their thinking.

Following this the children were asked to write down their own questions from their observations. Morven then developed this as they shared their ideas and

(Continued)

(Continued)

questions with the rest of the class. Morven used this sequence of events as an opportunity for assessment of their ideas and questions. This was a great opportunity for assessment for learning in action!

The next part of the lesson involved the children exploring light with a range of equipment. Morven had created an iMovie using one of the newly acquired class set of iPads to show the class the available equipment. She used this as an opportunity to suggest starting points for investigations. The class needed to handle the equipment and make further observations to refine their questions.

Observing the children exploring and manipulating the equipment, there was no doubt that their curiosity had been aroused. Every child in the class was interested and engaged, and moving forward in their skills of being investigative scientists. Children explored the equipment available to them that had been set up around the room; this helped them to raise more questions and to refine them as they thought about what might be investigated.

As the children considered what aspect of light they could investigate, they found it relatively easy to ask 'how' and 'why' questions. However, it was a real challenge for the children to raise questions that could be investigated and answered through practical enquiry. Issues arose from not understanding the idea of identifying variables. They struggled with this, deciding what they could change and what they could measure within their investigation. Morven collected and shared the raised questions to extend their learning further, providing

Figure 3.7   Recording an investigation collaboratively answering the question: Will the light creep through when you use different materials?

examples of the types of question they could ask. When the children were clearer about what they were being asked to do, they amended their questions and were ready to investigate.

Morven explained that they were allowed to record in whatever way they wished. Some chose to write and some chose to record collaboratively on large pieces of paper (see Figure 3.7). In this way, the children were given ownership of their scientific enquiry – investigating light.

Some groups used an iPad to record, in lux the light intensity within their investigation of, for example, when shadows were cast on a plain surface (Figure 3.8).

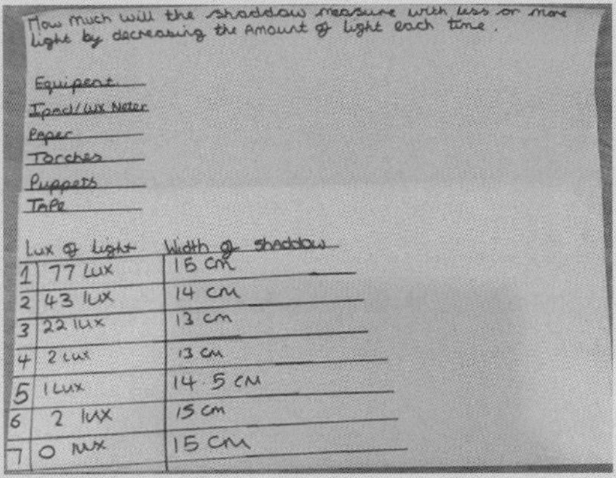

Figure 3.8   Recording the results of an investigation into the formation of shadows

Reflecting on the whole investigation, Olivia said, 'It's probably been one of the best science lessons I have ever had ... being able to ask questions that I didn't know the answer to. Today has been really exciting; we have had a lot of looking into things that I haven't known before and answering questions.' Ownership of learning was the key here. Morven gave children ownership; this was not very comfortable for them or for Morven at times, but the effort and the investment of time were worth it.

Reflecting after the lesson, Morven said that it had been a good experience for all of them and there had been great progression in learning during the lesson. Together, they had adopted a very different approach, which was a brave choice. Morven said it was 'fantastic' to see her children 'so engrossed, so engaged carrying out their investigations sensibly' and without her prescribing exactly what they had to do, with the emphasis on scientific enquiry.

(Continued)

(Continued)

Key to the success of the lesson was proper planning. The children had had an open-ended lesson and in their eyes had had full ownership of their learning, but actually Morven had broken the potential learning down to structure it by the equipment she had provided and the way in which she had interacted with them as individuals working in groups and the whole class. She said that they were keen to raise questions, but they needed support to get away from factual-type enquiries; they responded well to what they were shown. It was important to provide the children with time to raise questions and to develop their own investigation. She thought that there had been too much to cover in one lesson. In future lessons, she needed to focus learning more on what types of questions could be investigated.

At the end of the lesson many were able to explain what an investigative question was, and were able to take ownership, not having to ask permission to investigate in particular ways. They had responded really, really well to that approach.

Morven had assessed learning during the lesson in a number of ways using a range of methods: questioning, listening to them, collaboration and use of Post-it notes. All this told her much about their ideas and she was also able to identify misconceptions about light. For example, someone had mentioned the colour at the bottom of the flame which provided a great talking point. Using Post-it notes was a good way of collecting evidence about their observations and their ability to raise investigative questions. Morven had noticed how the children were developing their scientific skills and their use of scientific vocabulary, such as shadows and reflection. Drawing conclusions for the class involved them in deciding what they had found out and explaining this to others in a coherent way. The children were very good at determining the next steps in terms of further possible investigations and at applying their existing scientific knowledge to try to explain their results. Discussing these aspects allowed many learning points to be drawn out and, importantly, identified key areas where the learning needed further planning for progression of learning.

This experience has subsequently impacted positively on Morven's approach to teaching science and on the learning of her children working scientifically. During a topic on the heart, the children were given the opportunity to investigate the way 'pulse' varies. Once again, the children were completely engrossed throughout the lesson. As a result of the light investigation, there was clear scaffolding for setting up investigative questions. This allowed the children to truly understand what was meant by an investigative question. Not only did they succeed in this, but they were able to describe the method and draw conclusions on their final results. They successfully applied their prior knowledge of the heart to do this. After completing more work like this, the next step for Morven and her class would be for her to give the children a wider field to discover, like light, in order to see how they hone their investigative skills on a wider topic once more.

Assessment

Unlike mathematics and English, national tests in science were removed in England in 2009. This responded to the view that the formal tests were detrimental not only to children's attitudes towards science as they got older, but also to the view that 'teaching' to the test was having an undesirable effect on the way that science was taught in primary schools, particularly in Years 5 and 6. The removal of tests did not change practice for the better. Indeed, it is generally agreed that science lost its previous status as a result. There remains a statutory requirement to report pupils' performance in science, but Ofsted (2013) reported evidence of relative weaknesses in pupils' skills of scientific enquiry, and that the NC levels recorded through teacher assessment for all schools appear to be too high (Ofsted 2013: 8).

Effective assessment in science needs to involve both aspects of science – working scientifically as well as assessing children's knowledge and understanding of scientific concepts. This requires teachers to think differently about the kind of evidence they collect. Teachers need to consider, for example, not just providing children with the opportunity to observe or sort things into groups, but also to assess how well they do these things. Children need to be given regular opportunities to raise questions, but their questions need to be assessed for the type and quality of questions raised, particularly in relation to those that lead to the answers being found by further observation or investigation. In other words, children need to be given the opportunity to improve and progress their scientific skills as well as their understanding of science in the world around them.

Given this and Ofsted's praise of practice in the EYFS, much could be learned in terms of how science achievement in later years is managed and recorded. Adopting strategies already common in many early years classrooms could provide a way forward for those teaching older children:

- observing the level of curiosity and interest in their surroundings
- observing whether the child can identify similarities and differences when observing objects and living things
- recording questions that are asked, including about why things happen and how things work

- recording what children say, including the ideas they express in discussion with their peers or a practitioner, for example when exploring understanding and explaining their ideas
- taking photographs of children as they work to be placed in their books for annotation by the child or practitioner
- noting whether the child investigates materials and living things by using all the senses as appropriate and can identify and talk about the features
- discussing with children their ideas when planning investigations, asking them why they have, for example, chosen particular equipment and recording this information as above
- formal writing up of investigations, such as writing to develop scientific literacy, perhaps in a notebook (Webb 2007, 2010)
- children's drawings, concept maps and KWHL grids (Ward et al. 2008)
- self and peer assessment.

Conclusion

This chapter has examined the nature of primary science and the need for children to be given the opportunity to read about science, to talk and argue in science, to plan practical investigations collaboratively and to develop understanding of the nature of science and scientific principles. It has examined how science can be a vehicle for learning in other subjects in the primary curriculum and how children's learning in science can be assessed. It has argued that science has a unique position in the primary curriculum, providing extensive opportunities for learning across the curriculum. In summary, primary science needs to:

- lay the foundations for producing a scientifically literate society where individuals can engage intelligently in everyday debate about scientific issues
- go beyond providing children with a 'fun' experience to ensure that children develop their knowledge and understanding of science and their ability to work scientifically
- ensure that children have the opportunity to think creatively and to demonstrate their own creativity
- maximise opportunities for learning science through other subjects, but especially through English, mathematics and design and technology.

 Reflection Points

1. Thinking about your own experience of observing and teaching science, can you identify how you can optimise learning in other subjects through science?

2. How could the organisation of resources in a school known to you be improved to facilitate increased pupil autonomy characterised by more choice and independence?
3. What have you learned from this chapter that will impact on your future practice in science?

Further Reading

Brunton, P. and Thornton, L. (2010) *Science in the Early Years: Building Firm Foundations from Birth to Five.* London: SAGE.

Johnston, J. (2014) *Emergent Science: Teaching Science from Birth to 8.* Abingdon: Routledge.

Loxley, P., Dawes, L., Nicholls, L. and Dore, B. (2014) *Teaching Primary Science: Promoting Enjoyment and Developing Understanding*, 2nd edn. Harlow: Pearson.

Roden, J. and Archer, J. (2014) *Primary Science for Trainee Teachers.* London: SAGE/ Learning Matters.

References

Alexander, R. (ed.) (2010) *Children, Their World, Their Education: Final Report and Recommendations of the Cambridge Primary Review.* Abingdon: Routledge.

Allen, M. (2010) *Misconception in Primary Science.* Maidenhead: Open University Press.

Archer, L., Osborne, J., Dewitt, J., Dillon, J., Wong, B. and Willis, B. (2013) *ASPIRES: Young People and Career Aspirations 10–14.* London: King's College London.

Bullock, K. and Muschamp, Y. (2006) 'Learning about learning in the primary school', *Cambridge Journal of Education* 36 (1): 49–62.

Davies, D. and Howe, A. (2003) *Teaching Science and Design and Technology in the Early Years.* London: David Fulton.

DfE (Department for Education) (2012) *Early Years Statutory Framework.* London: DfE.

DfE (Department for Education) (2013) *Science Programmes of Study: Key Stages 1 and 2. National Curriculum in England.* London: DfE.

Harlen, W. (2008) 'Science as a key component of the primary curriculum: a rationale with policy implications', in *Perspectives on Education: Primary Science 1.* London: Wellcome Trust. pp. 4–18.

Harlen, W. (ed.) (2012) *Principles and Big Ideas of Science Education.* Hatfield: Association for Science Education (ASE), available on the ASE website: www.ase.org.uk.

Harlen, W. and Qualter, A. (2009) 'Aims and outcomes of primary science education', in *The Teaching of Science in Primary Schools*, 5th edn. Abingdon: Routledge.

Johnson, J. (2009) 'What is creativity in science education?', in A. Wilson (ed.), *Creativity in Primary Education*, 2nd edn. Exeter: Learning Matters.

Loxley, P., Dawes, L., Nicholls, L. and Dore, B. (2014) *Teaching Primary Science: Promoting Enjoyment and Developing Understanding*, 2nd edn. Abingdon: Routledge.

Mercer, N., Dawes, L., Wegerif, R. and Sams, C. (2004) 'Reasoning as a scientist: ways of helping children to use language to learn science', *British Educational Research Journal* 30 (3): 359–77.

Newton, D.P. and Newton, L.D. (2009) 'Some student teachers' conceptions of creativity in school science', *Research in Science and Technological Education*, 27 (1): 45–60.

Newton, L.D. (2010) 'Improving primary science teaching', in M. Wenham and P. Ovens (eds), *Understanding Primary Science*, 3rd edn. London: SAGE.

Ofsted (Office for Standards in Education) (2008) *Success in Science*. London: Ofsted.

Ofsted (Office for Standards in Education) (2011) *Successful Science*. London: Ofsted.

Ofsted (Office for Standards in Education) (2013) *Maintaining Curiosity: A Survey into Science Education in Schools*. London: Ofsted.

Osborne, J. (2010) 'Arguing to learn in science: the role of collaborative, critical discourse', *Science* 328 (23): 463–6.

Pearson, P.D., Moje, E. and Greenleaf, C. (2010) 'Literacy and science: each in the service of each other', *Science* 328 (23): 459–63.

Roden, J. (2005) 'The role of practical work', in *Primary Science Reflective Reader*. Exeter: Learning Matters.

Silver, A. and Rushton, B.S. (2008) 'Primary-school children's attitudes towards science, engineering and technology and their images of scientists and engineers', *Education 3–13*, 36 (1): 51–67.

Tymms, P., Bolden, P. and Merrell, C. (2008) 'Science in English primary schools: trends in attainment, attitudes and approaches', in *Perspectives on Education: Primary Science 1*. London: Wellcome Trust. pp. 19–42.

Ward, H., Roden, J., Hewlett, C. and Foreman, J. (2008) *Teaching Science in the Primary Curriculum: A Practical Guide*, 2nd edn. London: SAGE.

Webb, P. (ed.) (2007) *Scientific Literacy: A New Synthesis*. Port Elizabeth, South Africa: Bay Books.

Webb, P. (2010) 'Science education and literacy: imperative for the developed and developing world', *Science* 328 (5977): 488–50.

Whitbread, D., Anderson, H., Coltman, P., Page, C., Pasternak, D.P. and Mehta, S. (2005) 'Developing independent learning in the early years', *Education 3–13*, March: 40–50.

CHAPTER 4

AN INTRODUCTION TO DESIGN AND TECHNOLOGY

James Archer

Chapter Aims

This chapter will:

- examine and explore the nature of creative design and technology

- establish what design and technology as a subject has been, is and could be in the future, highlighting its potential for teaching and learning within the primary curriculum

- consider the contribution that the adoption of a creative pedagogy in design and technology can make to children's learning

- highlight current and potential practice for teaching and learning in design and technology

Introduction

Design and technology (D&T) can be an exciting subject in the primary curriculum enjoyed by children and teachers alike. D&T is an essential element of the primary curriculum in that it provides opportunities for children to explore existing materials and to practise a range of practical skills. Engaging with D&T is a process of inventing or improving things to satisfy practical needs and solve practical problems (Newton 2005). D&T is often wrongly perceived as being just making models but this is a commonly held misconception (Hope 2006: 11). Instead, D&T involves children in making different products from similar starting points. The process, in terms of planning, designing and making, is as important as the final 'product'. The product may not necessarily be an object because D&T provides children with opportunities to design and plan in a much wider sense.

Amazingly, D&T encompasses a wide range of materials, applications and activities, from food to textiles, and from control technology to construction kits. It provides opportunities to develop children's creativity and understanding of the needs and problems of the world within which they are growing up. Such opportunities allow children to be authentically creative since 'the process' has the potential to involve autonomous and creative problem solving at all of its stages (Hope 2006). The higher-level thinking skill of problem solving is fundamental to D&T. Davies and Howe (2014a) remind us that:

> Design problems tend to be 'wicked' [involving] many factors such as materials, technology and human lifestyles. This sometimes makes them not look like problems at all: 'design and make sandwiches for a picnic' sounds more like an opportunity for trying out new combinations of fillings ... For a food technologist, designing a sandwich that will stick together, taste pleasant and not make the bread too soggy presents a whole range of problems – it's no picnic! (pp. 165–6).

Good practice in D&T involves many things including:

- play and exploration: where children gain knowledge and understanding of materials and their properties or existing products
- focused practical tasks (FPTs): where the child acquires or develops new skills
- the formalisation and making of a design (see, for example, Hope 2004, 2006; Newton 2005).

These different aspects of D&T together provide children with the opportunity to explore materials, to learn new skills through FPTs and to apply these in more open but formalised design challenges. Play and exploration are highly valued aspects of the Early Years Foundation Stage (EYFS), but often appear less often in the later primary years. Nevertheless, these are important for all primary-aged children because, through play and exploration, children are given the opportunity to be both inventive and explorative. Through playing and exploring with materials children can develop knowledge and skills that should enable them to imagine how the materials might be put to use.

Case Study 4.1

'Trashion'

A group of first-year BA (Hons) in Primary Education students were developing their knowledge of key principles of primary design and technology. They were asked to work in groups to create a new look for a well-known character, be that fictional or famous. The students were encouraged to consider how they could create a new look but enable their character to still be identifiable. The students went through a host of processes that led to each group creating new and unique products, all from the same starting point.

One group decided to redesign Cinderella. The students were allowed to play with the materials available and they explored the properties of the waste materials that they were going to reuse and recycle; they even started to model some ideas such as headdresses (*play and exploration*).

During the entire process the students engaged in *focused practical tasks* (FPTs). The students were given opportunities to develop skills including joining and construction techniques. In Figure 4.1 you can see the student practising joining

Figure 4.1   Students practising joining techniques

(Continued)

(Continued)

techniques to hold pleats in place. This important stage prepared the students for their final 'make'. Without engaging in this part of the process students would not have the specific knowledge required to create their design. By undertaking this task the students were expertly able to choose the best possible joining technique for their product informed by their experience.

Figure 4.2   Student making pleats

By engaging in this experience the students were able to appreciate that the phase in which the *formalisation and making of a design* occurs is a fluid and flexible one.

After engaging in the play, exploration and FPTs, the students were able to create a design that was informed by a design process. They sought to formalise this through a thought shower (see Figure 4.3). As they created their final design they reworked their thought shower, demonstrating changes and amendments that were made.

Each group sent their model down the class catwalk (Figure 4.4). The students not modelling the final product fed back and talked about the process and the product with their peers in a fashion-show style.

Through this experience the student teachers were able to develop their understanding of the nature of primary design and technology and how stimulating, complex and fascinating it can be.

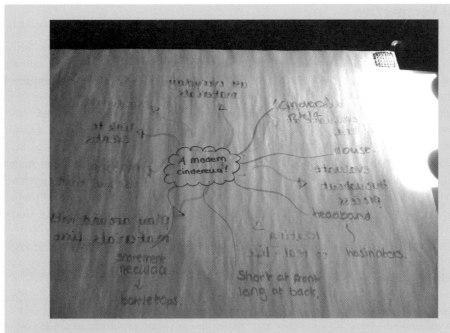

Figure 4.3   Thought shower

Figure 4.4   The fashion parade

A Historical Perspective

Design and technology (D&T) has changed and developed over the years. Most recently, attempts have been made to ensure that practice in England is at the cutting edge of innovation in the field (DfE 2013). Children in Key Stage 2 are now required to be taught to be 'innovative'; whether this is physically or neurologically possible is a question for further debate and research, nevertheless this represents a huge new challenge to the primary practitioner. Children are being required to develop a more in-depth knowledge of how things work with a new emphasis on mechanical and electrical systems (DfE 2013). It has not always been this way. D&T has faced many challenges in the past and will do so in the years to come. It is important therefore that we fully understand where D&T has come from in order for us to establish what it could be like in this new era we find ourselves in with the new programme of study (DfE 2013).

In 1988, D&T was born out of a belief that it could offer many new skills and contribute to new understandings across the curriculum. Academics wrote enthusiastically about the opportunities for society and the individual:

> design and technology has the potential to help create imaginative, thinking, tolerant and responsible adults better able to adapt and cope with day-to-day problems and aware of the effect of their actions. (Jarvis 1993: 1)

However, it was acknowledged that, inevitably, teaching D&T would place a high level of challenge on primary teachers. In 1989 the new curriculum was published and, consequently, there was considerable confusion about practice related to technological activity in the primary school (Ritchie 2001: 11). This became hugely apparent as there was little or no tradition of D&T in the primary classroom (Tickle 1990). Primary teachers were not familiar enough, either from their own teaching or from their personal education, with what was expected of them, which led to great unease:

> it was not uncommon to hear the fears and anxieties of student teachers and teachers who are not familiar with the territory of CDT being expressed loudly and clearly. At times one might think some teachers would rather handle a deadly cobra. (Tickle 1990: 29)

Looking back, even when professional development courses were provided in the 1980s and early 1990s, there had been a continued 'blurring' between both science and D&T. This may have added to the confusion about the nature of D&T and how it is separate from science. However, other factors also contributed, for example the lack of consultation with practitioners in the development of the original statutory orders for D&T (Hope 2004) and the lack of investment in terms of training, time and other resources. In addition, there was a lack of research within the field of D&T teaching. The continual and rising dominance of the core subjects, particularly English and mathematics, as a result of successive policies and strategies, also had an impact on teachers' attitudes, understanding and expertise in primary D&T. In most cases this had a knock-on impact on the amount and quality of D&T teaching seen within primary schools even up until this day.

Greater freedoms have been granted to the primary D&T practitioner in the National Curriculum 2014. Not only is there less content in the new programme of study but it is likely that there will be no further non-statutory guidance than what is given in the programme of study itself (DfE 2013). This could be the cause of great joy for some and terror for others. It is uncertain whether in the future local authorities will produce supporting materials websites, such as: www.expertsubjectgroups.co.uk; these were a good starting point for the creative primary practitioner.

The State of the Art in Pedagogy

D&T has continued to hold very low status in many schools to this present day. Little systematic research has been undertaken into the teaching and learning of D&T (Cross 2003: 126). Its representation on initial teacher training courses has often been minimal. The majority of students in training for primary education will have experienced, at best, a 12- or 20-hour course in D&T, with those in school-based training routes even less (Hope 2006). This low status might be attributed to a fundamental lack of understanding amongst teachers as to how D&T fits into the curriculum.

The teaching of D&T is successful when teachers understand the potential for children's learning arising out of the experience D&T brings. It is essential that teachers are provided with adequate support and resources. Sadly this support for the majority of primary teachers appears to have been lacking. It is no coincidence that the best examples of good practice have emerged from funded projects or have had special attention from enthusiasts within local authorities. Hence, good practice is currently not widespread in schools and D&T does not figure highly in literature. Additionally, while the Cambridge Review champions the linkage of science and technology, only one fleeting reference is made specifically to D&T in the whole final report (Alexander 2010: 180).

The Ofsted (2008) report on D&T in schools based on visits to 30 primary schools over a 3-year period paints a very depressing picture:

> In most of the primary schools ... design and technology continued to be on the margins of the curriculum. Only a third of schools offered a provision which rose above the bare minimum to be judged satisfactory. This lack of attention to the subject is related to the understandable focus on English, mathematics and science, as well as to the difficulties schools perceive in teaching a subject which is a complex amalgam of a number of formerly separate subjects, and includes substantial technical content ... (Ofsted 2008: 5)

The report referenced above also states that 'at least two-thirds of the primary schools ... have not realised the potential of design and technology to help all learners become confident and capable members of a technologically advanced society' (Ofsted 2008: 6). They recommended, amongst other things, that primary schools should improve teachers' subject knowledge in D&T and their awareness of teaching materials. Assessment and recording and reporting pupils' progress was also seen as an issue to be addressed.

While it could be argued that Ofsted reports are based on unrepresentative samples of schools, other evidence supports the low status and generally poor practice of D&T in primary schools. For example, in a survey of 175 final-year BA (Hons) in Primary Education students, when asked about their experience of D&T in the primary curriculum, most students stated that D&T held low status and it was typical for them not to have experienced D&T in their placement schools. Even if student teachers are keen to engage pupils in D&T there is some evidence that they are not given free rein to carry out their plans because of the need to 'fit in' with their class teacher's existing curriculum framework (Davies and Rogers 2000: 221). This is in itself worrying, because although current qualified teachers may well not be clear about good practice in D&T, novice teachers and those in the early stages of their teaching careers are the ones that ought to be able to make a considerable contribution to the development of D&T. They will also be the ones who, in the light of the new curriculum, should bring new expertise and an up-to-date knowledge of best practice, which means when teaching D&T they can support the development of the staff in the schools in which they are placed. This is particularly pertinent when thinking about a subject such as D&T, where it is rare for there to be development opportunities aimed at teachers in the field and even rarer still for these opportunities to be prioritised and taken up.

Creativity

D&T is an extremely creative subject. Many have sought to define creativity, but to little or no avail. The National Advisory Committee on Creative and Cultural Education (NACCCE) suggests that creativity is an 'imaginative activity fashioned so as to produce outcomes that are both original and of value (NACCCE 1999: 29)'. However, Sternberg and Lubart (1995) also suggest that creativity is shown if something or someone is both novel and appropriate. These definitions appear to imply that the act of creativity shows itself in a new final physical product or form. However, this view has been largely contested. Lucas (2001) suggests that creativity is a state of mind. Creativity should be seen as a golden thread that weaves its way through both the design process and a product. Design and Technology requires of its neophytes a great deal of thought, reflection and possibility thinking as well as the making and changing of materials. When making rafts that float there is much creativity to be seen in children testing, selecting and assembling materials. It could be argued that in this instance there is the potential for greater levels of creativity in the designing and making processes than in the final product. After all, when designing a raft, children often create something that looks like previous products they are aware of.

Educators need to be mindful of the discussion of 'high creativity' and 'ordinary creativity' (Craft 2001). Craft (2001) suggests that there are two main forms of creativity. The first addresses 'high creativity' or 'big C creativity', including those discoveries made by individuals that have the potential to affect themselves and others in a life-changing way. This type of creativity is original in as much as no other person has made such a discovery before (Craft 2001). The design and invention of the first sandwich, cars, A-line dresses and doors are clear examples. The second category is 'ordinary creativity' or 'little c creativity'. Craft (2001) suggests that this type of creativity typically impacts the individual only, as it is generally in the form of a revelation in an already accepted or explored notion, arena or product. This type of creativity, of the two, is the one most common in the primary classroom and is prolific within the teaching and learning of primary D&T. When children design and make their first pop-up car, moving toy or bag, they are exploring concepts and products that have already been established. However, when they use a split pin, create a motor or work out a successful stitch to join several pieces of material together, they enter a new world in which they are building up 'little c' creativity experience with the hope of one day being able to release 'big C' potential.

What Does Creative D&T Look Like?

Exploration in D&T is essential in developing children's creativity as it immerses them in the creative processes (including aspects of preparation, incubation, illumination or revelation and verification or reframing), thereby enabling children to work as designers in their own right (Davies and Howe 2014b). In addition, Roden (2005) seems to suggest that creative thought can derive from exploration. Exploration in D&T is a vital element in facilitating the revelation required for 'ordinary creativity' to occur. Davies and Howe (2014a) also concur with Hope (2006) when they say that:

> D&T is a hands-on activity in which children make real, tangible objects [and] also 'minds-on', involving a balance between doing and thinking, action and reflection. The act of designing inevitably involves imagining something that does not yet exist ... D&T offers children open-ended tasks which do not have a prescribed 'right answer' and involve an element of choice (of shape, colour, materials, function, etc.) ... their outcomes will be original. Evaluation is also central to the 'minds-on' dimension of D&T; children need to learn to appraise others' designs as well as their own ... [such creative processes] seem to echo those that designers or children might undertake in the course of a D&T project. (Davies and Howe 2014b: 164–5)

It could be argued that creative D&T teaching and learning is the only form of D&T that should be seen within our schools. Creative D&T teaching involves providing opportunities for exploration of materials as well as reflective periods for explorative thought. These two key elements are the ingredients that are essential in order to facilitate the child as a creative designer.

Contexts for Learning within D&T

Teaching D&T within contexts means:

> through themes, cycles, spirals and special events: the use of a specialist pedagogy involving experimental learning: and through the promotion of network learning, involving (an) interconnected multi-perspectival and multileveled learning (approach). (Jeffrey and Woods 2003: 78)

Here, real-life situations are utilised. These need to be 'real' to the child in terms of things they can relate to and experience, or made real, such as when a storybook is used as a starting point. For example, if children were inventing sweets, it would be appropriate to use a text that celebrates confectionery like Roald Dahl's *Charlie and the Chocolate Factory*. Younger children could design a wheelbarrow or a playground for a park motivated by one of the *Percy the Park Keeper* books by Nick Butterworth.

Both Johnston (2005) and Jeffrey and Woods (2003) advocate contextualised learning, for example setting tasks that challenge children to explore real places and situations, which increases the effectiveness of teaching and learning. By using contexts such as the immediate environment, the people, the places, the problems and events as springboards for learning, children are launched into a world of wonder, amazement and intrigue where learning is more purposeful and is established in the child for longer. When using the environment, teachers can encourage children to design and make a shelter for which the children would need to identify the needs and respond with practical solutions. Similarly, children could be asked to design a point of attraction to draw visitors to a particular area. There is a wide range of design opportunities here, from designing information stands to the children being involved in the design and planning of a playground that would support initiatives for children's well-being.

The creative practitioner therefore should identify relevant contexts within which design and technology learning can take place. There is a danger, however, that in an attempt to make learning purposeful by providing a context we do the reverse and in actuality alienate the child by choosing a poor, tenuous or irrelevant context. It is for this reason care should be taken to ensure that the context is relevant to the child's prior learning and experience. We should start with the child's immediate environment and work outwards; in the early years we would be looking for contexts that are immediate to the child, for example designing and developing new toys or using toys as starting points. This can be developed in wider contexts with the older child, for example a food product to be sold in the local bakery or as part of school meals or events.

 Case Study 4.2

Food, glorious food

The children of a joint Year 5 and 6 class in a small village school were challenged to consider how they could improve the school dinner provision. The school has had to make dramatic changes to its infrastructure and provision of school dinners, in particular in response to the new Universal Infant Free School Meal Policy. In addition, the school had decided to become an early adopter of the new primary curriculum (DfE 2013) and as such was aware of major changes to the subject. This included the fact that D&T is now split into two clear strands – designing and making, and cooking and nutrition. The class teacher was keen to ensure that the learning met the new requirements for the design process to be 'iterative'.

Working in small groups the children were encouraged to design a menu around a theme. They were to suggest a main meal and a pudding. The children were asked to produce a meal for the £2.30 guideline found in the new free school meal policy.

Initially the children looked at meals available within their price range. This included vegetarian wraps (under the theme of 'street food'), filled jacket potatoes (under the theme of 'winter warmers'), a stir-fry (under the theme of 'a taste of the orient') and a savoury bean and mince crumble (under the theme of 'food from fiction', the meal being inspired by Julia Donaldson's 'Gruffalo Crumble'). The children tasted and deconstructed these to discover the ingredients used. Each group selected one of these dishes to modify. The children then had an opportunity to work with adults and explore the processes required. The children went on a trip to the local farm shop to discover what foods were in season and try to find alternatives for those used in the meals that they had taken apart. After this, they designed a meal that used similar ingredients and modified processes. The children adapted their meals in light of their experimentation with ingredients and the processes.

The next stage involved the children undertaking practical market research with both parents and children at the school's termly parent share event. After evaluating

(Continued)

(Continued)

the feedback, the children made further modifications. This process was also replicated for the puddings to accompany the meals.

The final meals the children produced are now incorporated into the school's offer in its four-weekly menu cycle launched in September 2014. Not only did this experience provide a relevant context for the children's learning in which they were seeking to solve a real-life design dilemma but it also provided a rich source of learning within other subject areas. Strong links were made to English, mathematics and science throughout this topic and children were genuinely engaged in their learning.

Cross-Curricular Links

D&T is a true cross-curricular subject as clear links can be made easily with other subjects. One such subject is science. There is great controversy regarding whether D&T and science should be considered either as one subject or as two very separate entities. History is littered with designs and inventions that have occurred before any formula or scientific explanation (Hope 2006). As Hope (2006) highlights, however, the distinction between the two subjects comes from our understanding and perception of them. Is science, as Hope (2006) suggests, an unspecific formulised search for wide-reaching and generic rules or can it also be a specific voyage of discovery with the purpose of finding the solution to a specific problem? Looking at both these subjects we can see that not only are there factual overlaps but there are also clear correlations in the processes and ways of working that are undertaken. Science and D&T are closely linked in the early years curriculum (Davies and Howe 2014b). It is interesting that these subjects, which are interwoven at this early stage, are then separated for the rest of compulsory education and then rejoined at a higher education level or in the workforce.

Learners will not benefit from a diet of cross-curricular activities artificially flavoured and pre-packaged. The potential power of a cross-curricular approach or the strength of a discipline can be diluted or lost when too many links are made to too many subjects. The same can be said when tenuous or irrelevant links are made (Roth 2000) as the learner can find it hard to distinguish what it is they had learnt. There is a danger of delivering a compromised curriculum through forcing links which has a detrimental impact on the potential for learning. Care needs to be taken to ensure that adopting a cross-curricular approach enhances and enriches the learning experience for the child.

Applying this to D&T, for example, while children could be designing footwear, how much richer this experience could be if they also, simultaneously, explored both the concept of friction and materials and their properties. The danger in this is that through a scientific emphasis the D&T is lost. The skill of the practitioner here is in ensuring that when planning, ideas and subjects dovetail, and complement each other in a way that ensures progression in the learning of both subjects.

Health and Safety Issues: Preparation for Life

D&T can be a source of anxiety for many teachers on the grounds of health and safety. Children need to be safe, but this does not mean that they should be totally protected from any possible hazard; rather, they need to become aware of the dangers and potential hazards around them and develop an ability to stay safe. Indeed, in my experience, children today are less likely to actively explore their world, particularly out of doors, than countless previous generations of children have done. In this respect, parents and other significant adults too often ensure that their children face few, if any, potential hazards and are actively protected from even the most minor risk. The concern from parents about the potential risks and hazards, real or perceived, in the world outside of the home is sometimes reflected in school where teachers 'play safe' in the activities they provide for children inside the classroom, being either reluctant, or lacking in confidence, to provide such activities. This is despite the fact that never before have there been so many adults in the classroom regularly supporting the learning of individuals and groups, which should enable teachers to be more secure and adventurous in the nature of activities they provide for their children. One worrying undesirable consequence of this action is that many young people have not had to weigh up risk factors for themselves, as effectively adults have done much of their thinking for them. It is imperative, therefore, that children do undertake the sort of practical activities that characterise D&T, such as learning to use tools and other potentially hazardous materials within the relatively safe environment of the classroom. Time for discussion of the risks and hazards involved should be built into the scheme of work.

Providing opportunities for children to develop sound economic understanding is important for their future engagement with issues in society. D&T has a role here and as a subject can be strongly linked to the development of the child's economic well-being, as it exposes students to opportunities where they are:

> generating practical, cost-effective solutions that are relevant and fit for purpose; solving technical problems; responding creatively to briefs; developing proposals; working with designers; exploring career opportunities in design. (QCA 2008: 22)

As they develop some nations will arrive at an inevitable point where the mere trading of goods will not see the economic growth that will be required if standards of living are to be maintained or improved. Craft suggests that it is a nation's creativity, and the buying and selling thereof, that will ensure a nation's economic survival (Craft 2001).

Innovation in Creative D&T

Early on in the life of the National Curriculum, Smits (1990) forecast that D&T would:

> have an important part to play in providing a link between the cognitive and practical, in pulling together the threads of the curriculum and introduce relevance to children's learning. (Smits 1990: 30)

In some regards Smits is right. Good and innovative practice does involve pulling together threads of the curriculum to encourage relevance. However, it may be questionable as to whether D&T manages to bridge the gap between the cognitive and the practical. Education alone may not be able to bridge this gap. The ability to transform an abstract idea into a concrete reality is very demanding and requires a range of skills and abilities. Design heroes and champions are often people who can see the world in a different way. Questions as to whether current educational practice enables children to do this need to be asked (Robinson 2009). The current state of D&T education has resulted in a limitation of time available and a lack of confidence amongst primary teachers, resulting in a lack of opportunities for children to make choices and develop a genuine sense of autonomy in their design work.

When searching for innovation in the field we find that the advocated approaches to the teaching of D&T have changed little since 1989, despite minor revisions to the National Curriculum in 1995 and 1999. However, there have been suggestions as to how innovation could be brought about. Kimbell (2000) talks about the restrictive climate within the classroom, which is unhelpful in supporting risk-taking creativity. He states that creativity can be fostered in an environment of faith and trust. It is his opinion, however, that in an era of inspections, targets and league tables, as well as monitoring and accountability initiatives, a climate of 'naming and shaming' is cultivated. Government, school leadership and teaching staff are all responsible for creating the climate in which children learn. However, if school staff feel unsupported to take risks and fail to be pioneers in the area of creative D&T, we will see little to no progress and our teaching approaches will remain the same. As previously mentioned, children need D&T to be set in contexts real to them, including the fantasy world – for example, using an extract from a *Harry Potter* book to lead into the design and making of costumes; children love making costumes out of everyday materials such as bin liners.

The Limitations of a Creative Pedagogy in D&T

Haffenden (2004) has asked whether in a full timetable there is room for the development of creativity. She suggests that many practitioners are often torn between the requirement to meet goals and allowing children time to explore and deepen their understanding. She reasons that the ideal is to have both – to creatively teach what has to be taught. However, she also acknowledges that many teachers make a decision between the options of being compliant and being creative. Joubert (2001) echoes the belief that creativity is not the easy option. She is very careful to make us aware that creativity involves a certain amount of risk taking. She also asserts that for creativity to be successful in the primary school innovative thinking from the individual practitioner is required, and so too is visionary leadership.

Craft (2003) also lists numerous limitations to creativity. Her first concurs with Haffenden (2004) in regard to curriculum organisation. Craft (2003) furthers the argument surrounding the limited time for creativity in the primary sector by highlighting that it is not only restricted by subject content but by delivery as well. Another limitation, it is suggested, comes in the form of the centrally controlled pedagogy (Craft 2003). Unless there is a consensus amongst colleagues with regard to a whole-school approach, students will not progress.

The NACCCE (1999) report suggested that creativity may be connected with production and manufacturing. Children are interested in issues that can be seen at world-stage level, such as waste and pollution. These factors may have a positive limitation on children's creativity. Many design and make activities can be inherently wasteful, and children need to be given the opportunity to consider these issues when designing, which may result in the children imposing limits on their designs. Finally, it is important to acknowledge that creativity has the potential for destruction. When observing cases of Craft's 'big C' creativity, the production of lethal weapons would fit into this category. It is for this reason that ethical limitations may be required to be placed on creativity (Craft 2003). It is important that the children consider how their designs can be used for good.

As we have already explored above, there is real evidence to suggest that D&T as it currently stands is a marginalised subject that suffers from neglect in some already full timetables. Advocacy aimed at pedagogues to develop a creative approach to D&T may be the very thing that causes the subject to suffer yet another blow and D&T may once again become less attractive and further marginalised. A creative approach is not an easy option; planning and allowing time for creativity within D&T sessions is a highly skilled art that requires a strong and confident practitioner with the ability to remain true to their pedagogical beliefs.

Through bringing about creative learning opportunities we are providing the child with the chance to develop their own creative abilities. At appropriate times children must be made aware of the ethical implications that arise when we become creative individuals.

Assessment

Assessment within D&T is a key tool in seeing progression within the learner. Unfortunately, too often children are assessed on what they have made rather than on how they have made it. It is important that teachers take account of both the process and the product when assessing. Hope (2006) contends that assessment should focus on the development of process skills.

Stables (2002) argues that the child should be central and involved in the assessment process. Ritchie (2001) suggests that an important way of doing this is through children's own reflection and evaluations. It is important to note that evaluation should happen throughout the whole process and that unless children are taught how to evaluate, their evaluations can be limited in their value (Hope 2006).

The new programme of study for D&T (DfE 2013) is not at all aimed to be compatible with its previous incarnation. The security of level descriptors has been stripped away while the requirement of schools to report on progress ever increases. Replacing traditional assessment of the product with assessment of the process would appear to be a way forward. By doing this we need to consider how to look for evidence of progress. The importance of providing opportunities for reflective thought has been previously discussed in this chapter. Children need time to formalise their thinking when designing. This can be accomplished through modelling, drawing and redrawing, formal written work, conversations or the use of ICT, which could include photographs of the process (Hope 2006). The keeping of a process diary or a designer's log book is an excellent way for children to record their design process; it also provides the teacher with a rich source of evidence and the opportunity to move the learning on through the making of formative comments. A log that follows children throughout their school design journey, be it digital or in hard copy, would clearly demonstrate progression in design skill and ability.

Summary

D&T has much to contribute to a child's education. Taught well, it will develop the child to be a creative problem solver who is ready for the ever-changing world that is waiting for them after their compulsory education. D&T has suffered as a subject from neglect for many reasons, one of which is lack of teacher confidence in the subject, which in itself stems from lack of experience, expertise and training.

Creativity can be displayed through both a process and a product and both must begin to be valued equally. Creativity flourishes when faith and trust are used and displayed as foundational precepts. Within our classrooms and schools these environments must be established if we are to see creativity cultivated within our students. It has also been suggested that the development of creative abilities in the individual will also help students further ensure achievement of economic well-being in the future. This is especially demonstrated in areas such as D&T as we live in a world where the creation of the technology of tomorrow requires the child of today and their creativity.

Placing D&T in relevant, engaging and, on occasion, localised contexts helps to make learning purposeful. D&T is a subject that benefits from being taught through such an approach. D&T also profits from being taught in a cross-curricular fashion. It has been highlighted that links with D&T to other subjects can easily be made. Links to science can even provide the context for learning in D&T to take place.

Reflection Points

1. What are the benefits to adopting a creative approach to D&T? How can you as the teacher benefit? How can your children benefit?
2. Reflecting on your own experience of observing and teaching D&T, can you think of examples of how you can increase opportunities for creative learning in your future practice?
3. What have you gained from this chapter that will influence your approach to D&T?

Further Reading

Davies, D. and Howe, A. (2014) 'Creativity in primary design and technology', in A. Wilson (ed.), *Creativity in Primary Education*, 3rd edn. London: SAGE/Learning Matters.

Hope, G. (2006) *Teaching Design and Technology at Key Stages 1 and 2*. Exeter: Learning Matters.

Ritchie, R. (2012) *Primary Design and Technology: A Process for Learning*, 2nd edn. London: Fulton/Routledge.

References

Alexander, R. (ed.) (2010) *Children, Their World, Their Education: Final Report and Recommendations of the Cambridge Primary Review*. Abingdon: Routledge.

Craft, A. (2001) 'Little creativity', in A. Craft, B. Jeffrey and M. Liebling, *Creativity in Education*. London: Continuum.

Craft, A. (2003) 'The limits to creativity in education, dilemmas for the educator', *British Journal of Educational Studies*, 51 (2): 113–27.

Cross, A. (2003) 'Teacher influence on pupil autonomy in primary school design and technology', *Research in Science & Technological Education*, 21 (1): 123–35.

Davies, D. and Howe, A. (2014a) 'Creativity in primary design and technology', in A. Wilson (ed.), *Creativity in Primary Education*, 3rd edn. London: Learning Matters/SAGE.

Davies, D. and Howe, A. (2014b) *Teaching Science and Design and Technology in the Early Years*, 2nd edn. London: David Fulton.

Davies, D. and Rogers, M. (2000) 'Pre-service primary teachers' planning for science and technology activities: influences and constraints', *Research in Science and Technological Education*, 18 (2): 213–23.

DfE (Department for Education) (2013) *National Curriculum in England: Design and Technology Programmes of Study*. London: DfE.

Haffenden, D. (2004) 'Compliance and Creativity? Compliance or Creativity?' DATA conference paper, unpublished.

Hope, G. (2004) *Teaching Design and Technology 3–11*. London: Continuum.

Hope, G. (2006) *Teaching Design and Technology at Key Stages 1 and 2*. Exeter: Learning Matters.

Jarvis, T. (1993) *Teaching Design and Technology in the Primary School*. London: Routledge.

Jeffrey, B. and Woods, P. (2003) *The Creative School*. London: RoutledgeFalmer.

Johnston, J. (2005) *Early Explorations in Science*. Maidenhead: Open University Press.

Joubert, M. (2001) 'The art of creative teaching: the NACCCE and beyond', in A. Craft, B. Jeffrey and M. Liebling (eds), *Creativity in Education*. London: Continuum.

Kimbell, R. (2000) 'Creativity, risk and the curriculum', in R. Kimbell, *Footprints in Shifting Sands*. Wellesbourne: The Design and Technology Association.

Lucas, B. (2001) 'Creative teaching, teaching creativity and creative learning', in A. Craft, B. Jeffrey and M. Liebling (eds), *Creativity in Education*. London: Continuum.

NACCCE (1999) *All Our Futures: Creativity, Culture and Education: A Report*. London: DfEE.

Newton, D. (2005) *Teaching Design and Technology 3–11*. London: Paul Chapman Publishing.

Ofsted (2008) *Education for a Technologically Advanced Nation: Design and Technology in Schools 2004/07*. London: Ofsted.

QCA (2008) *Every Child Matters at the Heart of the Curriculum*. London: Qualifications and Curriculum Authority.

Ritchie, R. (2001) *Primary Design and Technology: A Process for Learning*, 2nd edn. London: David Fulton.

Robinson, K. (2009) *The Element: How Finding Your Passion Changes Everything*. London: Penguin

Roden, J. (2005) *Reflective Reader: Primary Science*. Exeter: Learning Matters.

Roth, K. (2000) 'The photosynthesis of Columbus – exploring interdisciplinary curriculum from the student's perspective', in S. Wineburg and P. Grossman (eds), *Interdisciplinary Curriculum Challenges to Implementation*. New York: Teachers College Press.

Smits, A. (1990) 'Primary school technology: where is it going?', in M. Bentley, J. Campbell, A. Lewis and M. Sullivan (eds), *Primary Design and Technology in Practice*. London: Longman.

Stables, K. (2002) 'Assessment in design and technology: authenticity and management issues', in S. Sayers, J. Morley and B. Barnes (eds), *Issues in Design and Technology Teaching*. London: Routledge.

Sternberg, R. and Lubart, T. (1995) *Defying the Crowd: Cultivating Creativity in a Culture of Conformity*. London: The Free Press.

Tickle, L. (ed.) (1990) *Design and Technology in Primary School Classrooms: Developing Teachers' Perspectives and Practices*. East Sussex: The Falmer Press.

CHAPTER 5

AN INTRODUCTION TO HISTORY

Rosemary Walters

Chapter Aims

This chapter will:

- introduce the main elements of the debate surrounding the nature and presence of history in the primary curriculum

- summarise the main strands of current thinking on effective pedagogy in history

- suggest practical ways of planning and implementing good practice in history in the context of creative innovation within the 2014 National Curriculum history programmes of study for Key Stage 1 and Key Stage 2

Introduction

The 2014 National Curriculum programme of study for history begins with a wide range of expectations for the subject.

A high-quality history education will help pupils gain a coherent knowledge and understanding of Britain's past and that of the wider world. It should inspire pupils' curiosity to know more about the past ... History helps pupils to understand the complexity of people's lives, the process of change, the diversities of societies and relationships between different groups, as well as their own identity and the challenges of their time. (DfE 2013: 1)

Certain questions arise from this affirmation:

- Which elements of Britain's past?
- How much of the wider world?
- What types of complexities and diversities?
- Which contemporary challenges?
- Who makes these decisions?

History teaching is a complex intellectual exercise that makes significant demands on the expertise and professionalism of history teachers (Pendry et al. 1998). This is particularly true where primary teachers are not specialists and have not had extensive exposure to historical method in their training, limiting their confidence and competence to experiment with more creative approaches to teaching and learning in the subject.

Teachers confronted with the expectations of the history curriculum for 2014 may well question the nature, purpose and role of teaching history and basic assumptions need to be explored:

- What is history for a twenty-first century curriculum?
- What is the nature of history in education in schools?
- Should pupils be taught to be historians or should they study history?
- How far can history in school replicate the activities of historians by engaging the pupils with evidence and interpretation?
- How should the history curriculum be organised, resourced and delivered?

Defining History

Even the youngest children need to be aware that history is an activity that seeks to recreate past times but cannot give direct access to the world of the past in the way in which geography, for example, can focus on a location which can then actually be visited. History teachers need to engage in the discussion of 'what is history?' just as thoroughly as university academics if they are to have any vision of the purpose and place of history in the primary curriculum. History shares with mathematics and science the process skills of hypothesising, investigating evidence and coming to conclusions. However, such conclusions cannot ultimately be verified by direct access to people or events. History is 'an imaginative reconstruction of the past' (Turner-Bisset 2005: 21) in which understanding the distinction between knowledge, hypothesis and the presence of imagination is appropriate and realistic for primary pupils. Ofsted's 2011 report *History for All* comments favourably on the best lessons in which: 'pupils started to become historical detectives … they refined their questioning skills and their thinking became more sophisticated. The demands placed on them, in terms of knowledge and thinking, became more challenging' (p. 19).

History in the Primary School

The introduction to the Report of the History Working Group on the founding National Curriculum in 1990 (DES 1990: 1) declared that 'History is a splendid subject for study'. However, academic historians have not always been so convinced that history is a valid ingredient of the school curriculum. Elton (2002) speculated as to whether the complexity of recreating the past can be done in any meaningful way when the intellectual capacity to judge the value of evidence is insufficiently developed.

Donaldson (cited in Arthur and Phillips 2000) argues that deductive reasoning is naturally embedded in the child's immediate concerns. Can children be historians? Should children be historians? Hayes (2007: 10) argues that young children are not sufficiently mature to begin grasping historical reality. He describes pseudo-history as dressing up, using cartoons and stories, and playing with archival material. Hayes articulates the vision of the 'need to convert imaginative perspectives into a properly conceived understanding of truth'. However, the value of play and imagination in absorbing young children into the world of the past can form a prelude to a lifelong fascination with history and a developing sophistication in seeking accuracy alongside a realistic understanding of the context of various forms of evidence. This surely validates the role of the teacher as an agent of induction into an interest in the past, at however basic a level?

The Function of History in the Primary School

Successive curriculum documents relating to history have concluded firmly that teaching and learning in history can:

- fire imagination, for example: How did the Roman soldiers feel when they landed in England?
- help the past to throw a constructive light on the present, for example: Why do we keep Remembrance Day?
- ultimately provide pupils with skills that will lead to employment that is fulfilling for them and economically productive for society, for example: I can investigate a problem and present my findings.

The limitations of the life experience of the pupils and the restrictions on their ability to work with the complexity of primary sources suggest that history is on the primary curriculum not only for the advancement of pure historical understanding but also for the personal, social and emotional development of the children. Waters (2008) speaks of the potential for history to equip children with the skill to detect what is relevant and meaningful for them in the subject and to experience history emotionally and spiritually. History, he argues (p. 5), has a particularly valuable role to play in the primary school curriculum. Waters claims that stories, artefacts, investigation, discovery, role play and interviews can give pupils a sense of where they have come from, their culture, their place in wider developments of human society and their relation to other people.

Barton and Levstik (2004: 241–2) argue that effective teaching and learning in history in the primary classroom will produce children whose skills in empathising with the characters and issues from history lessons whom they have lived with from the past will engender a sense of caring:

- *caring that*, looking at the moral judgements of the past: How did the Anglo-Saxons treat crime and punishment?
- *caring for* people in the past: What would it be like to be living in an Iron Age hill fort?
- *caring about* historical interests: Why is it important to care for our local historic buildings and monuments?
- *caring to apply* what they have learned in history to problems in the present so as to make a difference: What can we learn from the history of our local area that might affect planning for the future?

Hence history can be an agent of empowerment and change. It should be 'a human enterprise that the pupils can relate to on personal and ethical terms' (Levstik and Barton 2008: 50). History can foster the perspective of learning from a subject in which the pupils are encouraged to reflect on their own lives in the light of their knowledge and understanding of any given topic and is compatible with the range of opportunities detailed by Ofsted (2013: 37) supporting the inspection of spiritual, moral, social and cultural development in schools. These aspects of potential personal and emotional development run in parallel with the 2014 History curriculum's stated purpose to understand 'the complexity of people's lives and the diversity of societies and relationships between different groups'. The potential for fostering community cohesion and respect for diversity is a complicated process in the twenty-first century. There is a question over the reality of teaching a single, easily understood and transmitted culture, and as Pendry et al. (1998: 148) point out, the importance in a modern society of understanding diversity is an important part of understanding society itself.

A further consideration is whether the study of history has an implicit or explicit moral purpose and this is closely connected to the selection of content. Husbands et al. (2003)

raise the question of choosing to explicitly promote a moral purpose in the teaching of history or the hope that this purpose will somehow emerge from the material. Additionally, the ability to evaluate and approach 'facts' critically is of immense importance in a media-saturated society. Davies and Redmond (1998: 50) stress the role of history teachers in 'preparing their children for life in a society which increasingly presents opinions as facts, and half truths as gospel'.

Furedi (2009) is opposed to what he sees as the use history is being put to as an instrument of social policy: 'history is subordinated to the task of transmitting the latest fashionable cause or value, not history with its own integrity but a vehicle for promoting a version of multicultural Britain' (2009: 129). It is only if teachers have a clear conceptual understanding of how to guide pupils towards the integrity of history through key knowledge, skills and understandings that the criticism of using the subject for particular purposes can be avoided.

What Is the Relevance of History?

In contrast to the current demand for effective teaching and learning in history to be 'relevant' to the lives of the pupils, Furedi (2009) is scathing about the failure of current history teaching to deliver knowledge of the past. This, he argues, has arisen because of the emphasis on relevance and a lack of attention to rigour:

> A one sided obsession with making history less boring has led pedagogies to focus on making the subject more directly relevant to children. Since 1990 the curriculum has been stripped of chronology (the orderly sequencing in time) and a sense of historical process (causes and consequences) has been substituted by a thin gruel of storytelling and skills-led weighing up of evidence. (2009: 82)

The result he sees as disastrous for the discipline of history. A generation of pupils have no idea of chronology – for example, 'did the Romans come before or after 1066?' – and find 'relevance' is no more stimulating than the distant past: 'not the history of our town *again*!' For Furedi it is important that education brings knowledge that is external to the child's experience into the classroom (2009: 143). Children need to be transported to the world of people who lived in times and civilisations beyond their own immediate experience – the Bronze Age settlement, the Roman villa, the Viking invader.

Following the philosophy of starting where the pupil is, Nichol (2008), in a contribution to the debate about what might constitute a history curriculum for the twenty-first century, describes a strategy that starts with the contemporary issue and traces it back to the past instead of starting with the past – a possible compromise in the discussion on relevance.

The State of the Art in Pedagogy

The aim of any contemporary pedagogy must be to replace past horrors described by Davies and Redmond (1998: 39) as 'copying pages from textbooks, colouring in pictures and answering meaningless questions about unconnected stories'. Pedagogy in primary history has progressed from the transmission and regurgitation of second-hand knowledge and understanding, copying information and colouring pictures, to history as the acquisition of skills and understanding derived from the personal investigation of evidence.

The implications of constructivism for the primary history curriculum have been outlined by Littledyke and Huxford (1998) in the context of fieldwork. Translating their theory into general practice for the history teacher, the essential elements of planning can be summarised as:

- deciding on the key question and subsidiary questions for the lesson
- providing the accessible evidence for the pupils to investigate these questions
- devising creative tasks that engage the pupils in investigating the evidence and finding answers to the questions using effective understanding
- structuring plenary sessions so that the pupils organise their findings and communicate them relating to the key and substantive questions.

These stages of planning have the advantage of promoting enquiry skills by focusing each lesson on a question and its component parts, stimulating the evaluation of evidence, giving priority to tasks that facilitate thinking skills and providing the opportunity to confidently articulate the results of enquiry.

Addressing the needs of the child in learning about the past in order to strengthen their sense of identity in the present, Hoodless (2008) articulates a range of strategies that underpin approaches to pedagogy and have been expounded by various history educators:

- the study of sources and evidence in historical enquiry (Cooper 2012)
- the potential of narrative (Bage 1999)
- the importance of explicit teaching and learning in chronology (Hodkinson 2002)
- the role of historical imagination (Turner-Bisset 2005).

Waters (2008) advocates history for its potential to promote the enhancement of learning and thinking skills. Skills in questioning are an imperative and the hierarchy of questioning from data recall to synthesising is helpfully analysed by Nichol (1984, reproduced in Turner-Bisset 2005: 140).

How Should History Teaching be Organised?

Ofsted (2011: 5) emphasises the need for overall coherence in the planning of history within the curriculum:

> Although pupils in primary schools generally had good knowledge of particular topics and episodes in history, their chronological understanding and their ability to make links across the knowledge they had gained were weaker.

In an attempt to address these concerns, the 2014 History National Curriculum is structured with prehistory to 1066 as the basic chronological spine of primary history with opportunities for a wider world study, a local study and a study of an aspect or theme in British history to extend chronological knowledge beyond 1066. The aims of the 2014 curriculum also encourage the understanding of historical concepts as the basis for questioning and analyses.

Hoodless et al. (2009: 3) point to the general humanities concepts of:

- continuity and change
- cause and effect
- conflict and consensus

and suggest specific progression to wider substantive concepts such as power and war. Giving priority to the building up of concepts through careful planning of content that delivers them in each year group could help to address Ofsted's anxiety (Ofsted 2011) that primary school pupils at Key Stage 2 acquire pockets of knowledge rather than progressing through the key elements of understanding of chronology, varieties of evidence and reliability of interpretation.

History Is More than Facts Alone

Knowledge and understanding must go hand in hand for teacher and learner if historical understanding is to be achieved. There can be no understanding without an accurate factual base. To foster pupil engagement and enjoyment it is necessary to have a balance between teacher-directed and independent learning (Maddison 2008). For 'real history' to come into being there needs to be interaction between the guidelines set by the teacher and pupils with the skill to ask historical questions. These questions must be grounded in a context of factual competence. Pupils cannot investigate the importance of King Alfred unless they have a basic understanding of the need for stability and consolidation as the background to his reign.

A definition of 'facts' and 'knowledge' (Furedi 2009) which automatically includes understanding is an important one. There is no place for actually knowing about the past. Facts accompanied by understanding are not dull, boring and useless.

Skelton and Reeves (2009: 147) highlight three aspects of knowledge which can be developed in cross-curricular planning. Thinking through the balance of these aspects provides a useful tool for reflection in the process of devising creative primary history:

- essential knowledge (what pupils must know): for example, how roads developed in Roman times
- motivational knowledge (what excites pupils): for example, what difference would roads make to the lives of Roman armies and town and country dwellers?
- transformational knowledge (knowledge that expands thinking): for example, what effect has the development of roads had on our lives today? Should we build more?

The focus on thinking skills in the primary classroom (Kelly 2005) is well illustrated in the Philosophy for Children approach (www.philosophy4children.co.uk). The website states specifically that 'in history, children are required to understand how the past has been interpreted and represented by different people. They need to demonstrate an understanding of the results of change and how it affects us now'. An enquiry process with opportunity for pupil choice in selecting lines of enquiry stimulates creativity by rewarding curiosity and exploration, building internal motivation and encouraging risk-taking (Jones and Wyse 2005).

The Philosophy for Children approach is a prime example of a constructivist pedagogy that can be applied to history. It works with the natural curiosity of the children and delivers opportunities for connecting with personal experience, independent thinking and evaluation, and social interaction, which help the learner to 'know what knowledge means' (Selby 1999: 5), rather than having it pre-packaged and handed over as the finished article. Fleetham (2005: 52) aligns the Philosophy for Children approach to brainstorming, which follows the set pattern of pupils:

- choosing the question
- appointing a scribe
- forbidding both praise and criticism as the problem is considered
- giving a time limit to producing as many creative solutions as possible before evaluating these.

The collaborative aspect of historical enquiry should be organised so that all pupils can contribute meaningfully and have their contribution valued.

Early Years

The 2013 Early Years Outcomes document (DfE 2013: 28) encourages historical investigation in the early learning goal 'People and Communities'. It states that children should talk about past and present events in their own lives and in the lives of family members.

Starting with the immediate family world of the young child, an emerging sense of the past can focus on

- my family
- my toys
- my home
- my shops
- my holidays.

The scope can be broadened to encompass the local environment and beyond with oral history from family members or local residents as a powerful tool. Given that young children relate most effectively to the familiar, it is encouraging that there is a Key Stage 1 requirement to explore significant events, people and places in their own locality.

However, developing a curiosity beyond the immediate and therefore including the distant, is essential to progression of historical understanding in the early years curriculum. Refusing to look beyond the immediate experience of the child can stifle imagination and limit discovery of aspects of human nature and human endeavour. Barnaby Bear undertakes many exciting explorations in the interests of early years geography and there seems no reason why such a character cannot be utilised to engage very young children in historical discovery and an understanding of time. What questions would Barnaby Bear ask if he travelled through time? These would probably be the same questions asked by the children themselves, such as:

- What did people eat?
- What did people wear?
- What type of homes did people have?
- How did people travel?
- What type of toys did children play with?

A start can then be made on moving from the descriptive to simple analysis: What are the differences and similarities with now and why is this so?

The Key Stage 1 2014 History Curriculum moves on to the wider scope of:

- changes within living memory, hinting that some of these relate to national life
- events beyond living memory that are significant nationally or globally
- the lives of significant individuals who have contributed to national and international achievements.

Egan (2008: 13) insists that the 'first principle for teaching young children history is that the curriculum should consist of real events, real characters, real times, real places. The events should be dramatic, the characters heroic, the names and places strange and distant'. He has a powerful vision of history as 'the story of civilisation, the struggle against ignorance and against oppression'. Children need to learn early about the real heroes and heroines who did great things. For example, there are Key Stage 1 resources to help with the stories of:

- Grace Darling
- Rosa Parks
- Samuel Pepys
- Captain Scott

as well as the more usual choices of Florence Nightingale and Mary Seacole.

The Thinking History Classroom

A thinking classroom that is alive to the possibility of effective and challenging history teaching will at once impress itself on a visitor with possibilities such as:

- the key question and subsidiary questions on display
- chronological vocabulary cards as appropriate to the unit of study
- a family tree based on a symbolic child on display who accompanies whatever study is in progress and can be dressed in appropriate costume
- an interactive timeline as a work in progress continually refreshed by pupil contributions
- an artefact dustbin
- time hats
- a picture gallery with pictures labelled by the pupils to illustrate understanding of the significance of the picture
- an artefact living museum with labels written and produced by the pupils using ICT.

All these will testify to an environment peopled by working historians rather than a display of the thought processes and artistic priorities of the teacher. The Learning Wall will be continually changing as new evidence and new interpretations of the answers to key questions come to light.

There must be explicit historical questions to be answered relating to:

- location in time
- causation and consequence
- similarity and difference with the present, implications for the future
- the reliability of sources and evidence
- the effective organisation and communication of the results of the investigation reported in a way that highlights these historical priorities.

Teaching Time

Previous and current Ofsted reports (2007, 2011) are concerned that primary history does not deliver 'big picture' understanding or the ability to accurately place chronological periods within a large timescale. New topics should always begin with an artefact or picture from the period that is placed between items from periods immediately before and after to give a visual representation of the location in time of the events to be studied.

Specific teaching and learning about chronology is advocated by Hodkinson (2002). Here, strategies such as:

- time hats
- looking through time windows to determine prior knowledge
- short, snappy, numeracy tasks
- the interactive timeline

are shown to be stimulating and effective methods of ascertaining and developing a sense of time. Chronology is not treated as an element of historical understanding that will automatically happen but as one that needs to be deliberately included in planning and subsequent activities.

The development of chronological vocabulary also needs careful thought. There should be a clear understanding of the appropriate chronological vocabulary to be introduced at each key stage with the use of display cards in the classroom to reinforce this, some flexible suggestions being:

Early Years/Key Stage 1

- now, then, past, present, today, tomorrow
- the names of days, weeks and months

Key Stage 2

- annual, decade, century, millennium
- specific period terminology, for example the Victorians

The use of some cardboard cut-out children whose family tree goes back to their great-grandparents will be a powerful visual aid and these children can be clothed in the dress of whatever historical period is being explored, reinforcing their place in history. Early years practitioners might like to make a simple three-generational family tree for a soft toy character, which can also include relevant costumes. Their own family tree going back to grandparents is a visual stimulus to prompt under-standing of how generations fit in.

Telling the Story: the Heart of the Matter

The history task is one of making sense of the narrative of the past, explaining the causes and consequences of a narrative sequence of events. Bage (1999) points to the central importance of the children thinking about and recognising the heart of any story in terms of human experience. Reflection on elements of a story such as greed, ambition, power and kindness can be recorded on a cardboard cut-out heart from each child, which can be put on display.

Children are endlessly fascinated by stories and there are times when listening to a story delivered with passion can enthral and fire the imagination. The vast resource of literacy approaches to story can be transferred to history:

- role play
- hot seating
- conscience alley
- a variation on the story board is a request from a TV company to provide a brief for adapting the story for television. Pupils need to decide on the sequence of scenes, the location and props and particularly why viewers will both enjoy and learn history from the story. Finally, their portfolio presentation is performed to their peers and a decision is made as to whether or not to commission the series.

The Past Alive through Pictures and Artefacts

Pictures and artefacts need to be incorporated as sources of enquiry and a wide vari-ety of imaginative tasks relating to these and ways of expressing the results of historical investigation from historical sources through role play and drama have been described by Turner-Bisset (2005). Hodkinson (2008: 14) charts the cognitive stages through which an exploration of pictures can be used as:

- closed questions for information
- open questions to stimulate thinking
- interpretative questions to prompt making judgements
- evaluative questions: What does this tell us about living in the past? How reliable is it as evidence?

These stages can equally apply to artefacts.

Both artefacts and pictures need to be introduced as 'mystery'. After a sense of excitement has built up, the resource is revealed. In the case of artefacts they can be uncovered or dug carefully out of sand trays, while pictures can be placed from face down to face up. Then the investigation begins. I Spy is a popular strategy to stimulate close observation. Portraits can be examined for propaganda, pictures of events entered imaginatively by the pupils via the five senses and possible conversations between characters created. Similarities and differences with the past can be identified by placing 'Post-its' on the picture. The labels for both artefacts and pictures can be produced by the pupils using an appropriate ICT programme, the content of the labels to progress from naming to explaining clearly but concisely what the resources tell us about the past.

The Past in Cyberspace

Undoubtedly one of the greatest recent influences on the potential for constructivist history teaching is the phenomenal scope of IT to provide a range of primary and secondary sources. At the press of a key, pupils can access the collections of archives and museums in a world far removed from reliance on the class textbook, library books and worksheet. The National Archives Education website (www.national archives.gov.uk/education/) is an outstanding resource. For example, its material on the Trimdon Grange Explosion includes a song written at the time. The use of IT to record interviews with local people and to produce spreadsheets of specific information, such as census returns, points to its many opportunities to communicate findings. The BBC's History for Kids website (www.bbc.co.uk/history/forkids/) has subject knowledge through games and quizzes.

New skills are required to cope with this abundance of opportunity:

- how to select the relevant items
- how to detect bias and determine the source and agenda of some internet material
- how to categorise the material into primary and secondary sources and to understand how this categorisation may affect the use of evidence.

Websites should always be approached with a question that will contribute to the lesson key question and never be just browsed. A key resource for teaching the 2014 curriculum with its emphasis on Britain Before 1066 is the English Heritage teaching resources site Heritage Explorer, which includes access to an excellent prehistory teachers' handbook. Reliable subject knowledge for teachers is available from the BBC History pages (www.bbc.co.uk/history/0/) where there is an option on Ancient History. The Historical Association and the BBC Learning Zone clips have a wealth of resources to stimulate historical thinking. IT sites can link with items such as folksongs.

Teaching Place

The Cambridge Review (Alexander 2010: 272–5) has made an impressive case for curriculum time to be determined by local considerations. Learning across and outside the classroom is recognised as an effective way to engage pupils' interest by relating to their everyday lives and experience. This is a wonderful opportunity for local history to take the lead in stimulating learning experiences based on local issues, events and personalities of the past which can put the present in perspective.

The local area, whatever its superficial limitations seem to be, can provide the stimulation for much outreach into historical enquiry of a variety of chronological and thematic lines of investigation, including:

- place names
- street names
- industrial and domestic architecture
- urban and rural development in transport, land use and employment.

The lives of wealthy and influential families, the lives of all those who seem to be insignificant, the war memorials, the post boxes, the battlefields – pupils can make sense of the whole muddle of the past as part of their local heritage seen in the context of today and tomorrow. These are the bones of history, which cross-curricular learning and subject-specific experiences, planned as part of a whole-school curriculum offering continuity and progression with due regard for chronological understanding, can form into the skeleton of a historical framework that has unlimited scope for lifelong interest.

The case for fieldwork is made convincingly by Corbishley (2009: 8), when he states that unless children are inducted into an attitude of concern for the physical evidence of the past, it will be gone. There is no time to wait until children are 'old enough' to begin taking an interest in this aspect of history. He points to the link with citizenship and heritage as a global concern and suggests that issues of the protection of buildings and inappropriate development are all a part of the history agenda as children take their place as citizens who hold in their hands the power to preserve or destroy environmental evidence of the past. Concern for the historic environment is not limited to 'ancient' sites but is for history all around. Fieldwork is one of the defining characteristics of good historical practice and pupils should be introduced to this first through the study of their local area at various levels of sophistication. In the classroom children can use their memory to record a simple map of the area with any historical features before they go out to plot items relating to a general or more specific focus, such as domestic buildings, street names, letter boxes, place names and transport. The English Heritage Series 'A Teachers Guide To ...' (TES 2015) is invaluable here.

Recording findings from fieldwork is well exemplified by Coulson in the Teachers TV programme *Hidden House* (TES 2015) where the use of a simple plan of the village in which the school is situated is laid out in toilet roll and provides a context for displaying coloured diagrams of buildings based on their age. At a glance it is obvious how the village has developed through time and the pupils enjoy placing their diagrams and watching the streets of the village take chronological shape. Copies of historic maps may well be available from the local library and similarities and differences can be noted and explained.

It is imperative that learning outside the classroom is just that and not a wasted opportunity where tasks that can be done in the classroom are merely moved to another, albeit more exotic, location. Pupils visiting a museum do not need to spend the majority of their time sitting on the carpet being introduced to artefacts when they could be discovering, where possible handling, and asking questions about, those artefacts themselves.

Visits to historic sites and museums focus on key questions and on the investigations that will yield the answers to these questions in addition to discussion on the reliability of the evidence. Empathy can be fostered through role play and the pupils' IT skills used to record and present findings. Guides to the collections in a museum and the significant architectural, domestic and political issues through time of a historic site can all be produced on screen as well as on paper. Interviews with museum staff and archaeologists on site are a practical advantage of access to IT.

A dynamic cross-curricular learning experience based on the local area can incorporate local issues of planning, land use and transport, including a study of the past as a reference point for change. Dialogue with local councillors and their staff, and suggestions from the pupils regarding local issues, will make use of skills and understandings from a combination of disciplines in an interdisciplinary model of cross-curricular activity. Fieldwork is a key strategy here.

 Case Study 5.1

Draft long-term planning for Key Stage 2

Faced with the requirements of the 2014 National Curriculum History, Key Stage 2 teachers in a small rural school worked with the history co-ordinator to plan an effective chronological and conceptual curriculum that will allow for the maximum flexibility and use of existing resources. A small budget for new resources was available. There was considerable apprehension about both subject knowledge and appropriate pedagogy in working with pre-1066 content.

Following initial discussion, the long-term plan below emerged.

Chronological Spine (Autumn Terms)

- Year 3 Stone Age to Iron Age in Britain
- Year 4 Roman Empire and its impact on Britain

- Year 5 Anglo-Saxon and Scots settlement
- Year 6 Viking and Anglo-Saxon struggle for the Kingdom up to Edward the Confessor

World History Topics (Spring Terms)

- Year 3 Ancient Egypt
- Year 4 Ancient Greece
- Year 5 Mayan civilisation
- Year 6 Benin (West Africa)

Themes Beyond 1066 (Summer Terms)

As a priority, visits will be built into the curriculum where possible and any local history will be specifically planned around these, rather than having the visits as a bolt-on.

- Year 3 Significant people and events in the history of our locality
- Year 4 A significant turning point in the history of transport, nationally and locally, roads, railways and canals
- Year 5 A site from a period beyond 1066 in the locality
- Year 6 World War II nationally and locally, evacuation, the Home Front, the Battle of Britain

The co-ordinator introduced the English Heritage website (www.english-heritage. org.uk/education/), the Heritage Explorer site (www.heritage-explorer.co.uk/ web/he/default.aspx), the Primary History area on BBC Learning Zone Clips (www.bbc.co.uk/learningzone/clips/) and the Historical Association primary website (www.history.org) to address staff apprehension around resources for the focus of the curriculum up to 1066.

Teachers from each year group began to work on their own planning.

 Reflection Points

1. Do you think that this draft planning will help or hinder pupils' chronological understanding? Would you change it? If so, how?
2. Look up one of the websites listed above. Does it increase your confidence in planning for British History up to 1066?

Case Study 5.2

Year 3 Unit One planning

Year 3 teachers in a large urban school with little local archaeological context decided to plan an introduction to the Stone Age that focused on the work of archaeologists and types of evidence for pre-history. They produced a draft sequence of learning as below:

Key Questions

- What is an archaeologist?
- How and what does archaeology tell us about the past?

Archaeologists in Action

Choose a clip from the BBC Learning Zone Primary History Historical Enquiry selection to show archaeologists in action.

Discussion

- Why might it be exciting to be an archaeologist?
- What are the skills you need?
- What happens to the evidence after it has been excavated?
- How much can the evidence tell you about the past?

Follow-Up

Sand trays containing historic artefacts on each table and pupils to excavate, investigate them and make labels for them.

Visitor

Invite the pupils to think up questions they would like to ask an archaeologist and invite one in as a visitor to answer their questions.

Visit

- Visit a local museum and talk to the curator about how the exhibits are displayed. Pupils to make suggestions to enhance the exhibition.

Follow-Up

- Make an interactive timeline for the classroom. Pupils research the internet and bring in pictures of any aspect of life in the Stone, Bronze and Iron Age to start it off.
- Pupils decide on contents that have a particular significance for our time and make up a time capsule with a leaflet explaining the significance of each item.
- Year 3 pupils then lead an assembly, producing the items from the time capsule and explaining what an archaeologist might learn from each item if it was dug up in the future.

Assessment

The 2014 history curriculum document does not include a definite statement of the key elements of history, the Knowledge, Skills and Understanding (KSUs) that underpinned the study of primary history in the previous National Curriculum, but these remain a vital guide to assessment in history and can be summarised as:

- chronological understanding: engaging with the literacy and numeracy of time
- knowledge and understanding of events: people and changes, and the concepts of causation, change and consequences
- historical enquiry: the different types of evidence available
- historical interpretation: the reliability of sources
- organisation and communication of findings: text, electronic, visual, charts, diagrams, oral.

Focusing on these components of the historian's task will enable non-specialist history teachers to audit their planning to ensure that historical learning and teaching are taking place. Davies and Redmond (1998: 58) comment on school case studies based on these key elements that 'by switching away from the factual knowledge of a study unit and towards the skill required to be a historian, these teachers managed to construct an extremely worthwhile history topic which would enable the children to acquire historical skills', and continue, 'there was sufficient attention to the key elements, and therefore to progression of the children as historians, with the skills necessary to study the subject effectively' (Davies and Redmond, 1998: 58).

The definition of assessment as 'sitting alongside' provides a vision of the teacher and pupil sitting alongside each other as historians, evaluating what has been learnt about the story of the past, the variety of evidence and its reliability, and the teacher making judgements about the way in which the pupil can communicate this knowledge and understanding.

There are imaginative strategies for summative assessment which can be employed here, such as:

- postcards from the past, which spell out concisely why an event or person is significant
- invitations to past events, which indicate their significance in terms of cause and effect
- reasoning portrayed in chart form with bullet points for and against an opinion or decision using content with varying degrees of sophistication related to the age and ability of the class
- summative templates using a sheet of A4 paper with a space in the middle for the pupils to draw a logo that represents the unit of work for them. Around this are boxes for bullet points to be filled in, the titles of which can be decided by the teacher focused on the knowledge and understanding that has been set out in the key questions of each lesson
- understanding of the lesson key question to which the pupils individually or in groups contribute in the plenary or at the end of the unit of work in a variety of ways.

Fleetham (2005) has a range of suggestions for imaginative formative and summative assessment which can be adapted for primary history, including thinking forks, living graphs, thinking pictures, chain of events, choice pyramids, pros and cons charts and odd-one-out lists (Figure 5.1).

Fleetham's Thinking Fork

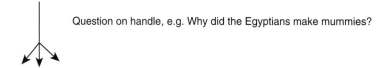

Question on handle, e.g. Why did the Egyptians make mummies?

Put possible answers on prongs; pupils to research and decide the most important.

Fleetham's Choice Pyramid

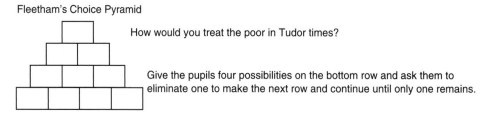

How would you treat the poor in Tudor times?

Give the pupils four possibilities on the bottom row and ask them to eliminate one to make the next row and continue until only one remains.

Figure 5.1   Fleetham's thinking fork and choice pyramid

In the absence of National Curriculum attainment target level descriptors to give a guide to building in continuity and progression, teachers still need a useful check to ensure that tasks are sufficiently challenging. Year 6 children should have gone beyond levels of historical understanding which restrict them to knowing and recounting episodes from stories about the past They should be aspiring to making links between events and changes and giving reasons for, and results of, these events and changes. Broad issues of progression are expressed as expectations in the History KS1 and KS2 areas of the DCSF Archived Standards site (webarchive.national archives.gov.uk).

Teachers need to plan for progression so that the pupils make progress in:

- a growing understanding of chronology
- an appreciation of the sources, the use and reliability of evidence
- a developing awareness of the nature of change and causation
- an articulate use of historical concepts.

Much attainment in history is mistakenly measured by subject knowledge alone but all the key skills should be progressing in the child's cognitive development. Peer and self-assessment can be activated using simple 'I can' statements. The latter can be used as a basis for 'Are you history smart?' attainment cards which can be hung over tables or kept by the pupils individually. For example, 'I can explain why hill forts were built in the Iron Age' can be further translated into a general 'I am history smart' card, 'I understand why events happen in time'.

Conclusion

This chapter has argued that in primary history pupils should be working as historians, that there are a variety of outcomes which history is expected to deliver in contemporary society and that history, whether planned as a discrete subject or within a cross-curricular learning experience, must include certain key elements if it is to enhance the world of understanding of the child. Assessment must be seen as the teacher and the pupil sitting alongside each other as fellow historians. Seemingly mechanistic devices such as attainment targets and level descriptors are effective in ensuring continuity and progression within the key elements if they are used in planning and not as bolt-ons of regurgitated material.

Encountering history gives children a sense of identity and becoming historians provides a context for acquiring and reinforcing the skills necessary for a post-modern, plural society. So where are the history teacher and learner going? An exciting question! As Bage comments mysteriously, 'No history should end at the present day but must go on to critically examine the different ways in which the future is currently represented' (Bage 2000: 155).

Reflection Points

1. What is the balance between subject knowledge and the process of investigation in primary history or is this a false dichotomy?
2. Is history what happened in the past or what is interpreted as having happened? Which of these applies the most in primary history?
3. How would you rank these functions of history at school:

   - to promote personal development
   - to provide pupils with skills which will lead to employment
   - to use the past to aid understanding of the present
   - to use the past to make a moral point
   - to encourage community cohesion and respect for diversity

4. How would you describe the 'value' of primary history for teachers and for pupils?
5. Look at Case Study 5.2. Do you think this is an effective way to begin Key Stage 2 history? Would you change it? If so, how?

Further Reading

Barnes, J. (2007) *Cross-Curricular Learning 3–14*. London: SAGE.

Boys, R. and Spink, E. (2008) *Teaching the Foundation Subjects*. London: Continuum.

Cooper, H. (1995) *History in the Early Years*. London: Routledge.

Cooper, H. (ed.) (2013) *Teaching History Creatively*. Abingdon: Routledge.

DfE (Department for Education) (2013) *Early Years Outcomes*. London: DfE.

Galton, M. (2007) *Learning and Teaching in the Primary Classroom*. London: SAGE.

Green, R. (2010) *Games, Ideas, Activities for Primary Humanities*. Harlow: Longman.

Fisher, R. and Williams, M. (2004) *Unlocking Creativity*. London: David Fulton.

Historical Association (2002) *Past Forward: A Vision for School History 2002–2012*. London: Historical Association.

Hoodless, P. (2008) *Achieving QTS: Teaching History in Primary Schools*. Exeter: Learning Matters.

Hughes, P., Cox, K. and Goddard, G. (2000) *Primary History Curriculum Guide*. London: David Fulton.

Kelly, P. (2005) *Using Thinking Skills in the Primary Classroom*. London: Paul Chapman.

Riley, M. and Harris, R. (2002) *Past Forward: A Vision for School History, 2002–2012*. Historical Association, www.history.org.uk (accessed 16 July 2014).

Turner-Bisset, R. (2005) *Creative Teaching: History in the Primary Classroom*. London: Fulton.

Wilson, A. (2009) *Creativity in Primary Education*, 2nd edn. Exeter: Learning Matters.

Wyse, D. and Dowson, P. (2009) *The Really Useful Creativity Book*. London: Routledge.

References

Alexander, R. (ed.) (2010) *Children, Their World, Their Education: Final Report and Recommendations of the Cambridge Primary Review*. Abingdon: Routledge.

Arthur, J. and Phillips, R. (2000) *Issues in History Teaching*. London: Routledge.

Bage, G. (1999) *Narrative Matters: Teaching and Learning History through Story*. London: Falmer.

Bage, G. (2000) *Thinking History 4–14*. London: RoutledgeFalmer.

Barton, K. and Levstik, L. (2004) *Teaching History for the Common Good*. London: Lawrence Erlbaum Associates.

Cooper, H. (2012) *History 5–11: A Guide For Teachers*, 2nd edn. Abingdon: Routledge.

Corbishley, M. (2009) 'Our heritage: use it or lose it', *Primary History*, 51: 8–9.

Davies, J. and Redmond, J. (1998) *Co-ordinating History Across the Primary School*. London: Falmer.

DES (Department of Education and Science) (1990) *History for Ages 5–16: National Curriculum Proposals of the Secretary of State for Education and Science*. London: DES.

DfE (Department for Education) (2013) *History Programmes of Study: Key Stages 1 and 2. National Curriculum in England*. London: DfE.

Egan, K. (2008) 'Teaching history to young children', *Primary History*, 50: 11–13.

Elton, G. (2002) *The Practice of History*. Oxford: Blackwell.

Fleetham, M. (2005) *How to Create and Develop a Thinking Classroom*. Cambridge: LDA.

Furedi, F. (2009) *Wasted: Why Education Isn't Educating*. London: Continuum.

Hayes, D. (2007) 'Consigning history to the history books', *Primary History*, 45: 10.

Hodkinson, A. (2002) Teachers TV KS1/2 Chronology Workshop at http://teachfind.com/teachers-tv/ks2-history-chronology-workshop?current_search=KS1%2F2%20Chronology%20Workshop (accessed 16 July 2014).

Hodkinson, A. (2008) 'Visual Literacy: Learning through pictures and images', *Primary History*, 49.

Hoodless, P. (2008) 'Every Child Matters: addressing the needs of the child in learning about the past', *Primary History*, 50: 14–17.

Hoodless, P., McCreery, E., Bermingham, S. and Bowen, P. (2009) *Teaching Humanities in Primary Schools*. Exeter: Learning Matters.

Husbands, C., Kitson, A. and Pendry, A. (2003) *Understanding History Teaching*. Maidenhead: Open University Press.

Jones, R. and Wyse, D. (2005) *Creativity in the Primary Curriculum*. London: David Fulton.

Kelly, P. (2005) *Using Thinking Skills in the Primary Classroom*. London: Paul Chapman.

Levstik, L. and Barton, K. (2008) *Researching History Education*. New York: Routledge.

Littledyke, M. and Huxford, L. (1998) *Teaching the Primary Curriculum for Constructivist Learning*. London: David Fulton.

Maddison, M. (2008) 'History in primary schools: an Ofsted perspective', *Primary History*, 50: 9.

Nichol, J. (2008) 'From Russia with love', *Primary History*, 50: 21–3.

Ofsted (2007) *History in the Balance*. London: Ofsted.

Ofsted (2011) *History for All*. London: Ofsted.

Ofsted (2013) *Subsidiary Guidance Supporting the Inspection of Maintained Schools and Academies*. London: Ofsted.

Pendry, A., Husbands, C., Arthur, J. and Davison, J. (1998) *History Teachers in the Making*. Buckingham: Open University Press.

Selby, N. (1999) *The Art of Constructivist Teaching in the Primary School*. London: David Fulton.

Skelton, M. and Reeves, G. (2009) 'What it means for primary-aged children to be internationally minded: the contribution of geography and history', in C. Rowley and H. Cooper (eds), *Cross-curricular Approaches to Teaching and Learning: Developing an Integrated Primary Curriculum*. London: SAGE.

TES (2015) Teachers TV Videos. Available at: www.tes.co.uk (Accessed 3 February 2015).

Turner-Bisset, R. (2005) *Creative Teaching: History in the Primary Classroom*. London: David Fulton.

Waters, M. (2008) 'History … about lives and living', *Primary History*, 50: 5–6.

Journals

Primary History. The primary education journal of the Historical Association, London.

Websites

BBC History for Kids: www.bbc.co.uk/history/forkids – useful ideas for creative activities

BBC Learning Zone: www.bbc.co.uk/learningzone/clips – short clips to introduce topics

English Heritage: www.heritage-explorer.co.uk

English Heritage Education: www.english-heritage.org.uk/education/

Historical Association: www.history.org – news and views about primary history with ideas for lessons

National Archives: www.nationalarchives.gov.uk/education – a wealth of primary source material

National Portrait Gallery: www.npg.org.uk – access to a wide variety of visual evidence

CHAPTER 6

AN INTRODUCTION TO GEOGRAPHY

Simon Hoult

Chapter Aims

This chapter will:

- introduce you to the current debates around the nature of geography in the primary curriculum
- outline key geographical pedagogic processes
- illustrate ways that geography can be taught within a creative and cross-curricular approach to the curriculum

Introduction

What Is Geography and Why Is It an Important Discipline?

'The study of geography is about more than just memorising places on a map. It's about understanding the complexity of our world: appreciating the diversity of cultures that exists across continents. And in the end, it's about using all that knowledge to help bridge divides and bring people together' (President Barack Obama, cited in Ballin 2013).

Geography enables study of, and active participation in, our local and global environments. This is through consideration of environmental changes and human actions, past, present and future and the implications of these for the well-being of our wider world. Heffernan argues that the 'deceptively simple word "geography" embraces a deeply contested intellectual project of great antiquity and extraordinary complexity' and positions geography as a 'distinct but complex field of intellectual enquiry at the interface between the natural environmental sciences, the social sciences and the humanities' (Heffernan 2003: 3, cited in Herbert and Matthews 2004: 3). As a consequence of this, it is difficult to define a discipline that spans such traditional curriculum groupings; however, reading geography as 'the study of the surface of the Earth [involving] the phenomena and processes of the Earth's natural and human environments and landscapes at local and global scales' (Herbert and Matthews 2004: 255) reflects the wide scope of the subject, not only in what is studied but in the way we learn to read our world with 'geographical eyes'.

'Geography underpins a lifelong "conversation" about the earth as the home of human kind. It contributes to a balanced education for all young people in schools, colleges and other settings' (Geographical Association 2009). Such learning develops a wealth of values, knowledge, understanding and skills that enable young people to understand and engage with their world. Geography as the discipline that helps children learn about their world could arguably be at the heart of any broad, balanced curriculum, however the Cambridge Review of Primary Education noted that geography (along with history) was 'widely regarded as being undervalued in primary education and under-represented in the curriculum' (Alexander 2010). This chapter helps to provide reasons and guidance as to how geography can reclaim a strong position in the primary curriculum.

Our geographical imagination is highlighted by Martin (2006), who illustrates this through an apparently simple decision of where to drink a cup of coffee. This may involve decisions about such matters as location (which cafe is nearest), place (where is best to drink coffee), micro-climate (where to sit to enjoy the sunshine or avoid a draught) and sustainability (which sell fairtrade coffee). Martin argues that geography is important in the primary curriculum because it 'raise[s] children's awareness of the geographical dimensions of our everyday experiences, so that they can make better, more informed decisions about how to live their lives' (2006: 3).

The merits of geography are well rehearsed amongst the professional and academic geography communities such as the Geographical Association (GA) and the Royal Geographical Society (RGS), but have been somewhat of an educational secret beyond such organisations at times. One reason for this is that there are some difficulties in thoughtfully answering the question of what geography really is and is for. This is not purely an academic question but one that is often posed in school 'all too urgently by students who demand to know what's the point?' (Morgan and Lambert 2005: 42).

The broad definitions of geography in the opening paragraph show simultaneously certain strengths and weakness of the subject. Such a broad and plural view of geography strengthens its ability to incorporate a wide, and apparently contrasting, range of specialisms such as climate science, population studies and behavioural geography within the discipline. Such a breadth gives the subject strength across the curriculum. Geography's curriculum flexibility enables almost any area of learning to have a geographical dimension, including curriculum areas given considerable time in the primary phase such as literacy and numeracy.

A weakness emerges, however, in the rather plural and wide-ranging view of the subject that can make it especially hard for non-specialist primary teachers to understand the nature of geography and geographical learning (Ofsted 2011) and particularly the concepts that underpin it. There is a danger that without a conceptual foundation the subject becomes diluted to a long list of content to 'cover' in a curriculum such as weather, our high street and tourism rather than exploring the concepts that underpin *and* connect the subject in pupils' minds. These concepts enable us to see things more broadly and deeply with 'geographical eyes'.

Open up a more thoughtful newspaper and look at the first few pages. It is near impossible *not* to find a story that does not have a geographical dimension. This may be more explicit in the article, such as a natural disaster, our carbon footprint or fair trade, or more implicit within stories about the closure of a pub, a community project to help immigrants or local crime. It is not the subject content that necessarily makes it geographical but the concepts that underpin it that enable its geography to be understood, knowledge to be developed, values to be explored and skills to be acquired.

There have been a number of proposals as to the nature of geographical concepts. Table 6.1 illustrates three such models of concepts which, to some degree, are determined by the intended focus and audience such as university geography or school geography (Taylor 2009). Although there is some consensus about key concepts such as place, space and scale, it is clear that geographical concepts are not a given and they will also change with time.

Table 6.1   Examples of geographical concepts

Holloway et al. (2003)	**Jackson (2006)**	**Lambert and Morgan (2010)**
Space	Space and place	Place
Time	Scale and connection	Space
Place	Proximity and distance	Scale
Scale	Relational thinking	Interdependence and development
Social formations		Cultural understanding and diversity
Physical systems		Environment, sustainability and futures
Landscape and environment		

Adapted from Taylor 2009

- *Place* (understanding the physical and human characteristics of places and developing 'geographical imaginations' of places).

- *Space* (understanding the interactions between places and the networks created by flows of information/people/goods, knowing where and why places and landscapes are located, the patterns and distributions they create, how and why these are changing and the implications for people).

- *Scale* (appreciating different scales and making links between scales to develop understanding of geographical ideas).

- *Interdependence* (exploring social, economic, environmental and political connections between places and understanding the significance of interdependence in change on all scales).

- *Physical and human processes* (understanding how sequences of events and activities in the physical and human worlds lead to change in places, landscapes and societies).

- *Environmental interaction and sustainable development* (understanding that the physical and human dimensions of the environment are interrelated and together influence environmental change; exploring sustainable development and its impact on environmental interaction and climate change).

- *Cultural understanding and diversity* (appreciating the differences and similarities between people, places, environments and cultures to inform an understanding of societies and economies; appreciating how people's values and attitudes differ and may influence social, environmental, economic and political issues, and developing one's own values and attitudes about such issues).

Figure 6.1   Geographical concepts briefly explained (adapted from QCA 2007)

Geographical concepts provide strong and explicit foundations upon which the primary curriculum can be built through our pedagogy and use of terminology to develop geographical knowledge, understanding, skills and values. Collectively, these concepts are the unique contribution that geography brings to the curriculum. Being explicit about the concepts in our preparation and teaching allows us to draw aspects of geography together rather than them remaining in separate knowledge domains of the discipline. To be a strong contributor to the cross-curricular curriculum, these concepts need to be understood by teachers *and* pupils so that geographical understanding can be built upon these explicit foundations within cross-curricular learning. Figure 6.1 provides a short explanation of some of the more commonly identified geographical concepts, although for further details and depth a text like Lambert and Morgan (2010) is advisable reading.

The previous geography national curriculum was explicit about its conceptual underpinnings and much less about the content that should be taught in schools which was locally determined. Ofsted (2011), however, commented that primary geography presented a 'polarised picture', with some outstanding geography teaching and learning, but where it was inadequate pupils' core geographical knowledge was often poor in the primary lessons observed. Ofsted defined core knowledge as the 'basic factual knowledge, vocabulary and the ability to locate, with a degree of accuracy, important places and human and physical features' (Ofsted 2011: 4). This evidence of some poor basic knowledge provides empirical support for the ideological change evident in the 2014 National Curriculum for England which has moved to a strong emphasis on required knowledge and which has removed all reference to key concepts. In addition to geographical skills and fieldwork, the curriculum (DfE 2013) focuses upon three forms of subject knowledge, namely:

Locational knowledge;
Place knowledge;
Human and physical geography.

In reading the new curriculum conceptually it is easy to see where concepts of place and human and physical processes are clearly evident. If, as the new curriculum requires in the outline of its aims, we consider places in the way they relate to other places through their local and global contexts, then concepts like scale and interdependence are also significant. Similarly the inter-related nature of physical and human processes draws on the concept of environmental interaction and sustainable development as well as interdependence. These all become potential curriculum foundations for your planning onto which you build your curriculum with associated geographical knowledge, understanding, skills and values. Crucially, in addition to this, your knowledge of the ways your pupils learn, and of the pupils themselves, will all affect the way you approach your geography teaching (Martin 2013), as well as the varied ways that you 'see' geography.

Seeing Geography in Different Ways

The way you see the world will have some bearing on the way that geography fits into your world order, whether this be a scientific view or one that is more about interpretation and human behaviour. Although often situated within the humanities subjects in school, geography can also be considered as a form of scientific study. The typical scientific or positivist approach to learning implies that there are 'truths' waiting to be discovered which then become the dominant argument until new evidence provides a compelling different explanation. This suggests that geographers are looking for theories that enable us to generalise things about the world, such as the causes and effects of climate change. 'The application of such knowledge is inherently conservative since it takes the existing organisation of society as a given' (Morgan and Lambert 2005: 44). More physical aspects of geography which are akin to the natural sciences, but also some approaches to human geography, are dominated by these large-scale scientific approaches. Morgan and Lambert (2005) argue that this approach to geography is highlighted by the use of textbooks that 'share its [scientific] assumptions about the world and how it can be known' (p. 44).

   On the other hand, geography can be learnt through more qualitative approaches that aim to make interpretations of individual processes or places rather than trying to prove points, or to generalise findings into theories. These geographical approaches, which apart from the natural science of physical geography are more common in higher education, seem less apparent in school geography. This approach emphasises the interpretations we make about our world through our thoughts and feelings, but where this may lack the quantity of broad-scale data it makes up for this in the depth of the enquiry and narrative. To exemplify, instead of developing a model describing how children use spaces to play, a more local interpretation might be a series of mood maps drawn by pupils to illustrate their thoughts and feelings. In no way can these findings be generalised, but they show potentially a deep insight into the minds of a small number of children about their play in one specific place and time.

Just like the way that you see the world can have a bearing on the approach you take to geography, the way that you construe the importance of education will have some bearing on the purpose of the curriculum you develop. Rawling (2001: 32) cites six 'ideological traditions' that have influenced the approach to and the significance of geography:

1. Utilitarian/informational: education primarily focused upon getting a job and having useful information and skills (such as basic literacy and map reading skills).
2. Cultural restorationism: restoring traditional areas of knowledge and skills to the curriculum (for example, understanding how parts of the British landscape were formed).
3. Liberal humanist: worthwhile knowledge which is 'passed onto' the next generation as a preparation for life (such as understanding the causes and effects of climate change).
4. Progressive educational: focus on self-development and developing autonomous individuals (for example, developing pupils' values about global poverty).
5. Reconstructionist or radical education as an agent to change society, encouraging challenge to existing knowledge (such as pupils looking at the carbon footprint of their school dinners and lobbying the headteacher to change policy after this research).
6. Vocationalist: providing pupils' knowledge and skills for the workplace (for example, enquiry skills and report writing).

Knowing aspects about the world and our environment has always been part of formal liberal classical education since the state system began, and many other ideologies have been present in the school curriculum for many decades. Since the early incarnations of the National Curriculum, geography has changed significantly in its nature and implementation. Initially the geography curriculum across the key stages was heavily prescriptive and content-driven, which in the primary phases 'presented considerable challenges and [with] little evidence of detailed curriculum or assessment planning' (Rawling 2001: 87). Later revisions of the National Curriculum reduced the complexity of its structure through removing some content, introducing geographical concepts and allowing schools to locally determine their curriculum much more.

'The purpose of studying geography' in Figure 6.2 is an extract from the geography programme of study for the 2014 National Curriculum in England. It is very much a statement about what pupils should know and be able to do rather than developing their position in the world as a global citizen or developing their values, as the more progressive previous curriculum emphasised or the opening quotation from Barack

A high-quality geography education should inspire in pupils a curiosity and fascination about the world and its people that will remain with them for the rest of their lives. Teaching should equip pupils with knowledge about diverse places, people, resources and natural and human environments, together with a deep understanding of the Earth's key physical and human processes. As pupils progress, their growing knowledge about the world should help them to deepen their understanding of the interaction between physical and human processes, and of the formation and use of landscapes and environments. Geographical knowledge, understanding and skills provide the framework and approaches that explain how the Earth's features at different scales are shaped, interconnected and change over time.

Figure 6.2   The purpose of studying geography (DfE 2013)

Obama suggested. The greater emphasis on knowledge is the key ingredient of the new curriculum, which suggests a liberal humanist position or perhaps a cultural restorationist stance, depending on how traditionally one views the content, such as locational knowledge more generally and topics such as glaciations at Key Stage 3 more specifically.

Despite the changing nature of the curriculum and the re-introduction of some prescriptive content, there are considerable opportunities for you to develop your own primary geography curriculum influenced by the ideologies that *you* value, and using the content that *you* know will stimulate your pupils. The knowledge base to the 2014 curriculum provides a 'skeleton curriculum' (Martin 2013: 9) with certain degrees of freedom for teachers to develop their own curriculum that empowers pupils to be active geographers based on their growing geographical values, knowledge, understanding and skills. A knowledge-based curriculum does not necessarily demand that we shy away from creative and stimulating lessons; its knowledge base perhaps cries out for creative approaches more than ever before! Martin's (2010) argument that 'the time for a more creative, integrated curriculum seems both ripe and opportune' still rings true. Seeing the world though geographical eyes means we can make a difference to the local environment and beyond while considering global issues such as climate change, world trade and aid, and developing knowledge, skills and promoting values in the process of learning.

The State of the Art in Pedagogy

Reforming Primary Geography

Discussions about what geography can provide within the curriculum are not new and there has been considerable national debate about the primary curriculum (Alexander 2010; Rose 2009). Perhaps it is not *what* geography can potentially do that has seen it marginalised in the curriculum, but understanding *how* to achieve this to ensure pupils

1. Me in the world (self in place; location; identity; global citizenship; participation).
2. Neighbourhood and community (local area; locality; place; features; social environment; physical/built environment; commerce and trade; sense of place).
3. Connecting with the wider world (links/relationships; places/locations; interdependence; travel and transport; technologies; commerce and trade; communication).
4. Other people, places and me (people in places; culture; diversity; global connections; identity; localities, regions and nations: local/global).
5. Seeing and representing the world (images; texts; pictures; maps; technologies).
6. Encountering 'big issues' (sustainability, poverty; water need, quality and use; migration; leisure; work and goods; responsiveness).
7. Seeing change and its effects (what and how changes occur; natural and social change; decision-making; impacts of change).
8. Caring for the world (environmental concern; environmental care and management; personal response; sustainable development; local/global).
9. Heading for the future (visions of the future; realism and future worlds; what if/what preferably).
10. The world today – near and far (news and topicality; participation; interaction; interdependence; cooperation and conflict; responsiveness).

Figure 6.3   Catling's ten threads of primary geography (Catling 2005)

learn an active, current subject in a creative and engaging manner that makes a difference to their lives.

Catling's ten threads of primary geography (see Figure 6.3) enable teachers to develop a framework for the curriculum beginning from the pupil and their immediate environment and exploring the connections of this to other people and environments on a growing scale and complexity. It enables geography to explore the present and the reasons for this and to consider the possible futures that await us and our world. This does not mean that we learn about our local environment at the expense of other places, but use local knowledge to compare and contrast other environments. For example, Horler et al. (2014) show how comparing our local landscape to David Hockney's vivid oil paintings of the Yorkshire countryside can develop our geographical thinking. Such a creative approach potentially fires the geographical imaginations of pupils. It allows them to first read Hockney's work in terms of matters like seasons of the year, longer-term change, what is natural or synthetic, but also to then regard their local environment in the same light and to imagine its potential futures using art. In short, it develops their geographical eyes in seeing their locality in a new and exciting light and links to Catling's threads such as 'me in the world', 'neighbourhood and community', 'seeing and representing the world' and 'seeing change and its effects'.

This creative example provokes pupils to ask questions and allows them to critique the resource and to consider different futures for the environments that they see. Pupils will probably need assistance in developing suitable geographical questions. Battersby and Hornby (2006) provide the following prompts which you can adapt to suit the situation of learning:

- What is it?
- Where is it?
- What is it like?
- How did it get like this?
- How and why is it changing?
- What are the implications of this?
- Who benefits and who loses?

Future thinking is another important and creative part of geography. Hicks provides a template for pupils to consider 'probable' and 'preferable' futures so that they can imagine alternative futures. In considering future scenarios, Hicks (2006: 47) proposes the following questions:

- Do you think people like living in this possible future?
- What are some of the good/difficult things about it?
- Who will benefit and who will lose in this future?
- Say why you would or would not like to live in this future.

Questioning and imagining our futures are important dimensions of geographical learning which are developed through geographical enquiry.

An Enquiry Approach to Geography

A pedagogical approach that is implicit with the previous example is enquiry-based learning. Enquiry is often at the heart of geography fieldwork but it should not be seen as just an approach for out-of-classroom learning. Enquiry is not necessarily well understood and taught in schools (Bell 2005; Ofsted 2011), however Ofsted noted that in the best examples of primary geography teaching the pedagogical emphasis was on 'discovery and enquiry' (Ofsted 2011: 12).

According to Roberts (2013), there are four dimensions to enquiry. Enquiry is question-driven, requires thinking geographically, is reflective and is supported by evidence. Roberts deliberately resists presenting these dimensions sequentially, arguing that each dimension could happen at any part of the enquiry process. The following four points therefore represent a *possible* route through enquiry and should not be seen as an absolute 'blueprint' for enquiry design, as we may return to or repeat many of these four dimensions during the enquiry process.

1. Good enquiry is about creating a need to know and thus developing pupils' curiosity. Speculation, made explicitly through *pupils'* questioning, is a key to developing pupil voice in this. Once questions are established then decisions on how to answer these questions can be made by considering what data to draw upon.

2. The data will probably be a range of primary and secondary data. Primary data are of the sort that is collected directly by the enquirer and will most likely be from outside of the classroom, but do not discount the potential to find out about issues from the pupils themselves via discussions or more systematically via short questionnaires or short focus group discussions. Primary data can be a mixture of quantitative data such as counts (for example, people, buildings or amounts of litter) or measurements (such as weather or footpath erosion) and qualitative data (for example, sketches, mapping, digital photography, open questionnaires and discussions). Secondary data are of the sort that has been collected by somebody else and can be examined in the classroom in forms such as a pamphlet or book, map, web-based document, artefact or picture. Pupils of all ages can influence or decide upon the data collection methods. Enquiry approaches move the teacher's role to more of a facilitator to support and challenge the pupils' learning rather than a 'fountain of all knowledge'.

3. Once the data are collected, pupils will develop their skills in representing this either through activities such as sketch or photograph labelling, report writing, tabling data and presentations, honing ICT skills such as graphical and digital imagery and report, poetry or story writing. Pupils will be encouraged to develop their geographical understanding in a variety of ways such as:

    o   developing questioning skills and enquiry approaches including data collection methods
    o   describing the data to compare and contrast findings
    o   analysing data and recognising relationships and different viewpoints and opinions
    o   reaching informed conclusions based on the original enquiry questions
    o   presenting findings using a range of communication skills.

4. Roberts' fourth dimension to enquiry is reflection on learning, which is arguably axiomatic with all learning throughout the process. The reflective role, however, develops pupils' criticality in order to develop an understanding of the learning process, what has been learnt, the reliability of the data, the approaches used to represent the data and how the enquiry could be improved (Roberts 2013: 9). Enquiry can be seen as a linear exploration of an issue, but a cyclical approach enables the learning to be explicitly taken forward from our reflections into either a deeper enquiry about the same issue or a new one entirely.

Contemporary Approaches to Geography

Like most subjects geography is difficult to teach well if you are not sure about what it offers and where it can take you. This has emerged as a significant issue for geography in schools – especially primary schools where few teachers have had much exposure to 'thinking geographically' during their own professional preparation. (Lambert 2005)

In response to the perceived lack of quality of geography teaching in primary and secondary schools and to the changing nature of the curriculum, an 'Action Plan for Geography' was developed by the Geographical Association (GA) and the Royal Geographical Society (RGS) with government support in 2006 and ran for five years. Its aim was 'to ensure that a clear vision for geography's educational potential [was] understood by all, including and that teaching professionals were enabled and equipped to realise this potential with pupils to engage them with geography in an enjoyable way that they value' (GA 2011: 3). Much of what underpins good geography practice can be gleaned from the ideas developed during the action plan period which are summarised in the GA's 'A Different View' (GA 2009). This manifesto draws the action plan together and 'in a statement of beliefs and priorities' it affirms 'geography's place in the curriculum' (GA 2009: 3). It proposes a form of pedagogy called 'living geography' which is a 'strong brand for school geography as a twenty-first century subject', bringing 'contemporary context and real world enquiry to the curriculum' (GA 2009: 13).

Living geography:

- is directly relevant to people's lives and the world of work
- is about change – recognizes that the past helps explain the present, but is current and futures oriented
- has a scale 'zoom lens', so that the local is always set in a global context
- is 'deeply observant' – it looks beneath the surface to identify the mechanisms that change environments and societies
- encourages a critical understanding of big ideas like 'sustainable development', 'interdependence' and 'globalization'. (GA 2009: 13)

The ideas within living geography strongly link to Catling's ten threads and the conceptual underpinnings of geography discussed earlier in this chapter.

Constructivist theories and the principle of pupil voice are implicit through 'young people's geographies' which is a further strand of A Different View to aid curriculum planning. Such a curriculum 'results when teachers are responsive to what students *make of* what they get in geography lessons' (GA 2009: 15) and is characterised by:

- a variety of conversations: between teachers, young people, teacher educators and academic geographers;

- pedagogies that encourage communication and exchange, such as argumentation, debate and decision making;

- young people's everyday experiences, as reported by themselves and from research in geography;

- extending young people's involvement in, and on, curriculum making. (GA 2009: 15)

A valuable resource to enable the planning and teaching of geography to learners that supports the aims of A Different View is the 'Making Geography Happen' section of the GA's website (GA 2010). The emphasis is on openly discussing curriculum making, the pupil voice is clear and the examples build on the principles of young people's geography and living geography (Totterdell 2010). The website exemplifies practice across a range of schools, illustrating their classrooms, what their pupils do and learn and how they use their creative skills. For each exemplified unit of work there is a commentary on the geographical thinking behind it, an outline of the process of curriculum making, the context of the school and a range of pupil stories and work, and pupil and teacher reflections about the unit (Totterdell 2010).

Cross-Curricular Perspectives

The essence of geographical learning can be greatly enhanced through considering it within the context of the whole curriculum, be this formal or informal, through its cross-curricular links to other disciplines and to cross-curricular themes. There are unique qualities that geography brings to the curriculum, for example developing pupils' awareness and understanding of 'sense of place' and the specific subject-based knowledge required within the 2014 curriculum, however the discipline is also strongly interdisciplinary. Geographical ideas can be taught in a range of thematic ways, however the term 'interdisciplinary' suggests that the curriculum stems from the various disciplines – '[y]ou can't have interdisciplinary, or multidisciplinary, unless you have disciplines' (Menand 2001: 11) – and thus any interdisciplinary approach should still be strongly geographical through the concepts that underpin it and the knowledge, understanding, skills and values that are developed.

The 2014 National Curriculum in England requires that a school:

- promotes the spiritual, moral, cultural, mental and physical development of pupils
- prepares pupils at the school for the opportunities, responsibilities and experiences of later life
- make[s] provision for personal, social, health and economic education (DfE 2013: 5)

and that teachers should develop pupils':

- numeracy and mathematical reasoning in all subjects (p. 9)
- spoken language, reading, writing and vocabulary as integral aspects of the teaching of every subject (p. 10).

Making sense of life is arguably what learning is about, and to do this we require our pupils to make connections across the curriculum in order to move towards a 'big picture' for learning rather than a series of 'pigeon holes', each constituting a particular subject. This is not to decry the important and specific role that geography plays in the curriculum, which includes contributing to the learning highlighted in the bullet points above, but to show the potential it has to be taught within an interdisciplinary curriculum that promotes geographical thinking while simultaneously enhancing our learning of this big picture.

An example of geography within a multidisciplinary approach is illustrated in Case Study 6.1, adapted from the 'Making Geography Happen' website, where Year 4 and 5 pupils from a school in north-west England were learning about Saudi Arabia. The school already had existing links with a school in Jeddah and developed a unit of work that was 'extremely *cross-curricular* and included literacy, art, drama, design and technology and science', as well as geography.

 Case Study 6.1

Approaches to learning about Saudi Arabia

'The aim of the unit was to develop the children's idea of place through the people who live there.' The following points summarise the activities undertaken over six weeks:

- locating the country and capital on a world map, then emailing fellow school pupils in Jeddah about things like lifestyle, sport, hobbies, fashion, animals, religion, festivals, weddings and writing
- pupils completing a mind map demonstrating prior knowledge that continued to be reviewed and amended (in a different colour) as the unit progressed
- pupils identifying three things they wanted to find out and then developing a fact file including location on the map and key facts about Saudi Arabia
- discussing Saudi Arabian food and making flatbread and a drink called laban; pupils discussed dietary restrictions on eating pork and drinking alcohol and developed an advert to advertise the food or a guide to the etiquette of eating at a Saudi Arabian feast
- researching jewellery, markets and clothes: children role play a scene at a market, which was filmed
- showing children a range of people's views on Saudi Arabia and discussing bias, including who might hold these views and which views describe the country best

(Continued)

(Continued)

- children examining a range of art and pottery and recreating these; photos were taken and sent to the Saudi school
- identifying the images that were in the pupils' minds when they thought about Saudi Arabia. What were their favourite things? What would you want to show a visitor to the country?
- making a guide to the country on either paper or electronically using images that they felt sum up the country; these will be used with the children's text to create the guide. (GA/RGS 2009)

As an example of living geography, it can be seen that the unit develops from existing knowledge and interest through the school's international link. It starts from the pupils' knowledge which is built with fellow pupils in Jeddah as well as their own research in the UK. It shows how the local is set in a global context, explores similar and different cultural elements such as food, jewellery and markets and appeals to a wide range of senses in doing so. It starts to explore complexities such as dietary ethics and pupils are encouraged to review sources of information such as the idea of bias in viewpoints and thus begin to develop a critical understanding of matters. The work is underpinned by geographical concepts such as place, interdependence and cultural understanding and diversity, and develops a range of locational and place knowledge during the unit of work, as well as aspects of human and physical geography outlined in the Key Stage 2 subject content, including climate zones, land use, economic activity and trade links (DfE 2013: 186).

    Case Study 6.2

'Feel Good, Learn Well'

In a research project entitled 'Feel Good, Learn Well', pupils' active learning of geography utilised their empathetic skills to also enhance their self-esteem. The approach focused upon geographical enquiry but the idea of considering a question, thinking about how to investigate it and planning some ways of undertaking this investigation can be employed in a wide range of single or multidisciplinary approaches. Cross-curricular learning does not just mean learning about aspects of different subjects under one themed lesson. In addition, our approach required pupils to consider their learning before, during and after the enquiry through six questions and to focus on a personal goal to help improve their own learning:

1. What is my goal for today?
2. What do I need to know and do to reach my goal?
3. What should I do when I find things difficult or uncomfortable?
4. When things are not going well, what choices will face me?
5. What have I learnt today?
6. What have I learnt about myself today?

Pupils were asked to explore a village close to the field study centre as a possible home for a fictitious family. They were 'introduced' to the members of the family in the classroom before embarking on the fieldwork. Empathy skills were required to consider the opinions of the various family members, however we felt that in order to do this effectively the pupils needed to first attend to their own feelings towards the place. This utilised a bi-polar grid that was completed by pupils outlining their 'emotional response to the village'.

The main focus of the fieldwork was geographical but it was also clear that through the pupils' perceived thoughts and feelings about the family, they considered aspects of village history in terms of its function and the nature of the architecture and citizenship in terms of understanding the nature of the local community.

Back in the classroom, groups of pupils worked on PowerPoint presentations to present to 'the family' in order to convince them of their choices. A depth of geographical understanding related to the needs and interests of 'the family' were developed as well as building pupils' written and verbal communication skills and self-esteem (Hoult and Ellis 2008).

'Geographical skills and fieldwork' are a long-argued important facet of geography and are an integral dimension of the geography programme of study for the 2014 National Curriculum in England. Pupils should 'use fieldwork to observe, measure, record and present the human and physical features in the local area using a range of methods, including sketch maps, plans and graphs and digital technologies' (DfE 2013: 187).

Case Study 6.2 illustrates enquiry-based fieldwork which formed a research project entitled 'Feel Good, Learn Well', undertaken with a colleague from a field studies centre (Hoult and Ellis 2008). We researched the effects of geography fieldwork that integrated social and emotional aspects of learning for Key Stage 2 and 3 pupils. The approach was based on pupils' active learning, which utilised their empathetic skills to also enhance their self-esteem.

Geography as a curriculum discipline cannot and should not stand alone. It is enhanced by its interdisciplinary and multidisciplinary capabilities, which in turn enrich the learning potential for pupils, as we have seen in two case studies in this chapter.

We should view the connections between disciplines in a more open manner that enables us to remove the 'straitjacket' that each subject can demand of 'its' knowledge while enabling the unique contribution of each subject to flourish (Mourad 1997).

Assessment

> [It is] axiomatic for good geography to provide access to rich and varied resources, opportunities for enquiry in the 'real world' and realise the full potential of technologies to aid data handling, processing and communication. Formative assessment strategies in geography should allow for this and be shaped by these curriculum priorities. In other words formative assessment is focussed on learning goals. (Weeden and Lambert 2006: 6)

As an integral part of teaching and learning, the principles that underpin good geography should also underpin good geography assessment. Weeden and Lambert (2006: 6–7) propose four principles of learning, which are:

1. Learning should start from where the learner is, recognising that pupils have to be active in reconstructing their ideas.
2. Learning has to be done by the pupils, not for them.
3. In order to learn pupils must understand their learning target and where they are in relation to that target.
4. Pupils should use and understand the vocabulary of the subject (key terminology) as well as express its grammar (concepts).

Assessment based on these principles therefore needs to consider the individual learner's position, with the child at the heart of assessment, and assess *what* the pupil knows, understands or can do rather than *whether* he or she knows something (Torrance and Pryor 1998) or even what he or she does *not* know or cannot do!

The play *The History Boys* (Bennett 2004) illustrates two highly contrasting teachers: one targets pupils' examination attainment and the other focuses on the intrinsic love of education. We should not purely follow either example. Learning can clearly take place where targets are not explicit, however in the outcome-focused culture of teacher performance it is not realistically possible to avoid these. In setting short-term targets to help improve an aspect of geographical learning such as photographic interpretation, developing detailed description or explaining points, it is important that pupils are also aware of the broader purpose of geography. Where assessment is integral to teaching and learning, and pupils understand their current learning position within the bigger picture of where their learning is aiming towards, we have the potential to develop scaffolding for effective progression in geography lessons. We then need to help pupils to understand what to do next and how to achieve this in order to aid their progress.

Paul Weeden (2009) asks the following questions about progression which act as effective prompts to review your geography units of work across the primary phase:

- Do students' *knowledge* and *understanding* of geography develop as they move through their school career?
- Can students, with increasing independence, use *geographical skills* in more complex and precise ways?
- Do students *broaden* their *scale* of study and explain the *links between places*?
- Do students develop a more mature approach to *issues* and recognise the importance of *values and attitudes* in shaping decision making?

Assessment must be built into the units of work with plentiful and regular opportunities for feedback from teachers, fellow pupils and individually in verbal or written form. By understanding the expected pupil progression through the curriculum, an effective primary geography curriculum can be constructed based on the ideas discussed earlier in this chapter.

As a pupil makes progress, you would expect to see a growing awareness of geographical processes, an enlarging of pupils' awareness of their environment and its links with the world and of their ability to enquire and make reasoned and growingly autonomous judgements. The assessment and progression framework for geography (GA 2014) sets out clear expectations about pupil progress and identifies age-related expectations for pupils in geography at key points during the primary and secondary phases. It is an important development to understanding pupil assessment and progression in the National Curriculum and should be used to support good practice in assessing pupils' learning in geography.

One final thought regarding geographical assessment. Lambert and Morgan outline the potential of pupils' 'capability'. Capabilities include skills but also enhancing people's individual freedoms, particularly with regard to making choices about how to live. Thus a potentially empowering subject like geography has a contribution to make to developing pupils' capabilities, including:

- senses, imagination and thought: being able to use senses to imagine, think and reason;
- practical reason, being able to form a conception of the good and to engage in critical reflection about the planning of one's life;
- affiliation, for example being able to live with and towards others, showing concern for others and to engage in various forms of social interaction and to be able to empathise;
- control over one's environment, for example the political environment, by participating effectively in political choices that govern one's life. (Lambert and Morgan 2010: 63)

Perhaps in the future, instead of considering a range of knowledge, understanding and skills, we will be developing pupils' capabilities within the curriculum and assessing them on these, with an emphasis on developing thoughtful, active global citizens that make a difference to their world.

Conclusion

This chapter has outlined the nature of geography and illustrated that there is no single definition of such a wide-ranging discipline. It has shown that the subject has importance within the curriculum in its own right but also as a contributor to the wider knowledge and skills in the primary phase and more generally to a broad, balanced curriculum. Having said this, the subject has gone though some difficult times during the initial era of the National Curriculum and perhaps the subject is misunderstood in parts as a series of disconnected content, rather than understood as a discipline that is underpinned by key geographical concepts and where geographical knowledge is valued.

It is reassuring to see that geography remains explicit within the 2014 National Curriculum in England; however, there is some danger that its knowledge base may not help teachers to see geography as a whole conceptual discipline. A geography curriculum that has clear concepts at its foundations and that is built upon sound geographical knowledge has the potential to develop into a strong, exciting and meaningful discipline as part of the new primary curriculum, which the examples and case studies demonstrate throughout this chapter.

Reflection Points

1. How can you use Catling's ten threads of primary geography to help you plan 'Living Geography' lessons and units of work?
2. How can you make geographical concepts explicit within a cross-curricular curriculum that is likely to be focused on knowledge outlined in the 2014 National Curriculum?
3. How can using geographical concepts in planning your geography curriculum help you to assess pupils' progress in geography?

Further Reading

Martin, F. (2006) *Teaching Geography in Primary Schools: Learning to Live in the World*. London: Chris Kington Publishing.

North, W. and Hamblen, A. (2012) *Geography Plus: Primary Teachers' Toolkit. Australia Here We Come! Exploring a Distant Place*. Sheffield: Geographical Association.

Richardson, P. and Richardson, T. (2012) *Geography Plus: Primary Teachers' Toolkit. Living in the Freezer: Investigating Polar Environments.* Sheffield: Geographical Association.

Scoffham, S. (ed.) (2010) *Primary Geography Handbook*, rev. edn. Sheffield: Geographical Association.

Scoffham, S. (ed.) (2013) *Teaching Geography Creatively*. London: Routledge.

References

Alexander, R. (ed.) (2010) *Children, Their World, Their Education: Final Report and Recommendations of the Cambridge Primary Review*. Abingdon: Routledge.

Ballin, B. (2013) 'Editorial', *Primary Geographer*, 80: 4.

Battersby, J. with Hornby, N. (2006) 'Inspiring disaffected pupils', in D. Balderstone (ed.), *Secondary Geography Handbook*. Sheffield: Geographical Association.

Bell, D. (2005) 'The value and importance of geography', *Primary Geographer*, 56: 5.

Bennett, A. (2004) *The History Boys*. London: Faber & Faber.

Catling, S. (2005) *Children, Space and Environment*. Available at: www.geography.org.uk/download/EVcatling1.doc (accessed 4 August 2010).

DfE (Department for Education) (2013) *Geography Programme of Study: Key Stages 1 and 2. National Curriculum in England*. London: DfE.

GA (Geographical Association) (2009) *A Different View*. A manifesto from the Geographical Association. Sheffield: Geographical Association.

GA (Geographical Association) (2010) *Making Geography Happen*. Available at: www.geography.org.uk/projects/makinggeographyhappen (accessed 2 March 2014).

GA (Geographical Association) (2011) *The Action Plan for Geography 2006–2011: Final Report and Evaluation*. Sheffield: Geographical Association.

GA (Geographical Association) (2014) *An Assessment and Progression Framework for Geography*. Sheffield: Geographical Association.

Heffernan, M. (2003) 'Histories of geography', in S. Holloway, S. Rice and G. Valentine (eds), *Key Concepts in Geography*. London: SAGE.

Herbert, J. and Matthews, D. (eds.) (2004) *Unifying Geography: Common Heritage, Shared Future*. London: Routledge.

Hicks, D. (2006) *Lessons for the Future: The Missing Dimension in Education*. Oxford: Trafford Publishing.

Holloway, S., Rice, S. and Valentine, G. (eds) (2003) *Key Concepts in Geography*. London: SAGE.

Horler, T. with Mackintosh, M., Kavanagh, P. and Kent, G. (2014) 'The art of perceiving landscape', *Primary Geographer*, 83: 8–10.

Hoult, S. and Ellis, S. (2008) 'Feel Good, Learn Well', *Teaching Geography*, 33 (3): 143–6.

Jackson, P. (2006) 'Thinking geographically', *Geography*, 91 (3): 199–204.

Lambert, D. (2005) *Opinion Piece: Why Subjects Really Matter*. Available at: www.geography.org.uk/download/NPOGMatter.doc (accessed 4 August 2010).

Lambert, D. and Morgan, J. (2010) *Teaching Geography 11–18: A Conceptual Approach*. Maidenhead: Open University Press.

Martin, F. (2006) *Teaching Geography in Primary Schools: Learning to Live in the World*. London: Chris Kington Publishing.

Martin, F. (2010) 'Editorial', *Primary Geographer*, 72: 4.

Martin, F. (2013) 'The place of knowledge in the new curriculum', *Primary Geographer*, 82: 9–11.

Menand, L. (2001) *The Marketplace of Ideas*. American Council of Learned Societies. Occasional Paper No. 49.

Morgan, J. and Lambert, D. (2005) *Geography: Teaching School Subjects 11–19*. London: Routledge.

Mourad, R. (1997) *Postmodern Philosophical Critique and the Pursuit of Knowledge in Higher Education*. Westport, CT and London: Bergin and Garvey.

Ofsted (2011) *Geography: Learning to Make a World of Difference*. Manchester: Ofsted.

QCA (2007) National Curriculum for Geography. Available at: http://teachfind.com/qcda/geography-exemplification-standards-file-level-7-geography-standards-files-exemplification-1?current_search=geography%20concepts (accessed 2 March 2014).

Rawling, E. (2001) *Changing the Subject: The Impact of National School Policy on School Geography, 1980–2000*. Sheffield: Geographical Association.

Roberts, M. (2013) *Geography Through Enquiry: Approaches to Teaching and Learning in the Secondary School*. Sheffield: Geographical Association.

Rose, J. (2009) *Independent Review of the Primary Curriculum*. London: DCSF.

Taylor, L. (2009) *GTIP Think Piece Concepts in Geography*. Available at: www.geography.org.uk/gtip/thinkpieces/concepts/#top (accessed 4 August 2010).

Torrance, H. and Pryor, J. (1998) *Investigating Formative Assessment*. Buckingham: Open University Press.

Totterdell, R. (2010) 'Making geography happen', *The Geographical Association Magazine*, Spring, No. 14, Geographical Association.

Weeden, P. (2009) *Thinking about Progression in Geography*. Available at: www.geography.org.uk/projects/makinggeographyhappen/progression (accessed 4 August 2010).

Weeden, P. and Lambert, D. (2006) *Geography Inside the Black Box: Assessment for Learning in the Geography Classroom*. London: NFER Nelson.

CHAPTER 7

AN INTRODUCTION TO PHYSICAL EDUCATION

Kristy Howells

Chapter Aims

This chapter will:

- highlight the crucial role physical education has in inspiring all, promoting physical activity, engaging in competition and developing competence

- examine some innovative curriculum initiatives and case studies focusing on the aims of the National Curriculum

- consider strategies for assessment, focusing on movement concepts

---

Introduction

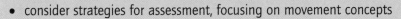

Primary physical education (PE) has recently received extra governmental funding for 2013–2015 to improve the provision of PE and sport. This increase in funding is particularly welcome as School Sports Partnerships were axed in 2010. These partnerships were a way of local networks of schools and PE teachers getting pupils to be more physically active during the school day and also included inter- and intra-school competitions. The new additional funding, however, also includes accountability. Since September 2013, Ofsted inspections of primary schools have included scrutiny of how the additional funding is being spent to improve PE and school sport. This initiative has increased the potential importance of PE within the primary school curriculum. Therefore within this chapter, the state of the art of pedagogy will be examined through the lens of looking at the purpose of study and the aims of the PE National Curriculum (DfE 2013). Suggestions will be proposed on ways to incorporate the purpose of study and aims into teaching and learning within the primary school setting. The focus of the chapter will be on:

- inspiring all
- competition
- sustained physical activity
- developing competence
- cross-curricular perspectives
- assessment.

Inspiring All

Lord Coe (2011) summarised the vision of the Olympic Games as 'changing the lives of young people through sport, to inspire young people around the world to choose sport' (p. 21). This philosophy links to the purpose of the PE programme of study within the new National Curriculum (DfE 2013), which focuses on inspiring 'all pupils to succeed and excel'. In 2012 many schools became an Olympic Games school as part of the *Get Set* programme, which was started as the official London 2012 education programme. This programme has continued to the Sochi 2014 Winter Olympics, with the vision of inspiring children to take up physical activity, resource areas for teachers to help within the curriculum and building a community of positive change. The programme includes activities that are physical, interactive and academically linked, in a cross-curricular way, to the values of the games. This has led to an increase in 'Sport Weeks' and 'Olympic Weeks' within the primary school year and opportunities for children to try both Olympic and Paralympic sports from the summer and winter games. The House of Commons Education Committee (2013) suggested that the use of elite athletes to visit schools would inspire pupils. Initiatives like Sport into Schools have linked elite athletes to particular schools, the aim being to inspire and encourage children within sport and PE lessons. In Kent, for example, the England women's cricket team who retained the Women's Ashes in 2014 visited primary schools to inspire girls in particular and to share their success stories. The impact of such visits can be significant and long-reaching: Lizzy Yarnold, the first GB gold medal winner of the Sochi Winter Olympics, stated that she 'wants to inspire the way that I was inspired by Denise Lewis when I was younger'. After the games she planned to visit schools in Kent, where she grew up, and also in Bath, where she lives.

Howells (2007) suggested that there is a need for positive, motivated and enthusiastic role models. These role models can be class teachers within primary school settings and within Physical Education lessons, but can also be elite athletes as it is important to show children how they too can be successful. Howells (2012) also proposed that since primary schools, and in particular PE lessons, are places where early forms of socialisation, habits, likes and dislikes are developed, it is important to recognise the potential opportunities that primary schools have not only to inspire but to engage children in physical activity, sport and PE lessons. Class teachers need to ensure that all the children understand why physical activity and PE lessons are important and to ensure that all children are able to access opportunities to develop skills, tactics and activities within the school day. This would ensure that a primary school setting was not a 'sparse' place for physical activity, as previously suggested by Dale et al. (2000: 240). However, it could be questioned whether children can be inspired to enjoy PE and sport, within the primary school setting, especially since advice given by the DfE (2013) to headteachers and school staff within their behaviour and discipline in schools document suggests that 'extra physical activity such as running around a playing field' (p. 8) be used as a behaviour and sanction method.

Competition

Within the new National Curriculum (DfE 2013) there has been a shift in focus from stating within the *breadth of study for games activities* that children should play competitive games, towards specifically stating as part of the *aims* of PE that all pupils should 'engage in competitive sports and activities'. This may well be linked to the legacy of the London 2012 Olympic Games. Additional funding (DfE 2013) has been ring-fenced by the current Coalition government for the provision of PE and sport within schools until 2015 and one of the suggestions for possible use of the funding is 'running sport competitions, or increasing pupils' participation in the School Games'. The Prime Minister (at time of writing) has also proposed that school sport has an important role in building 'confidence and a sense of achievement'. He further stated that if he remains as Prime Minister after the next election, the funding will continue for primary schools until 2020 (BBC 2014).

The School Games initiative has been described as a '2012 legacy activity for sporty young people' and has been criticised for 'not providing opportunities for everyone' (House of Commons Education Committee 2013: 11). However, within the School Games programme, Project Ability has been developed by the Youth Sport Trust as a way to build on the legacy of the Paralympics, to make a difference for young pupils with special education needs or disabilities (SEN/D) to enable them to take part in competitive sport within 50 lead schools. Also, within the School Games format there are inclusive sports formats designed in conjunction with national governing bodies and Project Ability to enable SEN/D and non-SEN/D pupils to compete against each other (Sainsbury's School Games 2014).

Laker (2001) champions the idea that PE lessons could be an ideal place for children to explore how to cope with winning and losing and to develop sporting behaviour. This strategy might well counteract a current trend towards unwanted behaviour, since it has been reported that two-thirds of school children between 8 and 16 reacted badly when they lost, in particular when playing cricket; sulking, getting angry and crying were all common behaviours (Richardson 2011). Therefore this key area of emotional development could be enhanced through primary PE. Yet competition is not perceived as inspiring or including all. The House of Commons Education Committee (2013) proposed that competition in school sport 'deters some young people from participating in sport and physical activity' (p. 2). Furthermore, there is also the danger of the negative aspects of competition, as the variable outcomes of competitive situations could overwhelm children and inhibit them from performing to their full potential, while at the same time competition is important as it is a key means by which it is possible to assess competence (Passer and Wilson 2002).

Another way to overcome potential negativity of competition is recommended by the House of Commons Education Committee (2013), who suggested that Change4Life Clubs could be offered within schools as a 'way of reaching the least active, including those who may not be attracted to competitive sport' (p. 2). The Change4Life programme, a relatively recent initiative (DH 2009), involves a multidisciplinary approach to being more physically active, coupled with consideration of diet and behavioural changes that can help children to live longer. The message to children, families and schools was to '*Eat well, Move more and Live longer*'.

Therefore it is the way in which competition is perceived that is important. Woods (1998) approached the idea of competition as a way of developing the idea of achievement motivation where an individual has motivation to strive for success. Encouragement and inspiration to succeed are what is needed, and what class teachers need to help children to develop. Developing this attitude would enable children to persist even when they meet an obstacle or lose a competition (Woods 1998). This attitude encourages persistence and determination to succeed and has been seen to benefit other academic disciplines within school. Research suggests that 'more than one third of 206 separate reports statistically show a significant correlation between increased competition and higher achievement' (Belfield and Levin 2002: 283).

There are two main ways in which competition could be developed and used within primary PE lessons. First, individual target setting, where the child is trying to beat personal goals, could be influential in developing positive aspects of competition. Second, competing against another child, or being part of a team and competing against another team, has a focus on improving performance and skill level, not just on winning and losing the competition (Martens 1981). One way of introducing competing against another or others is through the use of the Teaching Games for Understanding (TGfU) approach to game play (Griffin and Butler 2005). This allows children to experience low pressure competition against an opponent in order to help them develop their cognitive skills and abilities such as decision making and problem solving.

Case Study 7.1

Primary school competition

Joe Pellett is a Year 5/6 class teacher at Hamstreet Primary School, near Ashford in Kent.

Joe undertook a case study investigation to examine the effect of competition on performance in throwing. Ten children in Year 5 of mixed ability were observed throwing individually towards a target and then they were observed throwing against a partner towards a target. They had previously taken part in lessons on throwing and catching and could articulate techniques needed to throw towards a target. The children completed 10 throws to a variety of different hoops approximately 6 metres away. In the individual competition setting, their aim was to throw the balls as accurately as possible into the hoops. In the competition against a partner, they had to compete against a partner and were told to see who could get the most balls into the hoops.

In the individual target throwing, the children alternated overarm and under-arm techniques to find which was the more effective. Children observed each other and were able to replicate in their own throwing what they had seen to be the most successful technique. Time was taken over the throwing of the balls at the target and the children reported that they felt unpressurised and able to concentrate on consistency and replication.

Within the competition against a partner, it was observed that the children's focus moved away from their own individual throwing and onto their partner's success or failure at reaching the target. There was a split in the emotions with some of the pairs becoming excited when the other missed, whilst other pairs encouraged each other and highlighted how well they had done. This was particularly noted when one child who had been praised for their performance practised the throwing motion whilst waiting for their turn. More smiling and laughter were observed during the second activity. Joe concluded that, for his class, there was an improvement in skill development when children were exposed to competition with others, however he was concerned that the focus on others was missing. On reflection, he proposed that next time when competing with others, the children should have time to observe each other's performance. He would provide a checklist as Mosston and Ashworth (2002) use in their recipro-cal teaching style, so the focus would be on developing the actual skill to prevent any unsportsmanlike behaviour.

Sustained Physical Activity

Another new aim of the PE curriculum within the National Curriculum (DfE 2013) is that all pupils 'are physically active for sustained periods of time'. Views differ as to what is meant by physical activity, yet most have agreed and viewed physical activity as a 'complex' term. It has been recommended by the DH (2005) and the World Health Organization (WHO 2010) that children are physically active for 60 minutes a day at an intensity of at least moderate level, with any physical activity over 60 minutes providing additional health benefits. The WHO (2010) describes physical activity for children aged 5–17 as including: 'play, games, sports, transportation, recreation, physical education or planned exercise, in the context of the family, school and community' (p. 7). Official recommendations (DH 2005) have in the view of some writers, such as Stratton and Watson (2009), evolved from 'expert opinion with limited scientific evidence to support them' (p. 153). The WHO (2008) suggested that increasing the number of PE lessons the students have is the most direct way to increase students' physical activity, but PE lessons are not just about being physically active; as this chapter highlights, PE is also about inspiring all, developing competence and participating in competition. McKenzie and Kahan (2004) extended this suggestion by proposing that the teaching profession is obliged to provide pupils with adequate moderate to vigorous physical activity within PE lessons, especially if this was the main source of physical activity for a child within the school day.

According to Hills et al. (2007: 533), 'today's generation of children will be the first for over a century for whom life expectancy falls'. This prediction, however, is uncertain. The DfES (2004) has speculated that by 2020 1 in 2 youngsters will be obese. Once children have become obese there is a tendency for this to continue into adulthood which then links to life-threatening diseases that impact on health services. The global problem of obesity ('globesity') is now such a prominent feature within society that consequently increasing pressure has been put upon the education system and in particular primary schools to rectify this serious problem (Waring et al. 2007). Johns (2005) suggests that when children are mentioned in relation to being obese and overweight 'school PE, [physical development, health and well-being] ... are implicated immediately, both as a source of and as a possible solution to the problem' (p. 122). McMinn et al. (2010) support this by suggesting that 'school settings have been identified as key social establishments in which to promote physical activity and well-being, particularly through the medium of school clubs and PE lessons' (p. 68). Trost (2007) echoes this suggestion that 'schools serve as an excellent venue to provide students with the opportunities' (p. 1), but he highlights that this is often not the case and that 'most children get little or no physical activity in school' (p. 1), therefore impacting on the child's physical development, health and well-being. Green (2002) also emphasised the importance of PE and suggested that it is 'the most suitable vehicle for the encouragement of a lifestyle which is both healthy and physically active'. Trudeau et al. (1999) found that primary school children's participation in daily PE had a long-term effect on physical activity throughout the school day and later on in life (Howells et al. 2010).

Research into physical activity levels is important, as the actual physical activity levels that can be achieved by children are not easily visible. Harrington and Donnelly (2008) believe that 'before any strategies to increase physical activity can be employed, the activity levels of children need to be known' (p. 66). It is not easy to question or to examine whether children are actually achieving a moderate to intense level of physical activity for 60 minutes a day in line with WHO (2010) recommendations. Without this information schools cannot possibly ensure that they take on this type of responsibility for children's physical activity. Neither can they question whether PE lessons are the suitable place within the school day to enhance or encourage physical activity. Several studies have examined actual physical activity levels in school, but these took place over a short period of time and failed to take account of the broader influences of the daily varied school curriculum. Duncan et al. (2007), for example, considered children's physical activity over a period of three days. Another study, by Belton et al. (2009) in Ireland, looked at the physical activity of children aged 7–9 over seven days. They found that children chose physically active activities during school break time and immediately after school and they also found that children regarded PE as their favourite subject, which the authors suggested may indicate enjoyment. Children within the study were able to meet the recommended Tudor-Locke step count threshold (Tudor-Locke and Bassett 2004) for health benefits, which is the number of steps measured by a pedometer during the school day, but they recommended further research on a greater number of children to confirm their results. Daley et al. (2008) considered whether general practitioners (GPs) knew about these recommended levels of physical activity in order to achieve health benefits. Interestingly, only 60% of GPs were able 'to provide the correct answer regarding the minimum duration in minutes of physical activity required for health benefits, relatively few were aware of the minimum number of days per week adults should engage in moderate intensity physical activity'. These results are worrying. If GPs are not able to correctly describe the current physical activity recommendations for prevention and treatment of medical conditions, should this responsibility really be passed onto primary school teachers, who cannot do this alone, and where should the training come from to aid all practitioners? However, on a positive note, these results were a dramatic improvement on similar research, conducted in Scotland, where only 13% of GPs were able to correctly identify the recommendations for physical activity (Douglas et al. 2006).

The DfE (2013), however, does not stipulate the intensity level of the physical activity required within the National Curriculum so decisions around this are left to the school. There is a need for practitioners to examine how best to keep children at the maximum level of activity, whilst also developing competence and being physically active for sustained periods of time. This requires close examination of and reflection on how active children actually are during PE lessons. The way that the learning environment is set up, what apparatus is provided and the use of the learning space are all factors that require careful consideration. In gymnastics, the way that apparatus is set up can significantly alter the level of activity children can engage in. Queuing for 'turns' on apparatus often means that children spend much time inactive during a gymnastics lesson. Using a circuit might provide more opportunities for activity and less time spent getting on and off apparatus. Reflection on current practice is necessary because, as Broomfield (2011) highlighted, gymnastics is perceived by the children as containing less moderate to vigorous physical activity than games lessons. However, gymnastics is vitally important as it contributes to others areas of learning, in terms of mastering and developing decision-making which can be applied to different activity areas (Broomfield 2011). Pica (2004) also noted that gymnastics helps children to understand strength, suppleness and stamina and helps to promote spatial awareness, which again can be applied to different activities and skills; in particular, to learning skills in isolation within Key Stage 1 (DfE 2013) and to skills in combination within Key Stage 2 (DfE 2013).

Doherty and Brennan (2008) and Howells (2012) have questioned whether PE lessons are much more than just an opportunity to be physically active. They are also about educating the whole child, socially, emotionally, morally and cognitively, as well as providing opportunities for learning how to share and take turns, which is particularly important for Key Stage 1, listen to instructions, watch demonstrations and take active rest. Active rest is time when children are resting within the lesson, but are thinking, evaluating, analysing. It is time needed when developing and learning new physical skills as it allows for the skill being learnt, particularly in young children, to move from the cognitive stage of skill acquisition into the autonomous stage, where the children are able to complete the skill with more proficiency (Fitts and Posner 1979).

 Case Study 7.2

Illustrative example of improvements in physical activity in Kent and Medway

Within the Kent and Medway area the local authorities have focused on addressing and helping to improve PE to promote physical development, health and well-being within the primary school day. These examples are provided as an illustrative case study to show the reader how English local authorities are addressing physical activity beyond PE lessons. According to the Kent NHS Overview and Scrutiny Report (KNOSR 2006), providing hopscotch grids and basketball hoops in playgrounds helps increase levels of physical activity. By taking advantage of a money grant of £5000 to add facilities to school playgrounds, supplied by Kent County Council (KCC), it was possible to promote physical activity for children (KNOSR 2006), as improving school playgrounds 'increase[s] sporting opportunities, develop[s] skills based activity and raise[s] levels of physical activity'. Through providing access to small equipment it was possible to promote hopping, jumping, skipping with a rope, running, gymnastics, football, volleyball and tennis for break times too. All these activities were supported by the NHS (2011) as ways to promote physical activity for children during school time. KCC's (2006) evaluation found that 83% of schools within the scheme stated that, through the grant, they had increased sporting opportunities during playtime and that this had led to greater physical activity. However, it is important to note that lunchtime or mid-day playground supervisors who are looking after children during these playtimes may not be qualified or contracted to organise physical activities for the children. Therefore for the future, funding during break times needs to be considered as a way of promoting physical activity outside of PE lessons.

Developing Competence

Shaljean (2011) suggested that PE lessons should consist of high-quality learning experiences. For teachers of PE it is important to understand how different activities can help and 'develop competence' (DfE 2013) in a broad range of skills and activities. For example, gymnastics and dance are more than just locomotor skills. Swindlehurst and Chapman (2008) suggest that gymnastics and dance are also important for developing non-locomotor movement skills such as 'twisting, stretching, turning and bending' (p. 30). These skills help to develop the basic skills of balance and coordination (Jess and Dewar 2004). These, in turn, are then used within other activity areas such as athletics and games to improve overall performance of the child. Fairclough (2003) highlighted that 'children's perceptions of their competence and enjoyment in Physical Education are linked strongly' (p. 5). Therefore it is important for a teacher to be able to praise, feed back and feed forwards information about the skills, activity and setting to the children (see also Assessment section on page 147).

To be confident in ensuring that you as the teacher are developing the competence of the children to excel in a broad range of physical activities, there are two key factors. First is the lesson planning and planning in particular for the movement that occurs within each of the activities being taught. Being able to identify, for example, what parts of the body are involved in each part of the skill or physical activity, is a simple way of increasing your own confidence in identifying the learning that will occur and the progression that is planned for, both for the children and for the teacher in terms of teaching points. By breaking skills into body parts, for example – head, body, arms, legs, feet – it provides a template or a checklist that can be used to assess the children's competence and encourage the children to be physically confident, motivated and to understand how their body moves in action. This also increases teacher confidence when teaching in PE lessons. The second factor is knowledge – understanding the fundamental motor skills, as described by Gallahue (1996), as locomotor skills (such as running, jumping; see Assessment section), stability skills (such as bending, stretching) and manipulation skills (such as throwing and catching); how these can be developed both in isolation and combination; and how these can be developed to be mechanically efficient, coordinated and controlled (Gallahue and Ozmun 2002).

Cross-Curricular Perspectives

Another way to think creatively about the importance of PE lessons is by providing very positive opportunities through linkage within and across other subject areas where PE can become the centre of learning (Howells 2007). This is referred to as a whole-school approach when physical activity is encouraged in a wide variety of settings and situations throughout the school day. These opportunities are beyond the perhaps 'normally' considered cross-curricular links to other subject and curriculum areas. Research at St Edmund's School, Salisbury (online, n.d.) has shown that the use of a whole-school approach and the integration of PE into other lessons across the curriculum through physical activity techniques such as 'Wake and Shake', 'Take 10', skipping, seated sports and group juggling, improves physical and emotional well-being, concentration and academic performance. This was measured by improvements in both spelling and reading ages (Howells 2007).

These techniques have also shown acceleration in the children's progress, by the linking of the left and right hemispheres of the brain, caused by movements across the midline through whole-brain learning. Improvements also occur in co-ordination and self-esteem, and these can be naturally extended at play times (Teachers TV 2007a, 2007b), as well as the activities being fun. St Edmund's School, Salisbury (online, n.d.) found that using these particular cross-curricular links of Wake and Shake vastly improved the children's spelling over a three-month period with a dramatic improvement for one pupil with severe learning difficulties, whose spelling age increased by 52 months during this time (online, n.d.). Wake and Shake has also been used successfully and researched by the Youth Sport Trust in sport partnership with Callington School (online, n.d.). Here pupils showed improvements in behaviour, concentrating and learning. In particular, they found this was more profound after lunch. Increased self-esteem, increased enjoyment of physical activity, better rhythm, coordination and fitness were the results. In south Birmingham schools, 'Wake and Shake' techniques are being used to link physical activity and PE to healthy education and also to developing competence in a broad range of physical activities. Through 'Wake and Shake' not only the pupils but also the staff are benefiting from being more physically active; there have also been increases in confidence and self-esteem and the pupils are learning the benefits of regularly participating in physical activity (Howells 2007: ii).

These physical activity programmes and techniques have been shown to contribute to such improvements so it is vitally important that these non-traditional teaching approaches are also used to aid learning within PE. These have shown fundamentally how important the integration of physical activity is within the school day (Howells 2007). However, using these physical activity techniques to develop learning creates challenges for, in particular, non-PE specialists, who may be cynical about their value, but this brings an opportunity in itself, as there is no substitute for a good role model (Howells 2007). There is a skill in being able to successfully integrate physical activities into lessons across the whole curriculum and across all ages so they can be used effectively and efficiently as a learning tool. Some of the primary PE and sport funding could be used to support training on the use of physical activity programmes to help class teachers feel more confident in using these physical activity techniques with ease. The techniques need to be used without too much disruption and to reengage the children straight back into their work (Teachers TV 2007a, 2007b), not only to get rid of the wriggles and giggles, but also to reengage children with their learning after sitting, working or listening for prolonged periods of time.

Assessment

Within primary school the new curriculum (DfE 2013) aims for children to 'develop competence to excel in a broad range of physical activities', therefore it is important to be able to understand and know what the children are becoming competent in. This section is designed to illustrate how PE *can* be successfully and effectively assessed within a primary school setting. The example below illustrates one of the most effective processes by which to assess PE, in particular in early years learners. This process can be adapted for other movement concepts, age groups and areas of PE. The flow diagram in Figure 7.1 shows how the movement concept of 'moving with feet' is introduced and developed with the children and the processes involved in ensuring all children can be successful.

First, the movement concept is introduced to the children – in this illustration it is the movement of the feet. The children then explore the different ways in which the feet can move. This is then extended in two directions, first linked with art through the use of paint. The children stand in paint and then use their feet to record as many different ways to explore using their feet. The paint picture acts as a record of how they have been able to explore; the focus of the illustration is how they would land after jumping.

The children are then assessed on their ability to describe the foot patterns and movements that were used in the painting. The second direction is through the children

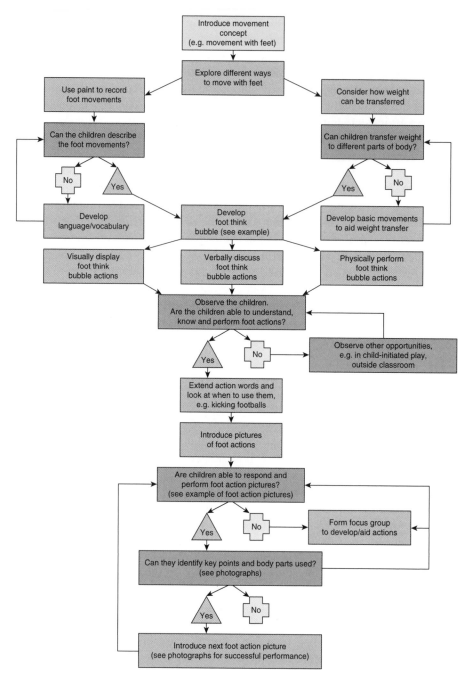

Figure 7.1   Flow chart diagram to illustrate the assessment process

considering how their own weight can be transferred, with the aim of them under-standing how their feet hold their weight. It may be that children need extra time to develop basic movements to aid weight transfer. When the children are able to describe both foot movements and how weight is transferred, then as a whole class a 'think foot bubble' (see Figure 7.2) is developed. This records all the different ways to move with the feet that the children have found and explored. For those children who are not able to describe immediately, the language and vocabulary are developed with them in focus groups, prior to the 'think foot bubble'.

The 'think foot bubble' is then visually displayed in the classroom and is verbally discussed as a class to help develop speaking, listening and physical literacy (an idea developed by Whitehead 2001), effectively linking to English within the curriculum. The next assessment is to observe the children performing the foot actions; this was completed through the use of photographs of the children. If they are not able to complete these movement concepts within the classroom setting, it is important to observe the children in other environments, such as child-initiated play and within the playground setting. Austin (2007) suggests that children 'learn best when what they are learning makes sense to them' so other opportunities to consider their jump-ing, for example, over a puddle in the playground, are as important as the classroom

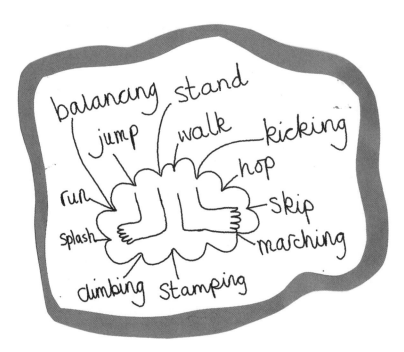

Figure 7.2   'Think foot bubble' (drawn by Emily Leggat)

setting. Once these have been observed, the foot actions are extended by using the actions in motion, such as kicking footballs, thereby moving from simple to more complex actions. It is here that pictures of the foot actions, for example jumping, can be shown to the children and the children can then copy and repeat the actions, a fundamental key assessment within the early years setting. If they are able to replicate the action of jumping, the actual parts of the body that are used in the action are explored further, such as how to land on the balls of the feet and with the knees bent. If individual children are unable to replicate the action or if the action is not fully accurate, for example landing with straight knees, then the teacher can work with those children in small groups to move them forward in their movement and thinking, to aid and develop the action. When the action is successful then the next movement concept can be introduced through the pictures and the assessment process is cyclic.

Conclusion

A true physically educated child will appreciate the benefits of PE and the fact that being physically active extends beyond the school gates. It is therefore vitally important that children have a positive experience of PE during school from primary onwards, to increase confidence, competence and self-esteem in particular. Pupils will then understand the benefits of regularly participating in physical activity and will become comfortable about wanting to continue with such activities throughout life. Therefore there is a need for positive, motivated and enthusiastic role models. It is important that PE is valued and that high-quality lessons are delivered both within the curriculum area and through links with other subjects. Teachers need to be able to inspire their children not only through lessons, but also through having stimulating physical playground environments (Howells 2007) that will extend and further encourage physical activity which the children will then want to continue into adulthood. This chapter has identified the importance of PE lessons, in particular how they can be an inspiration to all, how they can develop competence and how physical activity can be promoted and developed. The chapter has also offered alternatives outside the curriculum area, in which PE, physical activity, physical development, health and well-being opportunities can be developed, both in the classroom setting and within the outdoor environment (Austin 2007) through the use of 'Wake and Shake', 'Take 10', group juggling, skipping, seated sports and playground play. All of this has been shown to improve physical and emotional well-being (Howells 2007), reinforcing the idea that this particular curriculum area should not just be limited to curriculum time. This chapter has also illustrated how a fundamental movement such as jumping can be assessed through a flowing process, with ideas to develop and challenge the children further (see Figure 7.1), and how this idea of assessing movement concepts can be extrapolated to other movement concepts within PE.

Reflection Points

1. As a teacher, how will you increase your own confidence in teaching PE through developing planning and knowledge? How can you access professional development opportunities that are ring-fenced and funded by the primary school PE and sport funding?
2. What are the characteristics and qualities of a role model that you as a teacher need to ensure you promote positive PE?
3. How will you develop your assessment to be confident in developing the learning of movement concepts?

The following further reading is suggested to help extend your understanding and knowledge of PE, and to help you answer the previous questions.

Further Reading

Change4Life (2009) www.nhs.uk/change4life (accessed 29 July 2009).

Department of Health (DH) (2005) *Choosing Activity: A Physical Activity Action Plan*. Available at: http://webarchive.nationalarchives.gov.uk/20130107105354/http://www.dh.gov.uk/prod_consum_dh/groups/dh_digitalassets/@dh/@en/documents/digitalasset/dh_4105710.pdf (accessed 17 September 2014).

Doherty, J. and Brennan, P. (2008) *Physical Education and Development 3–11: A Guide for Teachers*. Abingdon: Routledge.

Howells, K. (2007) 'A critical reflection of the opportunities and challenges of integrating the Every Child Matters agenda into teaching physical education', *Primary Physical Education Matters*, Spring 2 (1): ii–iii.

Howells, K. (2012) 'Placing an importance on health and physical activity', in G. Griggs (ed.), *An Introduction to Primary Physical Education*. London: Routledge. pp. 207–20.

References

Austin, R. (2007) *Letting the Outside In: Developing Teaching and Learning Beyond the Early Years Classroom*. Stoke-on-Trent: Trentham Books.

Belfield, C.R. and Levin, H.M. (2002) *The Effects of Competition on Educational Outcomes: A Review of US Evidence*. New York: National Center for Study of Privatization in Education, Columbia University.

Belton, S.J., Meegan, S., Brady, P. and Woods, C. (2009) 'An examination of step count, BMI and physical activity participation in Irish primary school children', presented at Physical Education Physical Activity Youth Sport Conference, University of Limerick, June.

BBC (2014) Primary school sport £750 pledge. Available at: www.bbc.co.uk/news/education-26049332 (accessed 10 February 2014).

Broomfield, L. (2011) *Complete Guide to Primary Gymnastics*. Champaign, IL: Human Kinetics.

Callington School (no date) Wake Up and Shake Up (Callington School Sport Partnership). Accessed January 2007 at: www.youthsporttrust.org/page/casestudy-callington-wakeup/index.html.

Coe, S. (2011) 'It started with a bid', *Sport 217*, 9 September, pp. 19–26.

Dale, D., Corbin, C.B. and Dale, K.S. (2000) 'Restricting opportunities to be active during school time: do children compensate by increasing physical activity levels after school?', *Research Quarterly for Exercise and Sport*, 71 (3): 240–8.

Daley, A.J., Bassi, S., Hasanthi, R., Haththotuwa, T.H., Kalhan, M. and Rishi, S. (2008) '"Doctor, how much physical activity should I be doing?": How knowledgeable are general practitioners about the UK Chief Medical Officer's (2004) recommendations for active living to achieve health benefits?', *Public Health*, 122: 588–90.

DfE (Department for Education) (2013) *The National Curriculum in England. Framework Document for Consultation*. London: DfE.

DfES (Department for Education and Skills) (2004) *Healthy Living Blueprint for Schools*. Ref: DfES/0781/2004. London: DfES.

DH (Department of Health) (2005) *Choosing Activity: A Physical Activity Action Plan*. Available at: www.dh.gov.uk/prod_consum_dh/groups/dh_digitalassets/@dh/@en/documents/digitalasset/dh_4105710.pdf (accessed 26 October 2009).

DH (Department of Health) (2009) Change4Life Eat Well, Move More, Live Longer. Available at: www.nhs.uk/change4life/Pages/change-for-life.aspx (accessed 6 July 2009).

Doherty, J. and Brennan, P. (2008) *Physical Education and Development 3–11: A Guide for Teachers*. Abingdon: Routledge.

Douglas, F., Torrance, N. and van Teijlingen, E. (2006) 'Primary care staff's views and experiences related to routinely advising patients about physical activity: a questionnaire survey', *BMC Public Health*, 6: 138.

Duncan, M., Al-Nakeeb, Y., Woodfield, L. and Lyons, M. (2007) 'Pedometer determined physical activity levels in primary school children from central England', *Preventative Medicine*, 44: 416–20.

Fairclough, S. (2003) 'Physical activity, perceived competence and enjoyment during secondary school physical education', *European Journal of Physical Education*, 8 (1): 5–18.

Fitts, P.M. and Posner, I. (1979) *Human Performance*. Westport, CT: Greenwood Publishing Group.

Gallahue, D.L. (1996) *Developmental Physical Education for Today's Children*. Madison, WI: Brown and Benchmark.

Gallahue, D.L. and Ozmun, J.C. (2002) *Understanding Motor Development: Infants, Children, Adolescents, Adults*. New York: McGraw-Hill.

Green, K. (2002) 'Physical education and the "couch potato society"', *European Journal of Physical Education*, 7 (1): 95–107.

Griffin, L. and Butler, J. (2005) *Teaching Games for Understanding: Theory, Research and Practice*. Champaign, IL: Human Kinetics.

Harrington, D.M. and Donnelly, A.E. (2008) 'Physical activity levels of adolescent females using accelerometry: preliminary findings. Engaging young people in physical activity and sport'. Proceedings of 3rd Physical Education, Physical Activity and Youth Sport Forum, University of Limerick.

Hills, A., King, N. and Armstrong, T. (2007) 'The contribution of physical activity and sedentary behaviours to the growth and development of children and adolescents: implications for overweight and obesity', *Sports Medicine*, 37 (6): 533–45.

House of Commons Education Committee (2013) *School Sport Following London 2012: No More Political Football*. Government Response to the Committee's Third Report of Session 2013–14. House of Commons, London: TSO.

Howells, K. (2007) 'A critical reflection of the opportunities and challenges of integrating the Every Child Matters agenda into teaching physical education', *Primary Physical Education Matters*, Spring 2 (1): ii–iii.

Howells, K. (2012) 'Placing an importance on health and physical activity', in G. Griggs (ed.), *An Introduction to Primary Physical Education*. London: Routledge. pp. 207–20.

Howells, K., Caple, A. and Jones, M. (2010) 'Are boys more physically active than girls during a primary school day?', *Primary Physical Education Matters*, Autumn 5 (3): xvii–xix.

Jess, M. and Dewar, K. (2004) 'Basic moves, developing a foundation for lifelong physical activity', *British Journal of Teaching Physical Education*, 35 (2): 24–7.

Johns, D.P. (2005) cited in D. Kirk (2006) 'The "obesity crisis" and school physical education', *Sport, Education and Society*, 11 (2): 121–33.

KCC (Kent County Council) (2006) Sports Development Unit, PE and School Sport, Playground Improvement Scheme, Impact and Monitoring Report. Accessed 25 October 2009 at: http://209.85.229.132/search?q=cache:XZZ70sYYdygJ:www.kent-sport.org/schools/documents/PlaygroundMonitoringReportex-photos.doc+kent+children%27s+physical+activity+levels&cd=3&hl=en&ct=clnk&gl.

KNOSR (Kent NHS Overview and Scrutiny Report) (2006) *Tackling Obesity*. NHS Overview and Scrutiny Joint Select Committee Report, Parts I and II. Available at: https://shareweb.kent.gov.uk/Documents/Council-and-democracy/select%20committees/tackling-obesity-jan08.pdf (accessed August 2009).

Laker, A. (2001) *Developing Personal, Social and Moral Education through Physical Education: A Practical Guide for Teachers*. London: Routledge.

Martens, R. (1981) 'Stress or Distress?' Paper presented at the Guinness Conference of Sport, Towards Sporting Excellence, Ulster Polytechnic, 18–20 September.

McKenzie, T.L. and Kahan, D. (2004) 'Impact of the Surgeon General's report: through the eyes of physical education teacher educators', *Journal of Teaching in Physical Education*, 23 (4): 300–17.

McMinn, D., Rowe, D.A., Stark, M. and Nicol, L. (2010) 'Validity of the New Lifestyles NL-1000 accelerometer for measuring time spent in moderate-to-vigorous physical activity in school settings', *Measurement in Physical Education and Exercise Science*, 14: 67–78.

Mosston, M. and Ashworth, S. (2002) *Teaching Physical Education*. London: Benjamin Cummings.

NHS (National Health Service) (2011) *Physical Activity Guidelines for Children and Young People*. Available at: www.nhs.uk/Livewell/fitness/Pages/physical-activity-guidelines-for-young-people.aspx (accessed 17 August 2011).

Passer, M.W. and Wilson, B.J. (2002) 'Motivational, emotional, and cognitive determinants of children's age readiness for competition', in F.L. Smoll and R.E. Smith (eds), *Children and Youth in Sport*. Dubuque, IO: Kendall/Hunt Publishing Company. pp. 83–103.

Pica, R. (2004) *Experiences in Movement: Birth to Age 8*, 3rd edn. Albany, NY: Thomson, Delmar Learning.

Richardson, H. (2011) 'Britain's pupils are bad losers, survey suggests'. Available at: www.bbc.co.uk/news/education-12938578 (accessed 30 April 2011).

Sainsbury's School Games (2014) Inclusive Sports Formats. Available at: www.your-schoolgames.com/about-the-games/inclusive-competition/inclusive-sports-formats (accessed 17 February 2014).

Shaljean, J. (2011) 'Keeping your child active'. BBC Learning Parents Blog: Supporting your child's education. Available at: www.bbc.co.uk/blogs/parents/2011/03/adding-value-to-school-sport.shtml (accessed 30 April 2011).

St Edmund's School, Salisbury (no date) Wake and Shake! St Edmund's School Sports Partnership. Accessed January 2007 at: www.continyou.org.uk/content.php?CategoryID=585.

Stratton, G. and Watson, P. (2009) Chapter 8 – 'Young people and physical activity', in L. Dugdill, D. Crone and R. Murphy (eds), *Physical Activity and Health Promotion: Evidence-based Approaches to Practice*. Oxford: Wiley-Blackwell. pp. 150–73.

Swindlehurst, G. and Chapman, A. (2008) 'Teaching dance: a framework for creativity', in J. Lavin (ed.), *Creative Approaches to Physical Education: Helping Children to Achieve Their True Potential*. London: Routledge. pp. 29–54.

Teachers TV (2007a) KS2 PE 'The Morning: Waking Up – Waking and Shaking for Better Learning'. Available at: www.tes.co.uk/teaching-resource/Teachers-TV-The-Morning-Waking-Up-6082865/ (accessed September 2014).

Teachers TV (2007b) KS2 PE 'The Afternoon: Staying Awake – How to Get Students Moving During Sleepy Afternoons'. Available at: www.tes.co.uk/teaching-resource/Teachers-TV-The-Afternoon-Staying-Awake-6082866/ (accessed September 2014).

Trost, S.G. (2007) *Active Education, Physical Education, Physical Activity and Academic Performance*. Research Brief. Active Living Research. A national program of the Robert Wood Johnson Foundation. Available at: https://folio.iupui.edu/bitstream/handle/10244/587/Active_Ed.pdf?sequence=2 (accessed October 2010).

Trudeau, F., Laurencelle, L., Tremblay, J., Rajic, M. and Shepherd, R.J. (1999) 'Daily primary school physical education: effects on physical activity during adult life', *Medicine and Science in Sports and Exercise*, 31 (1): 111–17.

Tudor-Locke, C. and Bassett, D.R., Jr (2004) 'How many steps/day are enough? Preliminary pedometer indices for public health', *Sports Medicine*, 34: 1–8.

Waring, M., Warburton, P. and Coy, M. (2007) 'Observation of children's physical activity levels in primary school: is the school an ideal setting for meeting government activity targets?', *European Physical Education Review*, 13 (1): 25–40.

Whitehead, M. (2001) 'The concept of physical literacy', *Physical Education and Sport Pedagogy*, 6 (2): 127–38.

WHO (World Health Organization) (2008) *School Policy Framework: Implementation of the WHO Global Strategy on Diet, Physical Activity and Health*. Available at: www.who.int/dietphysicalactivity/SPF-en-2008.pdf (accessed October 2010).

WHO (World Health Organization) (2010) *Global Recommendations on Physical Activity for Health*. Available at: http://whqlibdoc.who.int/publications/2010/9789241599979_eng.pdf (accessed October 2010).

Woods, B. (1998) *Applying Psychology to Sport*. Oxford: Bookpoint.

CHAPTER 8

AN INTRODUCTION TO COMPUTING

Karl Bentley

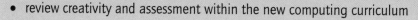

Chapter Aims

This chapter will:

- introduce the new computing curriculum for primary teachers
- highlight the greatest changes and challenges within the new computing curriculum
- review creativity and assessment within the new computing curriculum

Introduction

As of September 2014 'computing' replaced the previous National Curriculum subject 'information communication and technology' (ICT). Much discussion has happened across social media or within association meetings on this significant change and some teachers see this as a new subject while others see it more as a rebalancing and renaming. Whatever point of view one takes, the reality is that the new computing curriculum exists and is a lot briefer in terms of its programme of study and does not have the previous ICT's extended attainment targets, other than meeting the relevant scope of the programme of study. The other major difference is that there are no schemes of work planned by the Department for Education (DfE) to accompany the programme of study. Model lessons for teachers to consult will need to come directly from practitioners or education technology companies.

The new programme of study is so brief that it can be laid out below in its full detail. It is well worth reading through this and noting that a range of new terminology has been introduced and that a number of previous ICT aspects are still embedded within the new computing curriculum.

Computing programmes of study

Key Stages 1 and 2

National Curriculum in England

Purpose of study

A high-quality computing education equips pupils to use computational thinking and creativity to understand and change the world. Computing has deep links with mathematics, science, and design and technology, and provides insights into both natural and artificial systems. The core of computing is computer science, in which pupils are taught the principles of information and computation, how digital systems work, and how to put this knowledge to use through programming. Building on this knowledge and understanding, pupils are equipped to use information technology to create programs, systems and a range of content. Computing also ensures that pupils become digitally literate – able to use, and express themselves and develop their ideas through, information and communication technology – at a level suitable for the future workplace and as active participants in a digital world.

Aims

The national curriculum for computing aims to ensure that all pupils:

- can understand and apply the fundamental principles and concepts of computer science, including abstraction, logic, algorithms and data representation

- can analyse problems in computational terms, and have repeated practical experience of writing computer programs in order to solve such problems

(Continued)

(Continued)

- can evaluate and apply information technology, including new or unfamiliar technologies, analytically to solve problems
- are responsible, competent, confident and creative users of information and communication technology.

Attainment targets

By the end of each key stage, pupils are expected to know, apply and understand the matters, skills and processes specified in the relevant programme of study.

Subject content

Key Stage 1

Pupils should be taught to:

- understand what algorithms are; how they are implemented as programs on digital devices; and that programs execute by following precise and unambiguous instructions
- create and debug simple programs
- use logical reasoning to predict the behaviour of simple programs
- use technology purposefully to create, organise, store, manipulate and retrieve digital content
- recognise common uses of information technology beyond school
- use technology safely and respectfully, keeping personal information private; identify where to go for help and support when they have concerns about content or contact on the internet or other online technologies.

Key Stage 2

Pupils should be taught to:

- design, write and debug programs that accomplish specific goals, including controlling or simulating physical systems; solve problems by decomposing them into smaller parts

- use sequence, selection, and repetition in programs; work with variables and various forms of input and output

- use logical reasoning to explain how some simple algorithms work and to detect and correct errors in algorithms and programs

- understand computer networks including the internet; how they can provide multiple services, such as the world wide web; and the opportunities they offer for communication and collaboration

- use search technologies effectively, appreciate how results are selected and ranked, and be discerning in evaluating digital content

- select, use and combine a variety of software (including internet services) on a range of digital devices to design and create a range of programs, systems and content that accomplish given goals, including collecting, analysing, evaluating and presenting data and information

- use technology safely, respectfully and responsibly; recognise acceptable/unacceptable behaviour; identify a range of ways to report concerns about content and contact.

(DfE 2013)

It should be noted that in restructuring the ICT curriculum into the new computing curriculum the DfE has inherently made three major statements:

1. The new computing curriculum is more than just an 'add-on' or a subject to be embedded or lost within other subjects. Rather, it should be taught as a distinct subject where necessary and only merged within a cross-curricular form if that would enhance the teaching and learning of the subject.
2. The importance of 'computational thinking'; that is, a range of logical processes which can be used to achieve an intended outcome.
3. IT-safety runs across the whole computing curriculum.

We shall return to the above throughout this chapter.

No teacher can be unaware of the range of digital technologies that exist today within and beyond their classroom, no matter whether they are 'Digital Dreaming' (Fullan 2013: 40) or cursed by technology to be 'shallow thinkers' (Carr 2010: 55) or somewhere pragmatically in between. In most primary classrooms interactive whiteboards still hang on the walls and there is a variety of PCs, laptops or possibly tablets, such as iPads, all connected across much more reliable and readily available broadband connections, except for a few remote areas. Added to this are digital cameras, microscopes and a variety of digital sound recorders. Then there are the floor roamers (simple-to-program robots that respond to a basic array of commands inputted via simple keypads on the device or via a PC), digital construction kits, and more recently, basic micro-PCs such as the Raspberry Pi, which is a very cheap stripped-down computer for children to explore the basics of computing. Then there are micro controllers such as the Arduino, which is a simple micro-processor device that can be programmed via a computer to carry out a range of tasks that can make it the heart of computer projects such as building robots, weather stations and much, much more. We can also add to this the plethora of programs and apps from ever-expanding sources, including open source as well as more conventionally purchased licensed software titles.

Many pupils will be familiar with these objects, and very often so much more, at home with games consoles connected globally across ever-faster broadband. The rise in personal computing devices now includes phones that are more powerful than some home PCs of a few years ago and give the children of this age connectivity to the world that brings both choice and challenges to them and those that care for them, especially in terms of personal privacy, protection from those that would do us harm and harm that one might do either intentionally or otherwise to others connected to us across such devices. It is to respond to such challenges that the thread of e-safety, necessarily, runs right across the new computing curriculum for teachers, pupils and carers.

E-Safety

For any teacher the concept of e-safety must be paramount in the use of any modern technology, not only to protect pupils in their care but to protect themselves in their own careers. The majority of teachers will have gone through some form of safeguarding training (Ofsted 2014) and should be very much aware of the e-safety policies and policies regarding personal technology use within the school, but all teachers have a responsibility to maintain their levels of awareness of current trends and threats. Organisations such as the Child Exploitation and Online Protection Centre (CEOP), with their *Know IT all* site, and Childnet, with their *Think-U-Know* site (see links below), are ideal places for teachers to maintain their knowledge and skill levels in this ever-changing field. It is part of the teacher's role to ensure that pupils, parents and any other adults who form a part of their teaching and learning sphere are kept up to date and informed of current e-safety advice. There is no room for debate here: if you teach then you must safeguard those that you teach, and that includes e-safety.

Case Study 8.1

A group of pupils from a Year 5 class who had been identified as gifted and talented were tasked with using digital voice recorders to annotate the famous Japanese folk legend 'The 47 Ronin' so that their classmates could use the recorded narration to act out the play. The aspect of e-safety that was planned for review by the teacher here was personal ownership of material recorded, especially in this case where the narration was to be turned into a podcast published on an educational news site available to the pupils' parents and friends. Not only could the teacher review the previously explored idea of personal ownership and responsibility but extend this to the idea of permanence of material once posted on the internet. This allowed the discussion to move on to other forms of electronic communication across social media, including texting and how to report anything that might be upsetting.

Reflection Point

Which aspects of e-safety did this teacher focus on?

Pedagogic Demands of the Computing Curriculum

Many teachers viewed the old ICT curriculum as being built around three main aspects: digital literacy, information technology and, to a lesser degree, computer science. Digital literacy can be defined as the confident use of computers in such areas as office applications, word processing, spreadsheets and presentations, as well as making and editing video and sound. Developing from this and included in digital literacy is the safe use of email, internet searches and web browsers. Information technology (IT) focuses on how we can use technology effectively and how it can meet our needs. Computer science focuses on computational thinking, including logic, algorithms and data representation through designing, writing and debugging programs to accomplish specific goals.

Having worked with teachers who have reviewed the new curriculum at a variety of CPD workshops, seminars and conferences, some run by teaching associations such as NAACE (the National Association for ICT) and CAS (Computing at School), it was quite apparent that most of the concerns of teachers focused on computer science. Most were happy with the IT and digital literacy from their teaching of ICT, the main focus there being the need to update pedagogic practices around the use of tablets or iPads.

It is because of these common concerns that the next section will focus on computer science followed by shorter sections on IT and digital literacy, ending with a discussion on possible assessment strategies that could be used across the computing curriculum.

It should be noted that computer science, IT and digital literacy are not clear-cut aspects of the computing curriculum, nor are they terms used within that document. But they do serve as a starting point to help organise the content of the curriculum.

Computer Science

As was noted before, computer science focuses on the logical computation thinking that is at the heart of the new computing curriculum. Of all the changes in the computing curriculum the one that seems to be causing most worry to primary teachers is around computer science. To try to overcome this we can look at how computational thinking could be introduced from the Early Years Foundation Stage (EYFS) through to Year 6 in Key Stage 2 and possible transition to Key Stage 3 in secondary school.

Before we can introduce the idea of formal logical instructions we need to develop the language around it. In EYFS this would mean introducing the language of direction and command: left, right, forwards, backwards, stop, go, and so on. This could either be done by asking the children to act out being robots or by using simple remote control toys, starting off with the idea of basic commands and then extending this through more complex sequences to get around a track laid out on the floor or table top.

Reflection Point

Which of the EYFS areas would this cover? What other activities use these basic commands?

Once the children have a grasp of the language of direction and command, they can start to formulate plans for action. It is here that the basics of logical thinking that are key components to computational thinking are set out. Children can be asked to 'think through' their plans prior to carrying them out and to try to anticipate any challenges. Here we have the very basics of computational thinking: an algorithm – an unambiguous, step-by-step guide to achieving a known objective, a simple form of debugging or error correcting, and a sequence or set of instructions in an order to be carried out.

A simple way to check these basic algorithms is for the children to pass them on to each other for testing (Turvey et al. 2014). In order to do this there needs to be some form of recording and this is the start of programming.

This can be done using very simple symbols such as those used on floor roamers, for example the Bee-Bot's left, right, forward and back arrows either written down or on playing cards and placed in order. This can also be extended from simple Bee-Bot apps into using PC or tablet-based Turtle packages, a simple PC or tablet program that mimics early floor roamers and are so-called as the original object to be manipulated was an icon of a turtle. Most of these programs use simple Logo commands, which are very basic directional commands to manipulate the Turtle across the screen. These packages also allow the pupils to move from very simple arrow symbols to using key word commands and then key letter commands on a command line. The other aspect of this transition is that the pupil's work can now be saved and amended at a later date.

Reflection Point

What is available in your school? What floor roamers do you have? What PC/tablet software is available for you and your pupils to use?

Your own pedagogic principles and beliefs will determine how you introduce these ideas to your pupils. Would it be more beneficial to have some form of direct instruction to model how a Bee-Bot works, compared to a pupil just being given one and being allowed to explore for themselves? Your knowledge of your class and their capabilities added to your own teaching preferences will determine this. However, once the pupils do learn how to use a Bee-Bot, adding in real-life contexts, for example the Bee-Bot having to get from one location to another across a map or merging the activity within the structure of a story, adds context and challenge.

Reflection Point

What adventures could your Bee-Bot go on? What board games could it play?

The programming language Logo, created by Seymour Papert, a mathematician and computer scientist, not only moves the pupils to a more formal command line language, it also starts to engage them with the idea of accuracy in their inputting of commands. However, at this stage your pupils might find a series of Logo commands very difficult to debug (debugging is the term programmers use for error detecting and correcting) as it is very text rich. This is where educational software such as Flowol or Mimic can be useful as it allows your pupils to create an onscreen virtual simulation that is programmed using a flow chart. This allows the pupils easier access to the design of their algorithm and is a useful stepping stone, as it also allows them to visualise simple sub-routines.

Scratch is the next piece of educational software that you could introduce your pupils to. This is a programme created by Mitchel Resnick and researchers at the Massachusetts Institute of Technology (MIT) Media Labs. In this program pupils snap together graphical sequences of what look like blocks on the screen, each with their own action, movement or sound. This enables the pupils to build a program with a minimum of syntax into logical sequences to achieve planned outcomes to different keyboard and mouse inputs. When positioned in the right sequential order, the blocks can control sprites on the screen in terms of shape, size, colour, movement, sound and interactions when one sprite meets another.

Here the pupils have the opportunity to design, build and test far more elaborate sequences. The interaction of the sprites allows for quite complex games to be programmed quite quickly. This extended project allows children the scope to develop their computational thinking, especially in design and problem solving. There is a lot of online support for learning Scratch and it is easy to pick up the basics in a very short time using the MIT online getting started step-by-step guides (http://scratch.mit.edu/projects/editor/?tip_bar=getStarted).

Reflection Point

Is the key here learning the program or applying programming skills and knowledge?

At this stage most of the programming has been limited to manipulating graphics or sounds; the next stage is move to a more physical form of programming using devices such as Lego Mindstorm or WeDo, where the pupils will program an external device using their PC or tablet. Other physical programming devices are the low-cost Raspberry Pi computer, which is a single board mini computer or the Arduino Uno, an even simpler programmable micro-processor that comes with a host of input and output channels ready to be wired up to lights (including light-emitting diodes), motors, switches, input/output measuring devices or small LCD displays.

Both of these can be run using a form of operating software called Linux (so-called after its designer Linus Torvalds) as well as another higher-order program called Python. They are ideal for demonstrating how computers and their associated input and output devices are engineered and connected together. One of the final aspects of computer science is to understand how our computers are networked together and how they can do multiple things, but this is moving towards the area of IT. However, if you have got your class this far in programming then you will have easily covered the requirements of the computer science part of the computing curriculum.

Reflection Point

Map out the computer science part of the computing curriculum with the resources you have in your school from EYFS to Year 6. What additional resources and CPD do you need?

Information Technology

This is basically the purposeful use of technology to create, organise, store, manipulate and retrieve all forms of digital content. The creation part can overlap with digital literacy, as we will discuss later.

Most teachers will feel comfortable with this aspect of the computing curriculum as it is something that they do every day in terms of using technology; many of their pupils will come into school with some understanding of how to access, store and manipulate information from using games consoles or mobile phones. The change in the computing curriculum that needs to be highlighted is in the use of search engines – not only in terms of e-safety but also in terms of effective use of search engines; for example, how more precise use of key words or groups of words can enhance searches for specific information. The computing curriculum also asks that teachers make their pupils aware of how search engines such as Google 'rank' the results and how those results might not be the most relevant but might be top of the page due to a number of factors working behind the scenes. In Google's case an algorithm (PageRank) looks at perceived quality of a page determined by a quality ranking of pages linked to it. In addition to this, the computing curriculum asks that teachers enhance their pupils' critical evaluation skills when judging information obtained from the internet.

Reflection Point

Is this a transferable skill? If so, to which other subjects?

It is within the IT part of the computing curriculum where we also find the much derided 'office skills' (Gove 2012), such as using word processors, presentation and database software. While this aspect of the computing curriculum may seem to have lost favour due to the push for computer science knowledge and skills, the IT side of the curriculum links to the wide variety of tools used for communicating, collaboration and publication of ideas and information. With the rise of social networks, this side of IT has become the force that we know as 'social media' (Bazalgette 2010).

Reflection Point

What are the inherent challenges in relation to e-safety around 'social media'?

The difficulty for any class teacher is finding safe outlets for their pupils to use and practise social media. This will very much depend on the virtual learning environment (VLE) that teachers have at school. Some schools buy into secure online kids services such as Superclubsplus3, which provide moderated online spaces for primary children to communicate at the same time as learning e-safety skills and web page building skills. Other schools just buy into secure information sites such as Espresso. For basic blogging, schools use sites such as Edublogs, which are secure enough to provide children with teacher-moderated and modelled blogging experiences. Many schools lock down their internet search engines behind quality firewalls, but even so, every class teacher must know what to do when something unpleasant and unplanned for does appear on a class PC or tablet.

Reflection Point

What do you do if an inappropriate image appears on a class PC? What have you taught your pupils to do?

The danger here is that we forget the potential technology that enhanced learning and teaching (TELT) can offer. It is within IT and digital literacy that teachers and pupils can find the greatest possibilities in cross-curricular topics and projects. It is also the area where our pupils may well be using devices at home that they cannot have access to in school – devices such as mobile phones, iPads, tablets and internet-connected games machines and TVs. While some schools are heavily investing in iPads or tablets or have 'gone down the laptop route' previously, the results of such decisions, though initially promising, are not yet fully researched. So it is difficult to give a definitive answer as to the educational efficacy of them in primary education. The recent iPad Scotland Evaluation, led by Kevin Burden from the University of Hull, highlighted enhanced engagement by both students and teachers as well as many of the parents involved (Burden et al. 2012). However, the best advice is to go to a school near you that is using them and to experience it for yourself, or if you are fortunate enough to have gone down that route, invite other teachers in and work with your local university to set up an action research programme.

Digital Literacy

As was noted earlier, this covers the safe use of technology across a range of standard office software packages including word processing, databases, presentation software, as well as video and sound editing, and was a major strand under the old ICT curriculum. Under the old ICT curriculum it covered finding things out, sharing information and developing ideas, and tended to be focused on making films, recording and making music, as well as the fundamental how and why we use technology. In many ways this crosses over with IT. But where IT was concerned with the how, this is far more related to the why and to the quality and social ramifications that such digital communication entail. This also pulls into play the similar aspects to IT of e-safety but allows for a much broader discussion on why we need to be safe, as well as personal responsibility for our own interactions with social media as well as possible future challenges. Advances in technology mean that our pupils have far greater control over the editing process as well as being able to use multi-modal sources via single mobile devices such as iPads.

 Case Study 8.2

Previously, under the old ICT curriculum, to make a short film one child would have used a digital camera to capture pictures or a movie. Another child would have used a digital voice recorder to record the sounds. Then they would have got

(Continued)

(Continued)

together and transferred the sound and video to a computer and then edited them together using a specialised piece of software such as Windows Movie Maker. Once the editing process was complete they would then have saved the film in a suitable format and then, to show it to the class, taken it to a computer attached to a projector to display.

Now, doing the same activity using iPads in a classroom, a single child with an iPad using iMovie can do the same, but much faster, and then share it with their classmates using either AirDrop or AppleTV, which allows them instantaneously to share their work to other iPads in class.

Reflection Point

What has been gained and what has been lost in this recent development?

Creativity

Barnes (2015: 8) defines creativity as 'the ability in all humans imaginatively or practically to connect two or more ideas together to make a valued new idea'. Here the two or more ideas mentioned by Barnes will include one that is technology focused and others that may not be. In this way TELT has endless potential when it comes to creativity. The main challenge is ensuring that the pupils have the original ideas, skills and knowledge to which they can collaborate with others or with other subjects to develop 'new valued ideas'. Just as in the EYFS, where the teacher can subtly (or not so in some cases) manipulate the surroundings in order to guide the children in certain directions, so too can the pupils be guided in a TELT environment. The greatest challenge is not the initial ideas, but rather finding the time within the busy curriculum to undertake such projects. For example, if the Year 1 class is working with Bee-Bots and also making maps of the local area, the new idea could be a Bee-Bot going on a journey and his recounting of all the things he meets on this adventure. But then the most creative of teachers are those who can pull multiple assessments from single events.

Case Study 8.3

Year 1 pupils had been investigating their surrounding area and had drawn large maps which included local shops, parks and schools using a grid that corresponds to the Bee-Bot footprint (that is the distance a Bee-Bot moves for one command, which is the total length of the Bee-Bot). Following computer science sessions that enabled them to program Bee-Bots and record their basic program, they were then tasked in a lesson to program the Bee-Bots to make journeys from one location to another. The pupils worked in pairs and each pair drew up a route and program and wrote the program down in a very basic form using directional arrows and 'Go'. They tested out their program on the maps previously made. They then swapped their program for another pair's to test it out and likewise have theirs tested. The teacher and teaching assistant assessed not only their geographical knowledge, including understanding of local amenities, but they also assessed their computational thinking skills including their ability to debug and test a simple algorithm (a precise step-by-step guide to achieve a particular aim). In addition to the geographical and computer science knowledge and skills, there were a number of social skills as well as speaking and listening skills that were to be assessed as well, particularly in relation to a number of EAL children who were new to the class and were learning direction language and counting in English.

 Reflection Point

How would you record your assessments in such a lesson?

Assessment

Under the previous National Curriculum, Attainment Targets (ATs) were fully developed for every subject and were very specific as to the knowledge and skills a child had to demonstrate in each year. After the summer of 2014, National Curriculum Attainment Targets ceased to be mandatory and schools were given the freedom to develop their own assessment packages.

Freedom from ATs is freedom to be a teacher, as it allows us to create our own assessment instruments and it finally allows us to assess against the objectives set in our class for our pupils. No longer are we tied to some normative Department for Education view of what a 7-year-old child should or shouldn't be able to do in his or her computing lesson. Instead, that child will be assessed by the teacher who knows them best against an objective that was set for them based upon the teacher's knowledge of the subject, knowledge of the classroom environment where it will be taken and knowledge of that child using an assessment method to suit all of the previous. Against the objective the pupil will either have failed totally, be on track, achieved the target or exceeded it.

In terms of assessment instruments, these can be observations, discussions, grading work against a pre-set criterion or e-portfolios using mixed objectives for pupils to check off, as and when they are done. The important aspect is that they match the objective, and that for the child they help inform and motivate them to improve, by focusing not just on what they have learnt, but on how they learnt it as well.

CAS (Computing at School) also advocate something along similar lines, focussing on Assessment for Learning (AfL) techniques such as self-assessment, peer assessment, open questioning, discussion with peers, target setting (either by pupil or teacher) and KWL (what they already Know, what they Want to learn, and subsequently what they have Learned) (CAS 2013).

For both creative and cross-curricular approaches, 'performances of understanding', as described by Barnes (2015: Ch. 10), allow pupils to present their understanding in new situations, for example using their IT and digital literacy knowledge and skills to create an audio video exhibition or an interactive display in another subject. CAS has developed an excellent example of what progress might look like across the computing curriculum in its Computing Progression Pathways (2014) document and it is well worth reviewing this freely downloadable resource. Other educational companies such as Rising Stars and Espresso have also developed assessment packages that are worth investigating.

    Reflection Point

How else could your pupils demonstrate their learning via a 'performance of understanding'?

Conclusion

In this chapter we have highlighted the main changes and challenges to teaching the new computing curriculum in primary schools. Overall, the message has to be that computer science is as achievable for the primary teacher as is any other subject. The wealth of support being provided by fellow teachers via teacher organisations such as CAS or by other teacher groups sharing their CPD ideas online (see links below) has ensured that no teacher should feel isolated in preparing their computing classes. For the new teacher the freedom that the brevity of the programme of study provides should allow for both innovation and creativity. For the teacher who has already taught under the old ICT curriculum the coherence with the new computing curriculum is still there, meaning past knowledge and skills are still as valuable, and although coming to terms with the enhanced computer science aspect of the new curriculum is still a challenge, it is achievable. As ever, teachers, pupils and carers will be challenged by the constant demands of social media and the need to safeguard themselves and each other from those who would wish them harm. But as with computer science, the support is out there: we just need to remain up to date and constantly vigilant.

With any new curriculum there will be a short period where teachers, researchers and authors strive to make sense of the implementation of this new programme of study. This gives teachers an opportunity to carry out their own research into the effectiveness or otherwise of different aspects of the new curriculum and put their own mark upon it for future generations.

References

Barnes, J. (2015) *Cross-Curricular Learning 3–14,* 3rd edn. London: SAGE.

Bazalgette, C. (2010) *Teaching Media in Primary Schools.* London: SAGE.

Burden, K., Hopkins, P., Male, T., Martin, S. and Trala, C. (2012) iPad Scotland Final Evaluation Report. Available from: www2.hull.ac.uk/ifl/ipadresearchinschools.aspx (accessed July 2014).

Carr, N. (2010) *The Shallows: How the Internet Is Changing the Way We Think, Read and Remember.* New York: Norton.

CAS (2013) *Computing in the National Curriculum: A Guide for Primary Teachers.* Available at: www.computingatschool.org.uk/data/uploads/CASPrimaryComputing. pdf (accessed July 2014).

CAS (2014) Computing Progression Pathways. Available at: http://community.computingatschool.org.uk/resources (accessed July 2014).

DfE (2013) *National Curriculum in England: Computing Programmes of Study.* London: DfE.

Fullan, M. (2013) *Stratosphere: Integrating Technology, Pedagogy, and Change Knowledge.* Ontario: Pearson.

Gove, M. (2012) 'ICT in the curriculum', speech to Bett Show. Available at: www.gov. uk/government/speeches/michael-gove-speech-at-the-bett-show-2012 (accessed June 2014).

Ofsted (2014) Inspecting e-safety in schools. Available at: www.slideshare.net/ Ofstednews/inspecting-esafety-in-schools (accessed July 2014).

Turvey, K., Potter, J., Allan, J. and Sharp, J. (2014) *Primary Computing and ICT: Knowledge, Understanding and Practice.* London: SAGE.

Websites

Arduino	www.arduino.cc/
CAS	www.computingatschool.org.uk/
CEOP	www.thinkuknow.co.uk/
Childnet	www.childnet.com/resources/kia/
Computing ITT and CPD	https://sites.google.com/site/primaryictitt/
Edublogs	http://edublogs.org/
Espresso	www.espresso.co.uk/
iPad case studies	http://edfutures.net/IPad_case_studies_in_school
Naace	http://www.naace.co.uk/
Raspberry Pi	www.raspberrypi.org/
Scratch	http://scratch.mit.edu/projects/editor/?tip_bar=getStarted
Superclubsplus3	http://superclubsplus.com/

CHAPTER 9

AN INTRODUCTION TO MUSIC

Vanessa Young

Chapter Aims

The chapter will help you:

- to become aware of the values that underpin the music curriculum and the teaching of music in school

- to understand the key characteristics, skills and concepts of music

- to know how these can be translated into activities of musical engagement for children in the classroom

- to raise awareness of the current research interest into the ways that children learn in music

Introduction

Why is music in schools important? What should music in our primary schools look like? What 'counts' as school music? What does learning in music in the classroom involve? What implications does this have for the primary classroom teacher? Our perception of this as teachers will determine not just what we choose to teach – the content – but also how we choose to teach music – the pedagogy. This in turn will shape children's musical identities.

Prior to the introduction of the national curriculum in 1989, there were notions about what an effective music curriculum should look like, but these tended to be regionally initiated and therefore patchy. The Gulbenkian Report in 1982 commented that the arts in primary schools were 'widely perceived as pleasurable, occasionally cathartic but in the end frivolous and inessential – a far cry from what the arts at best can offer' (in Alexander 2010: 243). The inclusion of music as a subject in the national curriculum and the developments that followed were therefore highly important for primary music. This was a first real attempt to look at the music curriculum as a con-tinuum across the stages and phases of compulsory schooling, and the process involved an impressive range of interested parties. It is a shame that, due to a range of factors, the boost that this promised has not entirely been fulfilled. The new National Plan for Music (DfE 2011) and the new National Curriculum in England (DfE 2013) provide us with an opportunity to re-think our practice and ensure that music does indeed provide 'what the arts at best can offer'.

In order to understand the issues involved in developing and designing a curriculum, and the different ways that a curriculum subject can be conceived, it is worth remind-ing ourselves of some of the radical changes the programmes of study for music went through during the draft stages of developing the music national curriculum.

Following the Education Reform Act of 1988, the National Curriculum Music Working Group, which was set up to establish programmes of study and attainment targets for music, produced an initial report in 1991. This favoured practical participation by all children and included references to a wide range of musical styles and genres, includ-ing music from other countries and rock and pop music. Surprisingly, these two characteristics and the values that underpinned them were not accepted by all at the time, and music was immediately established as a controversial subject in the develop-ment of its programmes of study. It is worth remembering the grounds for the debate as this gives us an idea of what different models of music education might look like.

Shepherd and Vulliamy (1994) present us with a fairly comprehensive case study of what turned out to be a fascinating 'ideological struggle'. Kenneth Clarke, Secretary of State for Education at the time of the initial report, published a statement of con-cern about the emphasis placed on practical aspects of music. He felt that this would be at the expense of music history, theory and repertoire. A pressure group against the report entitled The Music Curriculum Association was formed, spear-headed by academic philosophers. The criticisms levelled by this Association were that European classical music was being replaced by 'inferior' pop music, coupled with an apparent failure of commitment to the teaching of music theory and history. The Music Working Group, they argued, was in the grip of 'political correctness'. A fierce debate ensued between those who supported a practical and multicultural approach, and those who favoured a more academic and theoretical approach with European classical music at its core. In spite of the overwhelming support for the former expressed by the teaching profession and music educationalists, fairly major changes were made to the report to appease The Music Curriculum Association. As a result, the music curriculum at this stage favoured learning about music at the expense of active participation in music-making. In response, many major figures in the music world wrote to the Secretary of State in protest, and ultimately active participation won the day.

This strength of feeling not only demonstrated the importance of music education in the eyes of the nation but also just how strongly people can feel about different approaches and the values that are implied. The struggle over musical repertoire therefore was much more significant than just a question of what children should listen to; it implied a whole set of values and ideas about what was important in music education. Arguably this 'victory' heralded a more progressive approach to music education. This flew in the face of government ideals at the time, which were focused on 'getting back to basics'. It is interesting to note that the 2014 National Curriculum in England, while retaining an emphasis on practical music-making, suggests an attempt to include a return to more traditional aspects of music.

There have always been differing views about the aims and purposes of education and the case for music is no exception. Although practices in school seem to have developed in a fairly pragmatic fashion, based on what works, the ideologies that underpin practice cannot be ignored. Two contrasting approaches in education, traditional and progressive, have been applied to music education (Philpott and Plummeridge 2001a). Each of these approaches will have an influence on what is included in the music curriculum; what repertoire is used; what activities are planned; what teaching styles and strategies are used; what kind of musical learning is recognised; how music is assessed. Table 9.1 sets out some of the key characteristics and approaches of each ideology applied to the context of music education.

As we can see, each approach would result in two very different kinds of music education. In the new primary curriculum for England current government thinking has shifted significantly towards a more traditional approach, with more emphasis on content knowledge and cultural heritage. In terms of music, this is reflected to some extent by the new inclusion of 'traditional staff notation', and listening to 'the best in the musical canon', meaning established (preferably British) classical composers. This statement from the National Plan for Music launched in 2011 gives a flavour of this:

> We have a long heritage in this country of creating some of the greatest music the world has ever heard. In every musical genre, composers and performers from England have made their mark. From Thomas Tallis and William Byrd in Elizabethan times, via Edward Elgar and Ralph Vaughan Williams in the 20th century, through to Peter Maxwell Davies, Thomas Adès and Howard Goodall today. (DfE 2011: 3)

Table 9.1   Two key ideologies and teaching approaches in music

	Traditional **Focus on the subject**	**Progressive** **Focus on the child**
Knowledge	Traditional principles, concepts and procedures of music hierarchically structured	Developing qualities of mind such as imaginativeness, creativeness, sense of the aesthetic
	Operational competence, aural, performing and literacy skills, such as traditional staff notation	Emphasis on creative self-expression; composing and improvising using a range of invented notations
Repertoire	Cultural heritage works of the great European composers; classical songs, British folk songs	Wide range of music including children's preferences
Teacher	Master/Instructor	Facilitator/Co-learner
Learner	Apprentice	Composer/Explorer
Differentiation	By task	By outcome
Teaching style	Instructional	Exploration; guided discovery
Assessment	Elitist; targets; testing; standards; summative assessment	Egalitarian; emphasis on practical; formative assessment of composition process

A key issue here of course is that only three of the composers cited are currently alive, and all of them are white male. Echoes of the initial debate about the values underpinning music education can be heard here.

So, what other initiatives have led up to our current position with the music national curriculum in primary schools? During the previous decade, there was some acknowledgement by the previous Labour government that music, alongside other foundation subjects, was being squeezed out of the curriculum to make room for subjects that 'counted' in terms of national tests and therefore league tables. Attempts were made to address the resulting impoverishment of the curriculum. The Music Manifesto of 2004 (DfES 2004) launched a number of practical initiatives, such as the Sing Up programme, which aimed to raise the status of singing and increase opportunities for primary school children to sing; and the Wider Opportunities Scheme was introduced to fulfil the pledge that over time all children at Key Stage 2 should have the opportunity to learn a musical instrument or have vocal tuition.

While welcoming the extra injection of resources available to schools, the Wider Opportunities Scheme in particular has raised questions as to why these were concentrated on instrumental tuition rather than on broader musical curriculum experiences. It could be argued that re-channelling the resource into the much-needed improvement of mainstream classroom teaching (through, for example, more CPD opportunities for teachers) would have been money better spent. The project also raised questions about continuity and progression. What happens when children reach the end of their year's tuition?

One of the strengths of such projects is, of course, that it raises the status of school music and enhances the life of the school. We also know that a good deal of musical learning takes place outside the classroom with extra-curricular provision, and indeed outside the school. The case for this kind of music, with its potential to 'showcase' the school, has seldom had to be made. Look at any school prospectus and you are likely to find a picture of a child playing an instrument! Indeed, 'good' primary schools for music are sometimes identified on the basis of their wonderful extra-curricular provision. Of greater concern is how such initiatives enhance what happens in the mainstream curriculum and the everyday primary classroom.

The National Plan for Music makes an attempt to bring instrumental and classroom music under one umbrella:

> Schools cannot do everything alone: they need the support of a wider local music structure. Central to our proposals is the creation of new music education hubs to take forward the work of local authority music services from September 2012. More children will experience a combination of classroom teaching, instrumental and vocal tuition, opportunities to play in ensembles and the chance to learn from professional musicians. Hubs will provide opportunities that reach beyond school boundaries and draw in the expertise of a range of education and arts partners. (DfE 2011: 3)

The outcome of this plan is that Music Hubs, funded by the Arts Council, have been set up across the country. We need to look at the implications of this kind of provision in the context of what might constitute effective musical learning for primary-aged children.

The State of the Art Pedagogy

If skills and understanding in music are best acquired through practical engagement, then children must *make* music rather than just *learn about* it. This engagement should fall within the key parameters of composing, performing, listening and evaluating. Children need to experience what it feels like to work as composers and to understand music 'from the inside'. Similarly, they need to know what it feels like to work as performers or as appraisers and critics of music.

Each of these key roles in musical engagement brings with it a set of specific musical skills, such as:

- performing: controlling sounds; keeping together; coming in on cue
- composing: selecting and manipulating sounds and ideas; organising and shaping
- listening and evaluating: recognising, identifying, distinguishing between, making judgements and decisions.

There are also specific musical concepts, previously referred to as the 'Musical Elements' and now 'Dimensions' in the current music curriculum, such as: duration and rhythm, pitch and melody, texture, timbre, tempo, structure and silence. It is also important to remember the attitudes or dispositions that children bring to music which need to be just as much a part of every music curriculum – being curious about music, for example; being open and prepared to listen to the 'unfamiliar' or to the music of other children; being prepared to aim for quality in their work. The diagram below encapsulates these parameters of musical engagement and how they relate:

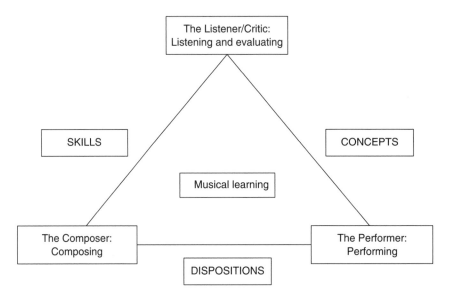

Figure 9.1 Parameters of musical engagement

It is important, however, that these parameters should be seen as integrated rather than 'stand alone' processes. It is not a case of 'covering' composing in the autumn term, performing in the spring term and listening and evaluating in the summer term. As an example, for composing decisions to be made children have to make musical judgements (evaluating). The following reflections exemplify this (key concepts are indicated in brackets):

  Case Study 9.1

The interrelationship between musical parameters and musical dimensions in practice

The children have been set a composing task. During their composing process, they also engage in trying out or performing their ideas. They listen to the ideas and evaluate them. They make aesthetic decisions on what they hear, selecting or rejecting those ideas so that the piece can be gradually shaped and refined. These are some of the decisions they will have to make:

- What will be the shape of our piece – how will we start/finish? Will we have some repetition/contrast? (Structure)
- What sound sources do we have available? What sounds will we select/reject? (Timbre)
- How fast do we want our piece to go? Do we want a strong beat? (Tempo)
- How many instruments do we want playing at any one time? Should we make use of silence? (Texture)
- Do we want a melody or will we stick to untuned percussion/chanting? (Pitch)

They rehearse their piece (by performing it) quite a few times, listening to and sometimes adjusting the composition as a result, or improving their performance of it.

Performing the final piece in turn requires careful listening so that the players can come in on cue, keep together rhythmically and control the dynamics to create a good balance of parts. They may even find themselves improvising (a form of composing) to some extent during the performance either because they can't remember quite what they practised or because they suddenly have a better idea during the performance!

Children working in this way are in a much better position to understand how professional composers and performers work, the constraints they might be working under and the opportunities open to them. This might lead the teacher to:

- focus the composing brief: You only have metal instruments to work with. You need to include this rhythmic pattern. You need to work within an ABA structure. You have this time limit.
- focus the children on important dimensions of performing: How will you keep together? How will you come in at the right place? How will you balance the parts and demonstrate confidence in your performance? What do you need to think about to perform to this small group, the class, the headteacher, a hall of parents? How will you position yourselves? How will you introduce your piece?
- focus the children's appraising of their music: Which sounds best? Is the drum too loud there? Should we make it longer? How could we make that sound lighter, more powerful, more sinister, funnier? How could we make the piece more interesting? How could we make the ending more effective? Could there be an element of surprise? What do we think of our piece? How would we improve it? Do we need to make changes to the composition or to the performance, or both? What do we think about the compositions of others?

The modes of performing and composing cannot effectively take place without listening and evaluating. Listening and evaluating, as we can see from the examples above, are crucial in supporting composing and performing. While listening and evaluating can only happen independently (we can listen to and make judgements about a piece of music without performing and composing), it would be a mistake to think it can be isolated from the other modes. The music of other composers can be used as a stimulus for practical work. It can illustrate concepts such as the expressive effects of increasing the tempo, or structures such as verse and chorus; these can then be incorporated into the children's own practical work, or indeed be used to enrich and inform evaluations of the children's own work. Ofsted (2009) pointed out that at Key Stage 3 too much creative work focused on students' demonstration of their knowledge of musical devices and structures; there was not enough listening to how composers and performers use these devices musically. This listening can start much earlier at the primary stage. For example, children, having invented their own piece, could then listen to a piece of music created by a composer who worked from the same 'brief'. This can be a powerful and insightful experience for children. Hearing different interpretations of common composition themes, or songs, perhaps from a range of music from different genres and styles, is crucial in developing children's open-mindedness and creativity and in making them aware of the richness and potential of the musical palette.

The role of 'notation' within these processes needs to be considered. Is learning to 'read' and 'write' music an end in itself or merely a tool to help achieve the key parameters of performing, composing, listening and evaluating? A valuable discussion can be had with the children as to why music is sometimes written down; why they might want to write it down; why some cultures (who rely on oral tradition) never write down their music. Why some kinds of notation might be more suitable to some kinds of music than to others could also be discussed. The new curriculum, for the first time, requires children to use and understand 'staff' notation at Key Stage 2. The inclusion of this traditional notation, as opposed to simply a range of ways of representing musical sound, here is specific. It is an area that generalist primary teachers could find worrying as it implies a specific knowledge base that they are unlikely to have. This does not have to be as intimidating as it first appears, as exemplified in the case study below.

 Case Study 9.2

Sounds, symbols and scores

The teachers played some contrasting sounds on classroom percussion instruments or the voice: a shake of a maraca; a glissando (slide) on the glockenspiel; a double scrape on the guiro (a ridged, wooden percussion instrument'); a long 'hum'; a series of taps on the woodblock. The children were asked to make some marks on their paper (symbols) to represent each of the sounds they heard. After doing this individually they then compared notes with their neighbour, discussing similarities and differences. The teacher pointed out that although their 'marks' were unlikely to be the same, there were probably similarities, such as a continuous line going diagonally upwards for the glockenspiel slide or three separate dots or crosses for the woodblock sounds. The class chose their favourite mark (symbol) to represent each sound. These were then put into a grid (see Figure 9.2) and performed:

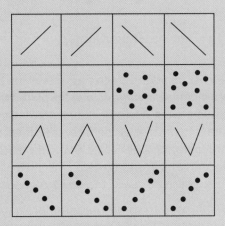

Figure 9.2   Example of grid with graphic symbols

They tried playing from left to right, down through the grid, and then experimented with playing from right to left or starting from the bottom. They also tried leaving some of the squares blank to represent silence. Having done this as a class, they worked on their own in groups, introducing new symbols and sounds. They rehearsed and performed these to the rest of the class. Lastly, they swapped notations so that another group had to 'read' and interpret their grid.

This led to a reflection on notation and its uses. They decided notation was helpful in recording their ideas and helping them to remember what to do during their performance. The limitations were that sometimes it was difficult to 'draw' the exact sound or rhythm, which meant that the other groups did not reproduce the piece accurately. Some children said it did not matter that the other group's interpretation was different. Sometimes it was better.

(Continued)

(Continued)

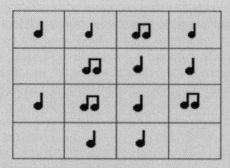

Figure 9.3   Example of grid with standard notation

This allowed the teacher to initiate a rich class discussion about when an exact realisation of the piece might be important, and the place for 'standard' notation. Some of the children who were having instrumental lessons were particularly interested in contributing to this discussion. They then tried a similar exercise but using simple 'standard' notation (see Figure 9.3). The teacher also showed the children some graphic notation scores created by contemporary composers and played extracts of their pieces to make the point that sometimes this kind of notation is more suitable.

Innovation in the Field

I once observed a student teacher in school with a Year 1 class who started her music lesson by asking the children: 'Who can tell me what rhythm is?'. This is highly problematic. Providing a succinct definition of an abstract noun of this nature would challenge most adults. Asking children of this age to define a musical concept in this way is inappropriate, not because they do not understand what 'rhythm' is, but rather that such concepts are difficult to articulate in words. We 'know more than we can tell' – what Polanyi refers to as 'tacit knowledge' (Polanyi 1967 in Swanwick 1988). We know things intuitively that we cannot explain or verbalise to others, such as the difference between two styles of music, or why we prefer one piece of music to another.

So how can children tell what they know? The very best (if not the only) way is through doing it. Those same Year 1 children had no problem recognizing and repeating rhythm patterns once they were clapped by the student teacher. They were even able to make up some patterns of their own, demonstrating that they had a clear understanding of what was meant by rhythm in this context. It was also not appropriate or necessary for the student teacher to define rhythm herself. In recent Ofsted reports for music a key criticism of practice in the primary classroom was that there was too much teacher talk and not enough demonstration (2009: 28; 2011: 3). Just as the music curriculum as experienced by children must be practical, it must also be taught in a practical way. As well as being critics, teachers must also be models and demonstrators, applying their understanding of music unmediated by words. Music is a non-verbal art. If we are going to be successful music teachers, we need to believe and understand that music has a power and meaning beyond words. Music takes over where words leave off.

Tacit knowledge coupled with the notion of intuition has a significant part to play in music. Indeed Folkestad (2006) argues that 'a music teacher never meets musically ignorant … pupils' (p. 136). They already possess a wealth of intuitive knowledge. The following example is taken from some research I carried out at a nursery in which I invited individual children to make up a song:

> Three-year-old Stacey chose to sing a song about her Barbie doll. Encouraged perhaps by the microphone which I gave her to hold, she made up a song about her doll. As well as using some of the usual musical conventions, it had many of the features of a pop song, with a strong sense of pulse, repeated riffs and slurred pitching; and the whole thing was sung with the slightly nasal 'twang' that is so characteristic of this genre. (Young 2003, unpublished research)

Davies' research (1986) into this area found that children were very able to 'sing it till a song comes' (the title of her paper), displaying many of the characteristics of Western song. Young children can improvise vocally with ease and confidence. Indeed, the urge to make songs, often as a narrative to activity, for example singing about their drawing or story, or getting changed for PE, is part of development at this age and happens daily and quite spontaneously often in the context of what are seen as 'playful behaviours'. These song utterances demonstrate the extensive knowledge children have already gained through enculturation: including song structures and conventions, cadences, scales, word rhythms and musical movement and gesture. Although these children may draw from songs they have been taught, or 'caught', they have not been 'instructed' in the composition of songs, so one might wonder how they are able to do this. Susan Young (2006) points out that children just know what a song is, how songs 'go'; they know intuitively how songs are structured and what people do with songs.

At the other end of the age spectrum, Green (2002) carried out some important research into how rock musicians learnt new songs or pieces. She found that imitation and careful listening combined with a strong personal imperative to learn were at the heart of the process, rather than any formal instruction.

So what is the significance of these examples? Swanwick (1988) draws an important distinction between what he calls 'instruction' and 'encounter'. Instruction suggests a clear plan of objectives and pre-determined learning outcomes, which indicates what input the teacher needs to give in order for those skills to be mastered, for that knowledge to be absorbed. It involves analysis, questioning and criticality. Encounter is much more of an intuitive, open-ended process that is allowed for rather than systematically planned and where children become deeply involved in musical experiences. Encounter allows children to apply what they know intuitively; they 'develop a relationship' with the music. While instruction has a part to play, we need to also give children significant encounter experiences.

So what are the implications of this for us as teachers? With very young children in particular it seems appropriate to encourage them to respond intuitively with minimal and careful intervention. As children get older, one could argue that they should be encouraged to make conscious what is unconscious, and move from intuition to analysis (see Figure 9.4), and that it is the teacher's role to help them through this process. This implies, however, that intuition is only 'for young children' whereas, as we have seen, intuition has a crucial part to play in engagement with the arts. We also need to allow for a constant interplay between intuition and analysis (Figure 9.5).

Directly related to notions of encounter and instruction is another current focus for research in music education: the place of informal learning in music. We know that a good deal of musical engagement happens outside the school or classroom context. There is a schism between music in school that is planned, formally structured and

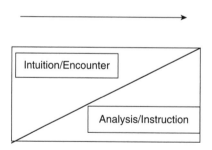

Figure 9.4   From intuition to analysis

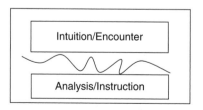

Figure 9.5   Interplay between intuition and analysis

prescribed by the teacher, and music that takes place outside the school in a more spontaneous, organic way (Hargreaves and Marshall 2003). This has been accentuated by access to the internet and the new technologies that are available to children and young people which enable them to engage musically with both the local and the global. A major factor associated with 'outside' music is the degree of freedom, autonomy and control that young people have over their music which they do not have 'inside' school. This is a significant point with implications for our pedagogy as music teachers.

Folkestad has looked at the relative merits of formal and informal learning in music. He challenges the assumption that children learn best where experiences are formal, structured and sequenced, and proposes that we need a shift in perspective away from teaching towards learning; from teacher towards learner and from how to teach towards what to learn (Folkestad 2006).

The formal approach involves conscious and explicit teaching to enable pupils to learn how to make music. The informal involves children in unconscious, or implicit, learning, which occurs as a result of making music. This is not to say that informal is 'good', formal is 'bad', but rather that we should look for ways of involving children in experiences that include opportunities for them to engage holistically as an informal learner, with autonomy of musical decision-making. A small-scale project was carried out by the well-known educationalist Bruner in a primary school back in 1983. He found that while an adult presence was essential to provide reassurance, encouragement and information, brusque intervention stole the initiative from the child: 'the children's play would become duller'. When the children were granted autonomy on the other hand, it seemed to increase not only their sense of personal responsibility but also their conscious awareness of how to improve their own learning (Green 2008: 107).

The message here about autonomy is important and needs to be explored much further in the primary context. This is especially important in a subject where teachers are clearly concerned about noise and its implications for classroom management. This can tempt teachers to place the emphasis on pre-determined outcomes or on 'presentable products', which may lead to too much intervention

Table 9.2   Typology: 'Formal and informal' approaches to learning in music

Formal (pedagogical framing) Emphasis on:	Informal (artistic/musical framing) Emphasis on:
Teaching	Learning
The teacher	The learner
How to teach	How to learn
Learning how to make music	Making music

Source: Based on Folkestad 2006

or over-structuring. We must allow children genuine time and space to be involved in significant experiences that demand genuine responsibility and autonomy in terms of musical decision-making.

Creativity

It is important to see music within the broader context of the arts. The arts inherently involve creativity; they provide us with a very specific and distinct way of looking at the world, involving both artistic and aesthetic perceptions. There are of course key differences and characteristics that make each art distinct and unique. Best (1992 in Philpott and Plummeridge 2001b) has argued controversially that because of their differences, the arts have very little in common and that mere 'expediency' brings them together, as expressive, creative, performing arts, perhaps to 'save time'. Indeed, Alexander states the importance of being alert to any form of 'reductionism' that could be the result of redefining the curriculum into fewer areas in an attempt to make it more manageable (Alexander 2010: 260).

To examine this more closely, it is important to recognise both what unifies the arts and what distinct contribution each has to make to children's education. Music, being auditory, draws on a different sense to the visual arts. Art works mostly in space whereas music works in time; the concepts of the visual arts (line, shape, tone) are different from those in dance (space, direction, level) and music again has essentially a palette of sounds and silence and specific musical concepts (melody, timbre, dynamics). 'Texture' as a concept in both music and the visual arts means something quite different. Skills acquired in one art cannot be immediately transferred to another art; a skilful dancer cannot become a skilful trumpet player without a great deal of hard work. Nevertheless, all arts draw upon and develop our affective as well as cognitive dimensions to form what Abbs refers to as a unique form of 'sensuous knowing' (Abbs 1994).

Crucially, the arts involve the common processes of making and evaluating. The creative process of 'making' is similar whatever the artistic medium. It involves having an expressive impulse or idea; working to shape the medium; realising the product in its final form; presenting it in some way at all stages in the whole process. The 'evaluating' process involves responding to and evaluating the work of art at all stages. Furthermore, while the sciences relate to 'objective' knowledge, the arts distinctively contribute to the growth of the pupil's 'inner world' of subjective knowledge or what has been called 'the life of feeling' (Plummeridge in Philpott and Plummeridge 2001a). In other words, the arts share a conceptual framework that is distinct and different from other disciplines.

In order to help teachers as well as children to understand each art form, it makes sense to consider what they have in common in this respect rather than just their distinctive natures. Since the first introduction of the national curriculum, there has been less concern to view the arts as related disciplines (Plummeridge in Philpott and Plummeridge, 2001a). Both Rose in the Rose Review (2009) and Alexander (2010) in the Cambridge Primary Review, made proposals to address this, with distinctive areas described respectively as: 'Understanding the Arts as an Area of Learning' (Rose 2009) and 'Arts and Creativity' (Alexander 2010). It is notable that no account of these recommendations has been taken in the new primary curriculum where even less is made of this shared relationship, with distinct subject disciplines for art and music being the order of the day.

Planning and Assessment

Differences between the 2014 National Curriculum in England (DfE 2013) and its predecessor concern emphasis rather than radical content change and largely affect Key Stage 2. As already stated, one shift is ensuring that children get opportunities to engage with the musical 'canon', 'works of the great composers'. Another is the introduction of 'staff' or traditional notation in Key Stage 2 in addition to other musical notations. The key parameters of performing, composing and listening, however, are still at the heart of the curriculum, although ensuring that children have the opportunity to learn a musical instrument is now a specific aim, suggesting an emphasis on performing. This has implications of course for the recently formed music hubs which have a responsibility to provide this kind of opportunity to schools.

The term 'elements' of music – pitch, duration, dynamics, tempo, timbre, texture, structure – has been changed to 'dimensions' and now includes 'appropriate musical notations'. There is an explicit reference to the idea that these dimensions are interrelated. This is important, as too often the musical elements under the previous curriculum were taught in isolation, or worse, decontextualised. These dimensions can be viewed both as key concepts within music and also as key skills (see Figure 9.1). In terms of planning and assessment, we need to understand that achieving one does not automatically mean that the other has also been achieved. For example, children may well have grasped the concept of pitch, but still not be able to sing accurately in tune or play a melody on the xylophone. Similarly, young children in particular may be able to show that they perceive a change in tempo or timbre, especially through movement, without fully understanding those concepts. Teachers need to be clear about this in their planning and assessment.

Because the parameters of performing, composing and listening are still central to the curriculum it can be regarded as 'spiral' in nature, where content is revisited at different levels of development. Children need to be involved in performing, composing and listening; understanding and applying the musical dimensions at every stage of their musical learning throughout their primary schooling, obviously through an age-appropriate repertoire. However, being involved in those processes year after year is not enough; indeed lack of musical progress in schools has been identified as a key issue by Ofsted (2009). Progression is less about *different* skills and concepts and more a matter of providing demand and expecting more in terms of depth, breadth or quality. It could be that the activity or task is made harder, for example singing the song in two or more parts (depth). It could be that there is greater range, for example playing the melody of the song on an instrument (breadth). It could be that simply improving how something is being sung or played is what is most needed, for example ensuring singing that is really 'in tune'; breathing through the phrases; legato singing; clear diction; better control of dynamics (quality). This crucial aspect of progression, improving quality, is too often neglected in favour of variety or repetition of old 'favourites'.

A key aspect of good progression is assessment. I have often heard student teachers say that there is no assessment for music. While what is implied is that there are no standardised national tests, the statement seems to indicate a worrying misconception. Even if we focus purely on summative assessment, at the mandatory end there are end of year reports to parents. For music it is much more important to focus on assessment for learning. The purpose of assessment is not to 'prove' but to 'improve'. An important realisation for any subject is that assessment is the flip side of the teaching coin. In other words: 'to teach is to assess'.

Swanwick goes further in declaring that arts teaching is arts criticism (Swanwick 1988). This is an important principle. Arts criteria will be different from scientific or mathematical criteria. Every time arts teachers make comments about children's music work in the classroom, such as those below, they should be based on artistic or aesthetic judgements. They are, in effect, formative assessment comments or questions:

- I wonder what would happen if you played it much slower?
- I really liked the way you got quieter and quieter in the middle, as it gave a real sense of suspense. What would it have been like if you'd had a short silence before you started up again?
- Did you think about repeating that section at the end?
- How could you have played more in time with each other?
- Could you have built the piece up more gradually?

These comments and questions are designed to move the children on in their thinking and understanding, not just through responding genuinely to children's work in order to encourage and challenge, but also by modelling the kind of questions that composers and performers ask of themselves or their performances. They also serve to model and consolidate key musical dimensions and their associated vocabulary and terminology.

Student teachers can often be nervous about making such comments, fearing that anything that is not perceived directly as unqualified praise might damage the important self-esteem of children. While the sentiment and the sensitivity behind it are understandable, this is misguided thinking. Children need much more than 'well done' and a round of applause if they are going to make progress. We should not be afraid of being a critic or indeed of helping children to develop their own powers of criticism. Indeed, this was highlighted by an Ofsted report:

> Too many of the teachers accepted pupils' first responses, praising their efforts indiscriminately with no correction of musical errors, or merely repeated the task without any emphasis on improvement, as in these examples:

> The staff divided pupils into groups and gave them the task of working out their own rhythmic pattern. The pupils worked together and then, at the end of the session, played what they had created. The teacher said, 'Well done,' and that is where it ended. The teacher did not know how to develop the ideas further, so the pupils' responses were not improved. (Ofsted 2009: 29)

One of the challenges for music, and the same is true of PE and much early years education, is that it is, by nature, ephemeral. Once a piece of music is played or a song sung, it has in effect 'disappeared'. This means that we have to find a way of capturing it, perhaps through audio or visual recording or through existing invented notations. The method of assessment therefore has to match the nature of the discipline. Of course, one could get children to complete worksheets, but this kind of approach is mostly only suited to factual learning about music, the instruments of the orchestra or the notes of a scale. If we want to really assess children's understanding, we need to do it through giving them opportunities to apply and demonstrate what they have learned in genuine musical contexts such as composing, performing, listening, responding to and evaluating

Table 9.3   Assessment

Sources of evidence	Examples of evidence	Method
What children 'do'	How the children communicate during performance/composing How well they clap in time to the beat How they hold their beaters How they approach inventing a notation	Observation Listening Questioning
What children 'say'	Technical vocabulary used (We need an instrument with a low pitch ...; I like the way it gradually gets louder ...; I can hear three different instruments playing ...; Let's have an ostinato) Expressive vocabulary used (It needs more suspense ... ; I like the way we have a silence in the middle ...; It sounds too happy for this story ...; Can we make it sound more shimmery?)	Observation Listening Questioning
What children 'produce'	Compositions Improvisations Performances Notations	Observation Listening Questioning Audio/video record Audio/video record Paper copies

music. Looking at the invented notations that children have produced to remember their piece will give us a much better insight into their thinking than whether they can name the notes on the stave. Hearing and observing the performances of their compositions and the processes that led up to them, will tell us even more. A helpful way of thinking about the evidence available to us is illustrated in Table 9.3.

Lastly, just as we need to develop our powers of criticism, we need to help children to do so as well. We need to engage them in both peer and self-assessment. Children are very good at knowing what they like and dislike in music, their own as well as other people's. What we need to help them to do is to understand why, and how their views relate to those of others. It is important for children to understand both the subjective, affective nature of music, that it can mean different things to all of us, and the more objective dimensions, including: the importance of playing in time; identifying where the piece gets louder or quieter; vocal techniques for controlling our breathing when singing a long line; holding a beater to get the best sound; and the relationship between rhythm and beat. The crucial point is to match our assessment approaches to the essentials of music as a discipline; to reflect the practical nature of the subject and resist at all cost the temptation to 'pin it down' to the written word.

Conclusion

This chapter has introduced the key parameters of engagement in music, which should frame all our music teaching and learning in schools and classrooms, and what good practice in classroom music might look like. The values that underpin any curriculum cannot be ignored and music is no exception. We need to understand not just what decisions there are to be made about the curriculum and our approach to teaching, but also what influences those decisions. We are currently at a 'watershed' time in terms of the primary curriculum, which makes it all the more important for us as teachers to be clear about our values and key principles in relation to what makes a good music education. The words of Philip Ball remind us of the fundamental nature of music to us as human beings:

> The human mind quite naturally possesses the mental apparatus for musicality, and it will make use of these tools whether we consciously will it or not. Music isn't something we as a species do by choice – it is ingrained in our auditory, cognitive and motor functions, and it is implicit in the way we construct our sonic landscape. (Ball 2010: 5)

There is significant innovation taking place arising out of recent research that makes it an exciting time to be teaching music. Whatever the apparent prescription in the curriculum, teachers are the key to ensuring children have a high-quality musical experience that will capitalise on this most natural of human instincts and help them to embrace the world of music with both knowledge and feeling.

Reflection Points

1. Think about three things you believe strongly in relation to teaching and learning in music. What does this tell you about your own values and ideology?
2. Think back to your own experiences of learning in music. Identify when you learnt formally and informally. What difference did it make to your learning?
3. Within a music lesson, identify when children are involved in performing, composing, listening and evaluating. How does each 'mode' support and inform the other?
4. Observe a range of musical activities in your school. When do you think children are learning best? Why? How do you know?

Further Reading

Bernard, P. and Murphy, R. (2013) *Teaching Music Creatively*. Abingdon: Routledge.

Finney, J. (2000) 'Stagnation: the case of singing in the English National Curriculum', *Music Education Research*, 2 (2): 203–11.

Glover, J. (2000) *Children Composing 4–14*. London: RoutledgeFalmer.

Jones, P. and Robson, C. (2008) *Teaching Music in Primary Schools*. Exeter: Learning Matters.

Mills, J. (2009) *Music in the Primary School*, 3rd edn. Oxford: Oxford University Press.

Ofsted (Office for Standards in Education) (2013) *Music in Schools – What Hubs Must Do*. London: Ofsted.

Philpott, C. and Spruce, G. (2012) *Debates in Music Teaching*. Abingdon: Routledge.

Pitts, S. (2000) 'Reasons to teach music: establishing a place in the contemporary curriculum', *British Journal of Music Education*, 17 (1): 33–42.

References

Abbs, P. (1994) *The Education Imperative*. London: Falmer Press.

Alexander, R. (ed.) (2010) *Children, Their World, Their Education: Final Report and Recommendations of the Cambridge Primary Review*. Abingdon: Routledge.

Ball, P. (2010) *The Music Instinct*. London: Bodley Head.

Best, D. (1992) 'Generic arts: an expedient myth', *Journal of Art and Design Education*, 11 (1): 27–44.

Davies, C. (1986) 'Say it 'til a song comes: reflections on songs invented by children 3–13', *British Journal of Music Education* 3 (3): 279–94.

DfE (Department for Education) (2011) The Importance of Music: A National Plan for Music Education. Ref: DFE-00086-2011. Available at: www.gov.uk/government/publications/the-importance-of-music-a-national-plan-for-music-education

DfE (Department for Education) (2013) *The National Curriculum in England Framework Document*. London: DfE.

DfES (Department for Education and Skills) (2004) *The Music Manifesto*. London: DfES.

Folkestad, G. (2006) 'Formal and informal learning situations or practices vs. formal and informal ways of learning', *British Journal of Music Education*, 23 (2): 135–45.

Green, L. (2002) *How Popular Musicians Learn: A Way Ahead for Music Education*. London: Ashgate Press.

Green, L. (2008) *Music, Informal Learning and the School: A New Classroom Pedagogy*. London: Ashgate Press.

Hargreaves, D.J. and Marshall, N.A. (2003) 'Developing identities in music education', *Music Education Research*, 5: 3.

Ofsted (Office for Standards in Education) (2009) *Making More of Music: An Evaluation of Music in School 2005–8*. London: Ofsted.

Ofsted (Office for Standards in Education) (2011) *Wider Still and Wider*. London: Ofsted.

Philpott, C. and Plummeridge, C. (2001a) *Issues in Music Teaching*. London: RoutledgeFalmer.

Philpott, C. and Plummeridge, C. (2001b) *Learning to Teach Music in the Secondary School*. London: RoutledgeFalmer.

Rose, J. (2009) *The Independent Review of the Primary Curriculum: Final Report*. London: DCSF.

Shepherd, J. and Vulliamy, G. (1994) 'The struggle for culture: a sociological case study of the development of a national music curriculum', *British Journal of Sociology of Education*, 15 (1): 27–40.

Snyder, S.R. (1996) *Integrate with Integrity: Music across the Curriculum*. Norwalk, CT: IDEAS Press.

Swanwick, K. (1988) *Music, Mind and Education*. London: Routledge.

Young, S. (2006) 'Seen but not heard: young children, improvised singing and educational practice', *Contemporary Issues in Early Childhood*, 7 (3): 270–80.

Websites

Musical Futures – www.musicalfutures.org.uk/about (accessed 4 March 2010)

Primary Music ITT – https://sites.google.com/site/primarymusicitt/home (accessed 21 February 2014)

Sing Up – www.sing-up.org (accessed 9 January 2008)

Teaching Music – www.teachingmusic.org.uk (accessed 9 January 2015)

Youth Music – www.youthmusic.org.uk/programmes-and-initiatives/Youthmusic_initiative/sing-up.html (accessed 30 December 2009)

CHAPTER 10

AN INTRODUCTION TO ART AND DESIGN

Claire Hewlett and Claire March

Chapter Aims

This chapter will:

- identify the different discourses that make art and design a distinctive subject within the primary curriculum

- summarise the key areas of current thinking on what constitutes effective pedagogy in art and design

- provide practical strategies for delivering a creative and innovative art, craft and design curriculum within the primary school

Introduction

With major changes to the structure of the primary curriculum following the 1988 Education Reform Act there has been increasing pressure on schools to deliver a broad and balanced curriculum. The introduction of testing and the drive to raise standards in core subjects has placed increasing pressure on teachers' accountability with relation to core subjects. The ever-increasing introduction of new initiatives has to be accommodated into what many feel is an over-packed curriculum. It is no surprise therefore that subject overload has resulted in some subjects being pushed further and further to the periphery of the curriculum, as has been the case for art and design.

Art has a unique role to play in children's learning in that it nurtures personal creative development that ultimately impacts on children's wider achievements. Just as in any other subject, schools should be aiming to improve standards within this area of the curriculum. Good practice is evident when art and design has a strong presence throughout the school and where the potential to support children's personal development is recognised. Where standards are high, schools have adopted a whole-school approach to ensure they are delivering an imaginative curriculum, enabling children to engage with a wide range of media for different purposes (Ofsted 2009, 2012). Good practice is exemplified when children work with both 2D and 3D forms whilst exploring materials and techniques beyond paint and paper, working with other materials such as fabric, clay and wood, and other art forms such as photography, printing and sculpture. Children will also be engaging with the work of artists and craftspeople from a range of cultures but also across a wide range of historical periods, including the present day.

Most importantly, quality planning in art and design provides children with the opportunity to experiment, explore and refine their own thoughts and ideas and to practise technical skills associated with the subject such as tone, line, form and colour. Good practice is embedded in the curriculum where schools are aware of local and national initiatives in art and design education. So, for example, where a creative partnership with a local artist is encouraged, both teachers and children are able to capitalise on the expertise they bring. Where the art and design curriculum is most effective, schools are aware of the importance of progression in learning, therefore this interaction is ongoing and purposely planned for throughout the year.

Delivering a well-rounded art and design curriculum presents many challenges for the primary classroom teacher. Though children's art, craft and design work may have a strong presence in schools, children are frequently subjected to an unimaginative curriculum where activities are limited and teaching fails to stimulate creativity (Ofsted 2009, 2012). It is important to consider why this might be.

State of the Art in Pedagogy

When art was introduced into the curriculum in the Victorian era of the mid-1800s, the objective was to equip children with competent technical drawing skills that valued accuracy and realism. Lessons would have involved fine tuning drawing skills, often by copying. This approach remained mainly unchallenged until the beginning of the twentieth century when there began a critical shift in thinking with the notion of children's artistic creativity and child art having value in its own right (Anning and Ring 2004; Hallam et al. 2007; Watts 2010). This more child-centred view came from the belief that children were able to produce art more naturally representational of their own self when freed from the restrictions imposed by the more traditional adult-orientated perception of art. It is this more child-centred view of learning that is now firmly embedded in current primary classroom practice with the teacher tending to adopt the role of the facilitator, rather than that of the traditional skills teacher.

Close inspection of the content of the 2014 National Curriculum for art and design in England (DfE 2013) reveals that both approaches continue to be firmly embedded in the provision of art education today. An open-ended approach is advocated with opportunities to develop knowledge, skills and understanding of a wide range of media, situations and contexts through investigating, making and evaluating. The role of the child as artist is clearly evident by the inclusion of opportunities to explore personal creativity and self-expression. However, look closely and the importance of mastering relevant art and design techniques, which centre on drawing, are clearly identified as an essential requirement right from Key Stage 1. It is important to be aware of this and how it impacts on the teacher's role. The teaching of skills continues to be of key importance if children are to be able to express themselves competently in all forms of art, craft and design. This is returned to later in the chapter.

Besides these two approaches to art, there is arguably a further dimension that needs consideration, making the teaching role even more complex. The 2014 National Curriculum for art and design (DfE 2013: 176) states that as pupils progress they should be able to 'think critically and develop a more rigorous understanding of art and design', clearly suggesting that teachers need to adopt the role of art historian (Gardner 1990; Hallam et al. 2007; Prentice 2003), with the ability to explore meaning in the work of artists and demonstrate aspects of critical awareness of the role and purpose of art and design. This presents possibly the greatest challenge for the classroom practitioner who might well struggle with their own understanding of the aesthetic, cultural and critical issues behind the meaning of art and design. It is not surprising that this continues to be an underdeveloped aspect of art and design teaching in the primary school.

These three different art discourses make art and design a distinct subject in its own right. Schools that reflect good practice are aware of how art and design, alongside other subjects classified as 'the arts', can be utilised to support wider areas of learning when given high status. Where priority is not so high, art and design can become an 'add-on' activity often included to enhance learning in other curriculum subjects – for example, making a version of an ancient Greek pot or painting a Tudor-style portrait may be included as part of a history topic. This in itself is not an issue; the value of identifying creative cross-curricular links to support children's wider contextual learning is not disputed. However, this form of isolated activity can be limiting, preventing children from being able to sustain any real level of art engagement (Prentice 2003). Prentice argues that such an approach leaves little opportunity for children to fully explore, develop and evaluate their own ideas with confidence and fails to allow the time to practise and explore handling materials, tools and processes (p. 34). It is important to highlight that processes include the process of thinking. For practising artists the thinking can be just as significant as the final visual product. This is particularly relevant when considering contemporary art, which has ideas and thoughts at its centre (Page et al. 2006). Children need time to engage with the thought process in order to progress and develop as artists in the long term. This add-on approach therefore makes this extremely difficult, forcing the focus of the teaching into becoming product- rather than process-led; in other words, teachers concentrate 'on what can be taught rather than what has to be learnt' (Steers 2003: 22).

Teachers frequently choose to look at works by well-known painters whom they personally feel comfortable with, Monet and his water-lilies being one such example. Artists who appear to have an easily interpretable style that children can replicate are also popular choices, such as Van Gogh for his brush strokes, Seurat for his pointillist dots or Mondrian for his blocks of primary colour. This narrow focus on the works of 'dead, white European men' (Steers 2004) can result in children's experiences of art being severely limited. Added to this, activities in the classroom may often involve replicating versions of famous images with the emphasis on producing a finished product, rather than being about exploring the learning process itself. Such activities often do little to encourage the development of evaluation, imagination, personal engagement or self-expression. Drawing and painting skills remain undeveloped, as does the critical appreciation aspect. This over-simplistic interpretation of the work of artists is argued by Prentice as being highly derivative, producing 'a proliferation of pastiche' (Prentice 2003: 34). Children need opportunities to learn about how artists develop into creative thinkers, honing their own style over a period of time. This should include looking at art in its different forms, including its place in a range of different historical periods and its significance within different cultures. The process of producing art needs to be experienced, so planning time for discussion related to colour, composition, light, mood, observational representation, movement, form, and so on needs to be explored, ensuring there are opportunities to evaluate at each stage of the process.

The Importance of Developing the Skill of Drawing

> [D]eveloping a broad range of drawing skills is central to progression in art, craft and design. Pupils can create effective work in two dimensional (2D), 3D and digital media, without apparently using traditional drawing skills. Nevertheless, the development of different drawing skills almost always underpinned the most impressive work seen in Key Stages 1 and 2. (Ofsted 2009: 10)

Drawing represents far more than a technical skill and more than just putting marks on paper. Think, for example, how the power of visual representation provides a tool for enabling young children to develop a sense of self. 'Drawing for children is an intentional and constructive process: thinking in action in a socio-cultural context' (Herne et al. 2009: 16). Children use drawing to help them to make sense of their world; it is one of the ways that they construct meaning and communicate their thinking. Drawing is a powerful tool that can be used in different ways to represent and help to articulate their world and the drawing process itself can involve quite complex modes of thinking and reasoning (Atkinson 2009). It is vital to be aware of the significance of this process, as a thinking tool as well as a means of self-expression. Children's drawing development is often overlooked when planning art and design activities; there are opportunities to draw but drawing skills are not often explicitly taught. This can result in children believing that drawing is something that is innate rather than something learned, that you can either draw or you can't. Children are not always aware that this is a skill that, with practice, can be refined and developed.

There are no clear guidelines for how to teach a progression of drawing skills within the art and design curriculum, though published schemes of work such as Art Express (Stanton 2009) may provide helpful frameworks. Online art-based websites provide a wealth of suggestions and approaches for teaching activities, including interactive resources that can be used in the classroom (see websites and resources listed later in the chapter). Rather than attempting to formally teach a progression of skills, it is more important to respond to children's drawing in context and engage with activities alongside the children, demonstrating how shading might be used, how shape may be represented, and so on. Seeing teachers modelling drawing techniques, as they might model writing styles in literacy, provides an incentive for children who need to see others also struggling with mastering skills. Again, online sources provide a useful learning resource to share with children, for example Van Gogh's letters to his brother clearly detail his ongoing struggle to master the processes of making art.

Further online initiatives are available to raise the profile of drawing in primary schools. The 'Big Draw' and the 'Campaign for Drawing' (both at www.campaign-fordrawing.org) have had an impact on schools, providing opportunities for children to engage with different skills for a range of purposes within different contexts. Such initiatives provide a valuable practical resource for teachers.

Effective Use of Sketchbooks

The regular use of sketchbooks remains a key requirement of the Key Stage 2 2014 curriculum, though a strong case can be put forward for using sketchbooks right from the Early Years Foundation Stage. Where primary schools are aware of the potential of the sketchbook as a tool for developing children's skills and knowledge, they are used productively and in a variety of ways. They have the potential to become a powerful learning resource, a place to 'reinforce a child's natural curiosity and propensity for discovery and exploration of ideas, whilst enhancing self-esteem' (Robinson 1995: 29).

Sketchbooks should take many different forms, with children being shown how they might use their books in a range of different ways and for different purposes, as artists do. Using them more as visual thinking books it is possible to begin to imagine the potential. Many artists keep 'themed' books; Henry Moore had one full of drawings of sheep (www. artjunction.org/sketchbooks), while Leonardo da Vinci used his to record first-hand observations and to problem solve his latest theories, recording his thought process, often writing his notes in his own shorthand and sometimes even recording his notes backwards so that only someone with a degree of intelligence could read them (www.unmuseum.org). Teachers and children can learn a great deal about how ideas and styles can be developed by engaging with sketchbooks of established artists. Examples can often be accessed through the major galleries online.

Modelling different methods of recording encourages children to understand how this becomes a place for experimentation and recording. Used as a resource in this way children can be supported to develop the language of art and design. Where schools encourage engagement with sketchbooks on a regular basis, children have opportunities to practise and develop their art skills by experimenting with manipulating different media and engaging with the creative process. Recording in this way provides children with a permanent record of their ongoing learning, whilst becoming a valuable resource that can be revisited and applied to different contexts.

For some children visual representation provides a starting point from which to stimulate and engage with the imaginative process of learning. This is not only relevant to art and design; in science, for example, conceptual understanding might be recorded through the use of symbols, words and images to help embed understanding and consolidate conceptual development. A sketchbook therefore has the potential to become a visual notebook supporting wider learning across the whole range of curriculum subjects.

 Case Study 10.1

Engaging with the creative process

Providing the children with a place where they can express themselves can provide opportunities for the imagination to spill onto the page. This often happens once children have gained confidence to use their books as a personal resource. Introducing sketchbooks for the first time to a Year 5 class, recording began slowly, even reluctantly, with many of the children unsure how to respond. Some stereotypical responses were noted: many of the boys drew cartoon characters, while the girls opted for representing family members and animals. Over time this changed for both groups as they were encouraged to use their sketchbooks to record in different ways and for different purposes. Most importantly, they

(Continued)

(Continued)

were encouraged to record for pleasure and were given time to return to their work. Both gender groups quickly began to adopt different attitudes and approaches. They became more focused when recording for a purpose, such as drawing images connected to their literacy work, and began to demonstrate deeper levels of engagement when undertaking art-based activities. Experimentation with mixing media and testing ideas was encouraged and their willingness to experiment also became more noticeable. Regular opportunities for feedback from peers, as well as the class teacher, showed the children that their efforts were being valued and children were able to learn from each other. As the sketchbooks became more established, some children elected to take their books home, where they recorded things of personal interest, such as the first spring flowers or the shell they found on the beach.

 Case Study 10.2

Developing drawing skills

A group of Year 2 children were working on still life. They found drawing the composition very difficult and drew each individual object without interrelation or spatial awareness. The teacher recognised the importance of the children observing a single object first. Gaining familiarisation of the object was done through quick sketches, sometimes only giving the children one or two minutes to record the form, with the emphasis on careful observation. The teacher then built up the composition by adding another object, again asking the children to observe both forms and how they related to one another. They continued to record what they could see. The children were then directed to look at the spaces between the objects and consider parts of the object that were not visible. The teacher then re-focused the children back on the complete composition. Their drawings began to show further understanding of the interrelationship between simple shape and form.

Critical studies of artists, genres or artefacts can be explored through encouraging children to build collections of images in their sketchbook, as they might a scrapbook. Images can be used as the basis of further research or for encouraging personal responses. For example, children might study the genres of landscapes through consideration of landscape compositions from different art genres or periods. Questions to encourage observational, emotional and enquiring responses could be asked to help shape the child's understanding, such as how are features presented or are there any common features? Possible meaning behind the artist's work might be recorded here. Exploring understanding in this way facilitates wider understanding of art appreciation.

Innovative Materials and Practice

Many contemporary artists and designers are moving away from the more traditional methods of producing art and using a range of ICT to create and exhibit their work. Computer technologies are therefore challenging teachers to re-think the way that skills, knowledge and understanding can be applied in the creative production of art and design and it is important that these approaches are reflected in the classroom (NSEAD 2007). With more and more schools investing in tablets and iPads, it is possible to move into the realms of filmmaking, animation, digital photography and dimensional printing, as well as using the technology to support more traditional aspects of art such as drawing and painting. There are a wide range of resources readily available, such as Artrage (see Table 10.2), that offer dynamic means of visual communication. This technology provides an exciting motivational tool for children to engage with art processes at greater speed as they explore, experiment, edit and review their work and take risks as they discover their own creativity.

Practitioners need to understand the importance of looking beyond the classroom to provide children with a more diverse range of learning experiences. With this in mind, it is important to consider how art and design practice might be shared beyond the classroom, particularly as Ofsted (2009) found that 'insufficient opportunities exist for the wider community to appreciate the achievements of students as young artists' (p. 6). One way schools have approached this is to hold art exhibitions of the children's work on school premises that are open to the public. Many local galleries, museums and libraries also offer space for schools to exhibit and this may provide an alternative if space is an issue. A creative use of the school's own website can also provide online opportunities where children's achievements can be celebrated. The local secondary school may also be encouraged to work collaboratively on projects if good links are established. Exhibiting online to an even wider audience is also possible. The National Gallery holds an exhibition of children's work annually based on the 'Take One Picture' project for that year (www.takeonepicture. org). This exciting project shares a range of resources and ideas online, suitable for both children and teachers, and supports the development of a wide range of art skills. Scotland has taken the contemporary gallery a stage further with 'room13.scotland'.

Here, children manage and run the online gallery themselves, supported by adult mentors, making all major decisions, such as managing budgets and hanging exhibitions. There are other similar initiatives being adopted on a smaller scale by schools around the country.

The 2014 art and design curriculum (DfE 2013) states that children should consider the 'contribution to the culture and creativity of our nation'. One way this might be approached is to provide children with opportunities to work alongside local artists and craftspeople. Through local projects with galleries and artists, parents and other members of the community can be encouraged into the school to engage with collaborative art works. Art is a visual medium free from the constraints of a language-based form of communication which makes it an ideal vehicle for breaking down community barriers and strengthening community involvement.

Artists in the Classroom

Besides strengthening links with the community there are other considerable benefits for children working alongside practising local artists on a regular basis. Visiting artists can have an immediate impact on pupils' aspirations and achievement. Ofsted (2009, 2012) cites this as being most successful where schools are able to sustain such links. Providing ongoing opportunities to interact with a range of artists enables children to engage with the wider processes of producing art, including all the decision-making that goes on when working towards a final piece, as previously mentioned. Many children hold stereotypical views of an artist, which is often linked to the media of paint. However, as artists today work within a wide range of media, such as photography, film, sound, ceramics, it is important that children engage with a range of creative processes. Different art forms require the artist to be proficient in different areas, but there remain many common skills such as the reflective and evaluative creative process. Children need these opportunities to experience a range of stimuli as a starting point for their own art.

Artists are often invited to work with children on short-term projects, such as a themed art week. Such projects generate valuable opportunities for children to immerse themselves in art and design for short periods. It is important that schools consider strategies for capitalising on the impetus created by such short intensive projects into more long-term commitments that ultimately can impact on art and design within the school. Utilising the local community resource is key to finding artists who might wish to form long-term links with a school. On a national level, the Arts Council (www.artscouncil.org.uk) is committed to investing in the development of arts and cultural practice and champions high-quality opportunities for children to enjoy the arts both in and out of school. More local organisations may also be available, including art galleries and museums that are likely to have good relationships with their exhibitors and may run regular workshops for schools.

Working with artists can have a positive impact on how schools deliver the curriculum. Evidence suggests that where long-term partnerships have been established, both children and teaching staff have benefited in terms of their conceptual and skills development. Working on projects provides opportunities to work collaboratively on group pieces, an area that remains underdeveloped in many schools. Facilitating experiences for both children and teachers to engage with the processes of creating art reinforces the understanding of what it is to be an artist. Involving artists from different cultural backgrounds can help reinforce this further, helping to develop understanding of cultural identity, socio-cultural issues or gender. As specific skills and processes develop they can be transferred to other art topics and learning in other curriculum areas. As there is little investment in professional development within art and design, working collaboratively in this manner is good practice that can be shared on many levels.

Developing an Understanding of Contemporary Art

Engaging with contemporary art is an area often neglected in primary schools. Websites, such as those of the Saatchi gallery and Tate Modern, provide a valuable resource for schools to involve themselves in contemporary art projects. The ideas behind contemporary artwork are often complex and multi-layered, requiring the audience to think and respond differently to how they might to the more traditional art forms (though all art is contemporary for its time – a concept that needs to be recognised when undertaking critical studies). Trying to make sense of the work may demand the questioning of personal beliefs and perceptions and this can be uncomfortable, difficult and ultimately challenging. Art can and should provoke questions that do not always have easy answers. It is understandable that the non-specialist teacher might choose not to tackle contemporary art head on, although children rarely approach such works with the same trepidation. Contact with community artists may well provide the opportunity to develop aspects of art that children might otherwise have little engagement with, such as working on very large-scale pieces or working with a range of materials not available in school.

Contemporary art often involves experimentation with a range of media, for example an installation might include different aspects of ICT to produce a multi-sensory, three-dimensional experience. Contemporary art engages children with the here and now and the technology of the future. It allows children to understand that 'art' is not only something from the past. 'Greyworld' (www.greyworld.org) is a collective of London-based artists interested in providing interactive installations in public places. Their work is designed to be experienced by a wide audience, many of whom might never choose to go to an art gallery. Their work is highly creative, playful and full of humour that encourages interaction in a non-threatening way. They are an excellent example of how contemporary art can be engaging and easily accessible and their work has great potential for sharing with primary-aged children.

Developing Cultural Diversity within Art and Design

With the increasing importance attached to teaching children about the global dimension, art is an ideal medium through which to learn about other cultures. Many cultures represent their traditions, history, religious or spiritual beliefs in highly visual forms and these can provide effective resources for capturing the interest of children and engaging their learning.

It is important to think about the images and artefacts used with children. It is easy to present stereotypical images through making broad assumptions about people's cultural heritage based on limited or superficial understanding. If using African masks as a stimulus, for example, be quite clear which African countries are being referenced and that masks have different cultural significance for different countries. The materials used and the way they are constructed will also differ greatly according to their origin. Contemporary artists from different cultures may be working with different media from their ancestors and may have strong modern messages behind their art. For example, El Anatsui, from Ghana, creates large-scale designs based on the traditional woven Kente cloth, only his cloth is made out of recycled materials such as wire and bottle tops. His chosen medium makes a bold statement about the modern-day disposable culture pertaining to Ghana, and how this is impacting on the inherited traditions. His work can be viewed in England: one of his pieces is on permanent display in the British Museum and The October Gallery, in London, regularly exhibits his work. Contemporary artists exhibit at this gallery from all five continents and workshops are available for schools, helping to develop cultural aspects of the art and design curriculum.

 Case Study 10.3

Exploring cultural diversity using the medium of batik

Children in a Year 6 class studied the craft of batik. They began by looking at batik prints from different continents (Africa and Asia) and explored similarities and differences alongside problem solving with relation to process. Children then explored the batik process of applying simple outlines to cartridge paper using wax. Testing the resist method of building up light to dark coloration, they used watercolours and further wax outlines to layer up and colour their designs (see Figure 10.1).

After this initial exploration of the batik technique, they undertook research into the history of batik textiles from Africa, learning, for example, that batik is

Figure 10.1   Testing the resist method

more highly developed amongst the Yoruba tribe in Nigeria. They found out that the Yoruba use cassava root ground into flour then mixed into a paste as a resist medium. The class returned to working on their own designs and experimented with making paste from flour and water, experimenting on samples of cotton fabric and repeating the coloration process using fabric paints. They looked at the symbolism of colour and the use of natural dyes in African batik, and applied personal symbolism to their own colour palate using fabric dyes and paints. Finally, they looked at the work of contemporary African batik artists and how many have adopted using wax resist methods, introduced into parts of Africa from Indonesia. They experimented with hot wax techniques using traditional *tjantings* (brass receptacles for drawing with wax). All their newly acquired knowledge was combined to produce wall hangings using a batik method of their choice. Their work was exhibited in the local library along with their sketch-books, reflecting their research and process.

Table 10.1   Art and science slab pots

Learning goals	Skill development	Exploration recording	Key vocabulary and teachers' notes
Art and design link: Develop an ability to manipulate clay	Ability to roll even slabs of clay to use in form-making	Rolling a range of different clay forms such as play dough, Plasticine, new clay and terracotta clay using 1cm-square batons (guide sticks or Dowling square sticks) as a guide in order to achieve even thickness. Experiment making different forms such as rolling sausage logs and balls etc.	New clay needs to be worked quickly and all clay needs to be worked with on a non-absorbent surface such as plastic otherwise it can stick. Limit the time you work with the clay.
	Skill: observation through manipulation	*Task:* Children compare and contrast the different materials at this stage, observing what properties each of the materials has, which is the easiest to roll, which would be the most effective for making their vessel. They record findings through drawings, words, photos or verbal recording dependent on age and ability	
Science link: Develop an ability to compare a range of materials through first-hand observations	Ability to make slip and use appropriately	*Focus task on joining clay:* Work with either new clay or terracotta. Introduce children to slip, which is just water mixed with the clay to form a single cream-like liquid which is used as glue. The easiest way to make slip is to take a ping pong ball size piece of clay, push your thumb in to make a vessel, pop some water in and mix with finger. Model to the children a range of joining techniques, i.e. two edges, vertical edge to horizontal surface, coil to flat surface. When joining, score both surfaces and apply slip, then smooth out joints. Leave joints to dry. Children can then evaluate their efforts	Real clay is the preferred medium as it doesn't dry out as quickly, and is easier to manipulate than new clay.
Art link: Explore and understand techniques for joining clay	Ability to join one piece of clay to another	*Task:* Children to develop an investigation that enables the collection of data on which conditions affect the way clay dries. Children record results. Results can be applied to final art task	Children can investigate a range of modelling clays or places that affect drying times. Does it dry out too quickly, crack or fall apart? Does it take too long to dry? What are the best conditions? These are questions to investigate
	Skill: planning investigation leading to reliable data		

Learning goals	Skill development	Exploration recording	Key vocabulary and teachers' notes
Science link: Develop planning skills. Plan an investigation to see which conditions affect clay drying	Make observations that inform simple designs	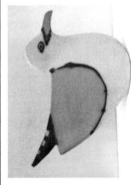 Figure 10.2 Ceramic by Terri Smart	Use a wide range of images from an artist (could be from local community) to provide children with ideas and discussion opportunities.
Art link: Create simple designs inspired by nature			
Develop an ability to make a simple vessel	Make a range of marks on clay using relevant tools	***Task:*** Design development (this example is based on animal pots by Terri Smart (see Figure 10.2), though any other stimulus can be used)	
Evaluate styles of vessels of artists, using these to problem-solve process techniques	Evaluate each part within the process	Look at a range of artwork by Terry Smart (see website) discussing shape, style, texture, form, etc. Consider what processes have been used to produce pieces. This could be recorded in sketchbooks in a variety of ways such as drawings and mind maps. Move on to looking at range of animal pictures as stimulus for developing own designs. Two-minute sketches to capture main features. Repeat activity with range of animals of child's choice. Evaluate sketches and select one animal to develop/design from	Evaluation is a key part of the process, so children should be encouraged to self- and peer-evaluate their work. Give time to develop designs further from their evaluations.
Develop ability to evaluate and further ideas		Mark-making on clay, give opportunities to explore a range of mark-making using different tools	
		Task: To make own vessel using all prior knowledge. Children select final design. Choose real or new clay as preferred medium. Use rolling, joining, drying and mark-making to produce final piece. Once dry, evaluate vessel, discuss how to create the final finish, i.e colour and PVA glue as varnish. Children could glaze these pots if firing is possible (local secondary school may help), otherwise finish with acrylic or poster paint which, when mixed with PVA, will leave a shiny finish	

Creativity

Adopting a cross-curricular approach to teaching art and design can provide deeper, more meaningful and more creative learning experiences. 'Kress (1997) suggests the world cannot be known only through written language but that we must recognize that children act multimodally' (Cox and Watts 2007: 14). Art and design provides alternative methods of communication for children, giving confidence to communicate through other channels.

Art and design seen as an 'add-on' activity was explored earlier in the chapter. However, it is imperative that art and design is seen as a subject in its own right, driving the learning experience as other subjects might do. One of the key aims of the 2014 curriculum is that children are encouraged to produce creative work based on the exploration of their own ideas. So what do we mean by creativity? Many educationalists define creativity as a process that enables the individual to generate new ideas and concepts from thought into existence (Csikszentmihalyi 1996; Edwards 2008; Robinson 2006). In relation to art and design, this means providing opportunities for children to experiment, problem-solve and take risks when producing their own artwork, as well as helping them master the skills and techniques needed in order to do this with some success. This has been touched upon in other sections of this chapter, in particular around using sketchbooks with children.

Tables 10.1 and 10.2 provide examples of how art and design can develop from a simple starting point and provide children with opportunities to both enjoy and learn

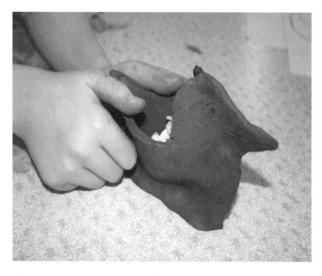

Figure 10.3   A child working on an animal: 'I like my finished shape. The bit that was the hardest was joining it together' – Year 5 child

Table 10.2 ICT and art

Learning goals	Skill development	Exploration recording	Key vocabulary and teachers' notes
ICT link: Review how contemporary artists are using ICT to develop their practice **Art link:** Evaluate work created by known artists	Evaluate and assess images of artists using ICT, support children with questions to develop thinking	Children explore the use of iPads and apps which allow them to draw, photo, film and develop digital sketchbooks Look at a range of artists who have use these skills, such as David Hockney, Emma Critchley or Andy Maitland. Both Hockney and Maitland use apps to support drawing in the environment, either using a stylus or finger. 'Artrage' or 'Brushes', teamed with 'Book Creator', will enable children to create online sketchbooks of their work. Below are aspects you might want to consider about creating artwork:	It is important when introducing children to a new genre (or artist) to provide a range of images. This develops understanding of different approaches and techniques. Use images to problem solve how they think they were created. Images by Critchley will immediately look strange and surreal to children and very different in style to Hockney's work
ICT: Explore a variety of ICT tools or apps **Art:** Experiment with a new medium to understand its potential **Art:** Explore the process of creating a composition	Be able to take images using digital cameras	How does the iPad complement the more traditional art processes? What processes might be introduced and developed specific to iPad technology? Identify a theme for the project, such as 'Water', that presents opportunities for further research and opportunities to explore personal freedom of expression ***Task:*** Creating a photo montage Encourage children to capture images (using digital cameras or the iPad). Complete a number of quick sketches either in the environment, or from selected images, on the iPads Peer-assess work at this stage	Children may need some instructions on how to use the different apps dependent on age, although older children may be more proficient, often able to teach the teacher. Digital cameras or Digital Blue cameras, which take video or stills, could be used
ICT: Use ICT to create, record and develop a number of compositions. Children should photograph their work as they go and re-work the image on the iPad. They can start on the iPad and build up a composition using layering (Artrage)	Evaluate and assess images Develop an understanding of composition	***Task:*** Creating a final piece. Select as appropriate: • create a montage of ideas as a collaborative activity • develop a collage of images layering images together • produce a final piece based on one selected image Experiment using different techniques to manipulate images, such as the range of drawing and painting media and tools. Explore how to use stencils from photographic images and how to work from these to develop different layered effects	You might also investgate using the iPhoto iPad app Allowing children opportunities to play and experiment is vital in order to understand the potential of the ICT media, to explore the processes of making art and to engage with the way contemporary artists are using them today

from established artists whilst also being encouraged to develop their own ideas. These examples also consciously combine learning from two curriculum areas in a multidisciplinary way (Barnes 2015), with the intention of providing children with meaningful, contextualised learning experiences that can deepen their overall learning. Both examples focus on the work of contemporary artists and identify relevant art processes that can be developed while working towards a final finished product.

Assessment

> One of the most significant aspects in the cycle of an art activity is assessment and evaluation, and more often than not, this is simply not considered by many primary teachers. (Herne et al. 2009: 93)

The role of assessment in promoting children's learning is nothing new but has taken on an increasingly important role in recent years. Despite this, there is no statutory requirement to document children's progress within art and design. Lack of guidance presents a challenge. Nevertheless, there are a number of ways teachers and pupils can engage with the assessment process. The main consideration involves identifying two key things: when an assessment activity is appropriate and what form the feedback might take. As already highlighted a number of times, it is important to provide opportunities for children to engage in the process of creating art. How these processes are assessed will involve looking at how competent children are in using a range of skills, how they choose to express themselves, how ideas develop and how they respond to art.

Both teacher and child have a role to play in the assessment process. Children need opportunities to peer- and self-evaluate their work, an area that continues to be highlighted by Ofsted (2009, 2012). Encouraging children to evaluate their own art elevates the standing of the art activity, giving it value. This can also help to develop self-confidence and a more positive attitude towards future art activities. However, there is a conflicting viewpoint worth noting, this being 'that any intervention from another person will impede an individual's creative will and in some way stifle expressive art work' (Key and Stillman 2009: 128). Teachers need to carefully consider the methods used when assessing art, ensuring children have understood the process and importance of assessment.

How Can Children's Art Be Assessed?

Sketchbooks, when used effectively, will provide an invaluable range of assessment information over the course of a year. A wealth of evidence will be accumulated, providing a record of development. By analysing work in the sketchbook it is possible to focus on the art processes of skills development, creative interpretation, use of media and problem solving, rather than being restricted to making judgements only on final pieces of work, where such processes may not be evident. This also reveals any gaps in learning that can then be addressed in later topics. For the subject leader, having access to this information across the whole school provides valuable evidence to track coverage of the breadth and balance of the art and design curriculum.

Critical engagement through discussion, peer sharing, or by including written feedback is to be encouraged. A useful strategy for developing critical skills is to provide a bank of possible reflective questions to support the evaluative process (see Table 10.3).

Table 10.3   Teacher questions

Simple questions suitable for Early Years and Key Stage 1	Higher-order questions suitable for Key Stage 2
How does it make you feel?	Explain your choice of medium.
What do you like about your piece of art?	Discuss how you could develop this work further
What might you change about this piece of art?	using a different medium.
What new skills have you developed?	How can you relate the work you have
Why have you chosen the colours you have used?	completed to the artist that we have studied?
Explain your art work.	How does this piece of art work represent your
Which media did you find difficult to work with and why?	personal thoughts, feeling and understanding?
What might it look like if ...?	Explain how you have developed your composition or sculpture.
How might you represent the light/tone?	What might happen if you combined ...?
How could you develop texture within this piece?	How have the colours you've used been selected or combined?
	Compare this with a piece of work you like.
	Decide what you could improve.

Recording Assessment

It is important to encourage a range of comments and questions from different sources, such as other children. Ensuring children are fully aware of the learning objective, along with the wider learning intentions, is imperative in order for effective evaluation to take place. Post-It notes can also be used for written feedback, allowing for comments to be removed at a later date. Questions such as those identified in Table 10.3 can be turned into 'can do' statements so that children can also monitor their own progress.

Other methods to consider could include keeping individual portfolios of selected work which move with the child through the school. Annotating this work in some way will be necessary to provide useful ongoing evidence. Photographic evidence of children engaging with the art process could accompany the work or form the basis of a display showing the sequenced stages of the learning process. Simple record sheets identifying the success criteria and the learning outcomes for specifically chosen tasks have been developed by some schools and are used to record children's achievements at certain times of the year. Whatever methods are used, it is important to ensure that it is the process of creating art and the mastery of skills, and not a simplistic judgement on the final product, that are being assessed, and that the assessment process supports other good practice within the school.

Conclusion

This chapter has identified some key issues in the teaching of art and design and has made suggestions for how non-specialist teachers might be able to address these with growing confidence in their own practice. In particular, the enormous potential of the sketchbook has been considered at some length as it is seen to provide a resource not only to support teaching of all aspects of the art and design curriculum, but indeed for engaging with learning across the wider curriculum.

Much of the discussion, along with suggestions for practical activities, centres around contemporary art, which has been identified as being underdeveloped in primary schools. This is therefore intentional and it is hoped that the examples suggested provide inspiration for how this genre might be used in innovative and creative ways to support the wider requirements of the curriculum that have also been explored. The strategies suggested are intended to be transferable and adaptable for teaching a variety of different topics and illustrate how opportunities for children to express their own personal creativity can be embedded in planning.

Assessment of art and design is regarded as a necessary requirement in order for schools to ensure progression across the curriculum. Opportunities for children to demonstrate their learning is vital. Peer- and self-assessment are viewed as being as important as teacher assessment. Strategies have been identified to support this process in a manageable form that will allow for the assessment of processes, attitudes and skills, thus ensuring all the requirements of the art and design curriculum can be addressed.

 Reflection Points

1. In light of what you have read, reflect upon to what extent a full range of artists, media and skills are explored within your own teaching.
2. How might you develop the potential of sketchbooks in your own practice?
3. Consider how the use of reflective questioning could impact on your teaching of art and design.

Further Reading

Herne, S., Cox, S. and Watts, R. (2009) *Readings in Primary Art Education*. Bristol: Intellect Books.

Robinson, G. (1995) *Sketch-books: Explore and Store*. London: Hodder and Stoughton.

Stillman, J. (2009) *Teaching Primary Art and Design*. Exeter: Learning Matters.

Watts, R. and Cox, S. (2007) *Teaching Art and Design 3–11*. London: Continuum.

References

Anning, A. and Ring, K. (2004) *Making Sense of Children's Drawings*. Buckingham: OUP.

Atkinson, D. (2009) 'How children use drawing', in S. Herne, S. Cox, and R. Watts (eds), *Readings in Primary Education*. Bristol: Intellect Books.

Barnes, J. (2015) *Cross-Curricular Learning 3–14*, 3rd edn. London: SAGE.

Cox, S. and Watts, R. (2007) *Teaching Art and Design 3-11: Reaching the Standard*. London: Continuum.

Csikszentmihalyi, M. (1996) *Creativity: Flow and the Psychology of Discovery and Invention*. New York: Harper Perennial.

DfE (Department for Education) (2013) The National Curriculum in England Framework Document. London: DfE.

Edwards, B. (2008) *Drawing on the Right Side of the Brain*. London: HarperCollins.

Gardner, H. (1990) *Art Education and Human Development*. Los Angeles, CA: Getty Publications.

Hallam, J., Lee, H. and DasGupta, M. (2007) 'An analysis of the presentation of art in the British primary school curriculum and its implications for teaching', *International Journal of Art and Design Education*, 26(2): 206–14.

Herne, S., Cox, S. and Watts, R. (2009) *Readings in Primary Education*. Bristol: Intellect Books.

Key, P. and Stillman, J. (2009) *Teaching Primary Art and Design*. Exeter: Learning Matters.

NSEAD (2007) Advocacy ICT in Art and Design. www.nsead.org/ict/about/about11.aspx

Ofsted (2009) *Drawing Together: Art, Craft and Design in Schools*. London: Ofsted.

Ofsted (2012) *Making a Mark: Art, Craft and Design Education 2008/2011*. London: Ofsted.

Page, T., Herne, S., Dash, P., Charman, H., Atkinson, D. and Adams, J. (2006) 'Teaching now with the living: A dialogue with teachers investigating contemporary art practices', *International Journal of Art Education*, 25(2).

Prentice, R. (2003) 'Changing places?', in N. Addison and L. Burgess (eds), *Issues in Art and Design Teaching*. London: RoutledgeFalmer.

Robinson, G. (1995) *Sketch-books: Explore and Store*. London: Hodder and Stoughton.

Robinson, K. (2006) 'How schools kill creativity', talk to TED conference. www.ted. com/talks/ken_robinson_says_schools_kill_creativity (accessed September 2014).

Stanton, J. (2009) *Art Express*. London: A & C Black.

Steers, J. (2003) 'Art and design in the UK: the theory gap', in N. Addison and L. Burgess (eds), *Issues in Art and Design Teaching*. London: RoutledgeFalmer.

Steers, J. (2004) 'Art and design', in J. White, *Rethinking the School Curriculum: Values, Aims and Purposes*. London: RoutledgeFalmer.

Watts, R. (2010) 'Responding to children's drawings', *Education 3–13*, 38 (2): 137–53.

Websites

www.accessart.org.uk – projects and skills information for teachers

www.artjunction.org/sketchbooks – Henry Moore's sketchbooks

www.artrage.com – iPad art app suitable for primary children

www.artscouncil.org.uk – Arts Council England champions a wide range of artistic and cultural experiences for adults and children

www.campaignfordrawing.org/bigdraw – national children's competition with teacher resources

www.gov.uki/government/publications/national-curriculum-in-england-art-and-design

www.greyworld.org – contemporary public installations

www.ipadapps4school.com – iPad app for creating narrated multimedia books

www.nationalgallery.org.uk – a range of resources for primary education

www.nsead.org – National Society for Education in Art and Design, a wealth of resources for both primary and secondary and links to current research

www.octobergallery.co.uk – a multicultural gallery offering workshops for schools

www.photographymuseum.com – photographic resources for cross-curricular planning

http://picassa.google.co.uk

www.room13scotland.com – children running their own online gallery

www.saatchi-gallery.co.uk/artroom/index.php – a range of contemporary art resources

www.starbeck.com – artefacts for teaching multicultural art and design

www.takeonepicture.org – maintained by the National Gallery and aimed at primary schools; takes a picture and looks at how to use in a cross-curricular manner

www.tate.org.uk – a useful site for teacher resources

www.terrismart.co.uk – artists' work used in the cross-curricular unit 10.1

www.unmuseum.org – Leonardo da Vinci's sketchbooks

www.wdwtwa.org.uk – Who do we think we are? website addressing community cohesion and diversity

CHAPTER 11

AN INTRODUCTION TO RELIGIOUS EDUCATION

Lynn Revell and Aidan Gillespie

Chapter Aims

This chapter will:

- introduce readers to the changes in contemporary RE and indicate some of the implications for teachers of RE
- examine the evolving educational and political climate in relation to RE
- encourage readers to consider new ways of considering the nature of RE and new forms of religiosity

Introduction

Religious education (RE) is a subject that embraces some of the most controversial and important questions that any child or adult will have to face in their lives: the nature of right and wrong, the origins of the universe, life after death or what it means to be human. It is a subject that is unavoidably topical (just turn on your television or open a newspaper) and a subject that introduces pupils to the world's most ancient and enduring traditions, cultures and beliefs. Yet RE is a curriculum subject that is not in the National Curriculum, the nature of its assessment is unique and, unlike every other subject, its curriculum is decided partly by the law and partly by local communities. This chapter will discuss some of the most recent developments in RE as well as advocating a challenging approach to RE.

Why Study Religion in Schools?

The curriculum is constantly under review by politicians and educationalists. If subjects wish to retain their place in the classroom then champions of those subjects need not only to defend their subjects but to encourage teachers to challenge their previous understanding of what that subject can bring to the curriculum and its rationale. A recent major three-year study into RE, 'Does RE Work?', concluded that the subject is often marginalised by government and that practice was often poor. The researchers argued that those committed to the subject need to ask difficult and challenging questions about the rigour and credibility of RE as a curriculum subject (Conroy et al. 2013).

Any really honest discussion of RE and the primary curriculum must acknowledge several factors that seriously impact on its place in the curriculum. The first is that in a secularised Britain, where church attendance is a minority activity and membership of other faith communities is tiny compared with the population as a whole, the argument that religion has no place in the primary classroom should at least be acknowledged.

One reason given by advocates for RE for maintaining the subject is that there should be a place in the curriculum for children to explore their own feelings and beliefs in relation to religion and religious questions. Most Agreed Syllabi and the Non-statutory Framework for Religious Education (NSFRE) recognise this element of the RE curriculum as important and it is reflected in the unusual approach that RE takes towards assessment. In RE teachers are expected to assess the progress of children as they learn about religion (Attainment 1) and as they learn from religion (Attainment 2). The second attainment is meant to support teachers' assessment of the depth and quality of children's personal reflection in RE.

An argument for the continued presence of religion in schools is that we are educating children to live in a society that is global and that global society is religious. Everyday billions of people engage in religious activities and live lives informed and shaped by religious beliefs. It is also religious in that every day there is conflict and possible violence influenced in some part by the clash of religions. The increasingly visible role of religion in global public life gives it a visible presence in contemporary society but one response may be to accept that these issues can be addressed as effectively in citizenship education as they can in RE. Citizenship education covers many of the skills, and demands a degree of empathy with and understanding of complex social and spiritual issues comparable with RE.

In light of the diminishing presence of religion in English life and the fact that citizenship education could embrace many of the topics and areas covered in RE, how can RE justify its place in a crowded curriculum? Two ways to approach this question are to ask what the study of religion brings to the education of the child that is unique (alternatively, what they would miss out on if they had no opportunity to learn about religion) and what is special to the study of religion in RE as opposed to religion as it is covered in other subjects.

John Hinnells (2005) argues that a true understanding of all culture is incomplete without an understanding of the role and significance of religion. However, he stresses that what makes the contribution of the study of religion to human society so invaluable is that the study of religion itself is so varied. Religion, he says, is like a diamond – it has many facets, no one discipline or way of studying it is enough to give us a true picture of just how varied, nuanced and multifaceted that thing really is. This then is one important reason for the study of religion in RE. It is the only subject in the curriculum where religious issues, traditions and practices can be learnt about directly. This is the place where children can begin to engage with some of the world's most devastating and powerful ideas and philosophies.

Even in the UK where organised Christianity is in decline, religious issues, conflict and celebration are still part of private and public life. It is not just that an understanding of the historical life of this country would be incomplete without an understanding of the religious past but that an understanding of the present and the future would be partial without knowledge of the forms and significance of contemporary religion.

Task

Using the National Curriculum, the Non-statutory Framework for RE and an Agreed Syllabus, map the skills and areas of subject knowledge that are common and distinct for RE, citizenship education and PSHE. Is it the case that everything that is covered in RE can also be covered elsewhere?

State of the Art in Pedagogy

Questions of Organisation and Change in RE

Although there is a distinction between the curriculum (what may be learned) and pedagogy (how it may be taught and learned), in reality the two are linked and this is certainly the case in RE (Stern 2006). For example, while pedagogies for other subjects may discuss the rationale for their subject, this is to a large extent dictated to RE because of the statutory requirements and involvement of faith groups in the creation of the curriculum. RE is so intimately linked with values education in England that it is easy to forget that there are ways of studying religion which do not seek to promote a particular ethos. The content of the RE curriculum in the NSFRE and Agreed Syllabi are informed by the values of the National Curriculum, the interests of the faith groups and the desire for RE to play a role in cultivating tolerance, which means that the pedagogies of RE are in many ways intimately and intrinsically intertwined with the organisation of RE as a subject.

This means that before we can discuss the role of pedagogy we need to fully understand the issues surrounding the unusual organisation of RE.

How Should RE Be Organised?

RE is in a state of flux and one of the most important areas of change is in the way it is organised. The creation of the National Curriculum released other subjects from the task of deciding how to organise their curriculum content. The way RE is organised is peculiar and the result of long-drawn-out historical and cultural forces, political and religious compromises and pragmatism.

The policies, laws and guidelines that inform the teaching of RE are the culmination of generations of debate and wrangling between Christian denominations, politicians and schools of thought representing different approaches to the teaching of religion in schools.

Currently there are two Acts of Parliament that regulate the provision of RE. The 1988 Education Reform Act made the provision of RE in all community schools mandatory. Within the boundaries of that Act, parents have a right to withdraw their children from RE and teachers also have the right to be excused from teaching RE on the grounds of conscience. A further unusual tenant is that it sets out the rules governing the way schools decide what should be taught in RE. While the 1988 Act brought the teaching of every other subject in the curriculum under the rubric of the National Curriculum, the teaching of RE was excluded. The given reason was that denominational schools would find it very difficult to fit in with a national system (Brown 2002). The omission of RE from the National Curriculum left the control of what was taught in the hands of local bodies called Standing Advisory Councils on RE (SACREs). These bodies are made up of local representatives from religious communities, the church and teachers, and their remit is to support the creation and delivery of RE in local schools.

The unusual approach to the formation of curriculum content is one of the factors that sets it apart from other subjects. While other subjects are determined centrally and by experts in the field, the content of RE is decided locally, and depends on the religious make-up and character of local regions. This means that the content of RE may be influenced by which faiths are present in that area, by people who are not experts in education, have no training on education or are aware of current standards or developments in education, and by the character of local faith communities.

The Agreed Syllabi vs a National Curriculum for RE

The new National Curriculum in England came into effect in September 2014 and was preceded by a surge of reports into the state of RE provision within primary education in England, such as the All Party Parliamentary Group on RE (APPGRE), the Religious Education Council (REC) and Ofsted, all of whom produced reports on RE in 2013. A lot of the material in the reports captures the decline of standards in RE across the sector and impressively all reports identify the same problem areas and reasons for the drop in standards.

One of the main problems facing RE is the slashing of budgets at local level, leading to the decline in support for primary school teachers with regards to specialist training and subject specialist forums. The REC in particular has been very outspoken in its opening statement within the National Curriculum Framework for RE (NCFRE 2013: 6–7). Within this report the Council outlines changes in the ways RE is assessed at secondary level which has led to fewer students taking RE at post-16 level and fewer applicants to university to train in Religious Education as well as fewer places being offered by universities (APPGRE 2013: 7). The lack of specialist teachers will ensure a continuing decline in the quality of RE that children will experience in schools.

Alongside this, Standing Advisory Councils for RE have had their budgets severely cut and the role of the national advisor for RE at the QCDA has been eliminated. This role was to ensure a coherent approach to RE across all SACREs; as a result of this they have become for the most part a formality within the local authorities in which they are placed and provide little or no effective support of RE, either at a school level, for CPD or in producing or disseminating RE materials. Within Kent, for example, the SACRE is now supported by an advisor who has been allocated 15 days a year to coordinate and advise on quality RE – no mean feat if they can do it. It is clear from this that the REC's framework, which should be used as a scaffold to the Agreed Syllabi produced by the various SACREs, may well not ever be looked at as there will be no funds to write or develop existing Agreed Syllabi.

However, despite all the doom and gloom there have been some voices that have drawn attention to the possibilities and opportunities that have arisen out of all the changes over the last year. Mark Chater and Clive Erricker outline ways in which the current state of RE curricula, as devised within the multitude of Agreed Syllabi and the outline within the RE Council's suggested framework, can be transformed (Chater and Erricker 2013: 137–41). They propose moving on from an over-reliance on Attainment Target 1 (*Learning About Religion*) and Attainment Target 2 (*Learning From Religion*) to a pedagogy that places the learner at the centre of the learning process. This would be a sea change from the current approach which, consciously or not, fragments RE into two separate approaches. Outstanding RE practitioners should aim to devise curricula that manage to give pupils a reference point in regards to religion in society but more importantly the conceptual tools to engage and critique the place and contribution of religion in their lives.

In 1992 one leading writer on RE noted that while some local authorities took their duties very lightly in relation to the provision of Agreed Syllabi others 'are clearly excellent' and that there is very little support for a national syllabus, because it would constitute a 'further centralisation of the curriculum' and 'take away more autonomy from local authorities' (Brown 2002: 5).

RE may not be in the National Curriculum but it is taught across the nation, it *is* a national subject. The idea that locally based syllabi allow RE teachers to engage with diversity that is particular to their local area presumes that not only is this a positive thing but that all the different religious communities are distributed around the country in a way that supports children's learning. An example of this is the teaching of Islam. Islam is Britain's fastest-growing religion. Its influence and impact on public life go far beyond the numbers in its communities. It is a religion that is rarely out of the news, both domestically and internationally, and there is a strong case that all primary children should be taught about Islam. According to the 2011 census, only 4.8% of the population of England and Wales are Muslim (ONS 2012); this means that relatively few children will be educated under a syllabus that prioritises the teaching of Islam. While it may make 'educational sense' for teachers to engage with children about Islam, the organisation of the curriculum through locally agreed syllabi could mean that their contact with this religion is minimal.

  Case Study 11.1

Year 3 in St Giles's RC primary school are exploring other faiths. Their teacher, Mr Kennedy, wants to invite some representatives of Islam to come and talk to the children about their faith and what it means to them.

The nearest mosque has a very active outreach and education team who are eager to help; however, the representatives coming to visit as well as the majority of worshippers are Sunni. Mr Kennedy is keen to have visitors who can help children to 'see' and experience what Islam means for people in their local area but also wants to present more than one Islamic tradition.

Do you think this is something that is integral to the teaching of this topic or is it a minor area that could be overlooked? Given your teaching context, what approach would you adopt for this issue? (Use another faith example if appropriate.)

Reflection Points

1. Look at a sample of Agreed Syllabi and the NSFRE. Do you think that the criticisms made in the APPGRE's report *The Truth Unmasked* are justified?
2. A key criticism made of the Agreed Syllabi in relation to primary RE is that many do not demonstrate progression. Do you think that the NSFRE is an improvement in this area?

Innovation

As we can see, the organisation of RE is not merely a technical question but one that influences the way teachers are expected to approach the teaching of religion. However, there is a range of pedagogies that embrace specific approaches to RE. The key resource for any student or teacher wishing to develop their understanding of RE pedagogy is *Pedagogies of Religious Education,* edited by Michael Grimmitt (2000). This excellent book provides case studies of the key pedagogies in the last 50 years and each case study is authored by an academic or professional who was instrumental in the development of that pedagogy.

The development of different pedagogies in RE is a relatively new phenomenon. In the post-war period the teaching of religion in schools was confessional, that is teachers and parents assumed that the purpose of religious teaching in schools was to nurture pupils in Christianity. The presumption that parents would support this is reflected in the 1944 Education Act, where the Act not only assumes that children will come from Christian families but it never mentions the word Christian in relation to religion precisely because in post-war Britain religion and Christianity were synonymous (Cox 1983). Today the key pedagogies reflect the fact that Britain is a multi-faith society and also one where Christianity is no longer a dominant force.

There is no room in this chapter to provide a summary of the main pedagogies outlined by Grimmitt but there are several good books and articles for any teacher who wishes to know more. Alongside Grimmitt (2000), Julian Stern provides a detailed summary and introduction to many of the key themes in *Teaching Religious Education* (2006). In 'Six Schools of Thought in RE', Lat Blaylock gives a funny, irreverent and accurate summary of what he identifies as the six main schools of thought in RE (2004).

Blaylock, Stern and Grimmitt all note that although the pedagogies may appear very different they share a common 'phenomenological platform'. They all promote an approach to RE that advocates teaching and learning that focus on the development of understanding different religious phenomena equally and without bias or prejudice. In this sense, it is a pedagogical platform that encourages pupils to view religions equally from a distance. It is a way of approaching subject areas, in this case religions, that attempts to 'do justice to their expressed meanings, and to reveal universal "essences" or "ideal types" to which specific examples of activity in different religious and cultural settings approximate' (Jackson 1997: 7).

Contemporary Issues for Pedagogy and RE

The pedagogies summarised by Grimmitt (2000) provide a comprehensive overview of the thinking that has underpinned RE in the post-war period, but it is worth considering whether these pedagogies are still relevant. A cursory glance at the six pedagogies shows that none is contemporary. It is also the case that all were developed during a period when it was presumed that the dominant religious experience of people would take place within religious traditions and communities and that the salient feature of religious life was one of worship, ritual or community.

One of the key challenges for RE is how to define what constitutes contemporary religious experience. Today no teacher can assume that just because pupils do not go to church they don't think of themselves as Christian, or that because they say they do not belong to a religious tradition they are not religious in some way.

In her review of the way religion is presented in the majority of classrooms, Linda Rudge (1998) noted that there is a tendency to define only those practices, traditions and beliefs that are commonly associated with traditional religious communities, like Christianity or Islam. What, she asks, is the child who does not belong to a religious community to make of this? Would they conclude that just because they are not members of one of the officially recognised six world religions they are not religious? Or they may decide that that the beliefs, questions and feelings they have about God, or about life after death, reincarnation or prayer, are not religious or even not important because they are not categorised as such in most Agreed Syllabi. She recounts a powerful story that illustrates her point. An inspector witnesses an RE lesson where the children are asked to write down a few lines about themselves. One pupil writes, 'I am Abdul; I am 11 years old; I have a mum and a dad and two brothers; I am a Muslim'; another wrote, 'I am Kawaljit Singh; I am 11 years old; I am a Sikh'; and another wrote 'I am John and I am nothing'. Pupils like John are part of what she refers to in RE as the 'silent majority', that broad swathe of children in every RE lesson whose own beliefs are rarely acknowledged (Rudge 1998).

Rudge believes that the way RE tends to describe religions as discrete communities with a series of observable factors means that children whose beliefs or customs fall outside those boundaries may feel excluded. This claim will ring true to every teacher who has heard a pupil demand to know why they have to do RE when they 'don't believe in God'. Rudge suggests that teachers need to find a way of opening up RE so that the term 'religious' is not so narrowly focused either on the 'big six' or on religions that have distinct traditions. The current definition of religion embedded within

English education presents organised religion as the norm – a view that may run counter to the experiences or world views of children and which may suggest that their own beliefs are possibly abnormal.

Creativity

Spiritual or Religious?

One approach to RE that seeks to make it more accessible to children who are not a part of a religious community is to redefine the parameters of the subject, to redefine what it means to be religious or what constitutes a religion. Clive and Jane Erricker (2000) have consistently argued that RE should engage with children's beliefs on their own terms. That is, it is not the job of the teacher to attempt to take children on a journey, intellectual or personal, that is defined by the values or beliefs of an established religion. Rather, the task of the teacher is to support the child as they embark on their own mysterious and personal journey. In this scenario, the teacher is the follower, the facilitator of a spiritual exploration initiated and shaped by the needs and desires of the child.

In this context the spiritual life of the child could literally be shaped by anything – their families, favourite pets, music, or equally Disney, Bratz or a McDonald's Happy Meal. It is not the job of the teacher to pass judgement on the child's spiritual experiences, only to support them as they ask their own questions.

Spiritual education is already a well-established cross-curricular theme in schools. Most teachers are aware that schools are meant to make spaces for children to experience an aspect of life that is contemplative, to grapple with 'big' questions and puzzles that they may encounter. Yet how is this different from RE? Many teachers and Agreed Syllabi may assume that the salient difference is that the term *religion* refers to organised religion, or those aspects of organised religion that relate to rules, authority and tradition, while the term *spirituality* refers to a more individual, or reflective, experience that can exist independently of religion. The problem with this understanding of religion and spirituality is that it sets up a distinction that Linda Rudge (1998) demonstrates in her article may hinder the way children engage with RE.

The final point to consider in relation to the changing nature of religion and pedagogy is that today one of the most pressing issues is not the way that children should be encouraged to approach religions but the way religions should be presented in the classroom. There is a growing consensus that the way religions are portrayed in the Agreed Syllabi misrepresents the way religions really are. This point has already been alluded to in the criticisms of many Agreed Syllabi and it is a good example of the way pedagogy and the organisation of RE are intimately intertwined. The phenomenological approach to religion embedded in most Agreed Syllabi is reflected in the way they define religions through a list of characteristics that will be familiar to any RE teacher: places of worship, special people, key ideas, special books or texts, and rituals and ceremonies. This standardised approach is designed to help teachers structure their teaching in a way that deals with each religion equally.

But this approach also serves to standardise religions themselves and creates artificial religious phenomena that exist nowhere outside of RE textbooks. It is this point that informs some of the most recent discussions on pedagogy and RE. Is it legitimate still to talk in the classroom of a universal Islam or Christianity, religions that have an essential, time essence? Or is it more honest and more accurate to teach about religions as they are locally located?

Case Study 11.2

Miss Walters is teaching a Year 4 class in a maintained school in the centre of a large town; her class has a mix of children from different ethnicities as well as from differing socio-economic backgrounds. RE sessions have always been creative but Miss Walters is unsure about how to teach a class on rites of passage to do with Christianity. The reason for this is that Miss Walters is from a liberal Christian background with few of the formal rites of passage that are mentioned in her locally Agreed Syllabus. However, she does know that there are children in her class with Roman Catholic and Anglican backgrounds, as well as children from other Christian denominations and other faiths.

Her lack of subject knowledge in this area, as well as the loose guidelines within the Agreed Syllabus, means that Miss Walters feels that she will at best misrepresent other denominations' traditions or, at worst, cause offence, albeit unintentionally.

What might one way forward be to address this issue?

Reflection Points

1. What criteria should be used to decide which religious traditions of communities are included in the curriculum?
2. What is the difference between religious and spiritual in terms of the curriculum? Is there a clear distinction and, if so, what are the advantages and disadvantages of maintaining this in the classroom?
3. Would redefining RE as spiritual education make it more inclusive? What would be the disadvantages of this change?

RE and Social Cohesion

For many people the salient impact of religion in society is one of divisiveness and conflict. Their familiarity with Islam may be intrinsically intertwined with images of fundamentalism, war and terrorism while their knowledge of Judaism may be a series of associations linked to the Holocaust or conflict in the Middle East. In the post-war period RE has often been associated with attempts to mitigate these negative images but recently RE has been the focus of a more specific strategy to enable children to see links between communities where possible conflict is an issue. In the wake of international and national developments, especially the 'war on terror', the government has prioritised policies and strategies in public life that draw communities together, generally called 'community cohesion'.

What Is Community Cohesion?

> By community cohesion, we mean working towards a society in which there is a common vision and sense of belonging by all communities; a society in which the diversity of people's backgrounds and circumstances is appreciated and valued; a society in which similar life opportunities are available to all; a society in which strong and positive relationships exist and continue to be developed in the workplace, in schools and the wider community. (Institute of Community Cohesion, submission to the Commission for Integration and Cohesion 2007: 1)

The government is committed to ensuring that all schools, whatever their ethnic or religious makeup, contribute to community cohesion in some way. It recognises that all schools will approach their duty towards community cohesion differently depending on the nature of their environment, the makeup of their pupils and their existing relationship with the community. A measure of how important the government perceives community cohesion to be is that it is an area that is inspected by Ofsted.

Guidelines published by Ofsted note that all schools, to successfully fulfil their duty to promote community cohesion, should focus on three strands:

- faith
- ethnicity and culture
- socio-economic factors.

Documents provided by Ofsted and the then DCSF identify a number of areas where they would expect to see evidence of community cohesion and where RE could contribute a great deal. There is a natural assumption that because RE is a subject where a variety of cultures, identities and religious traditions are considered, it is an ideal subject in which to engage with the priorities associated with the community cohesion agenda. The role of RE in social cohesion is disputed by some writers. Andrew Wright argues that in the mission to present all religions as equally true and valid, religions are misrepresented relativistic expressions of culture whose 'primary function is to point beyond itself to our common humanity' (Wright 2003: 287). Robert Jackson has argued against this view. He acknowledges that RE that sets out only to promote toler-ance or social cohesion is inadequate but that an RE that seeks to develop the necessary skills for children to gain a better understanding of the dynamics and gram-mar of religions will also develop the skills of self-reflection and self-awareness in pupils (Jackson 2004).

However, some of the most recent discussions within RE and by Ofsted suggest that RE as it exists at the moment may not be an effective vehicle for social cohesion. One reason for this is that the Agreed Syllabi are still statutorily obliged to privilege Christianity. The current guidelines for SACREs are that the Agreed Syllabi should allow children to study Christianity at each key stage whereas other religions must be studied in the course of their primary education. A circular published by the govern-ment in 1994 stated that the Agreed Syllabi shall 'reflect the fact that the religious traditions in Great Britain are in the main Christian while taking into account the teaching and practices of the other principal religions represented in Great Britain' (DfE 1994: 45). McCreery et al. (2008) believe that this privileging is more cultural than religious but the fact that it still exists sends a clear message that in the eyes of English education not all religions are equal.

A second reason is expressed repeatedly in the Ofsted report *Making Sense of Religion* (2007). Using inspection evidence, the report argues that many Agreed Syllabi simplify religion to such an extent that real engagement is unlikely. This critique is echoed by a growing debate within RE about the ways religions are represented to children as idealised pristine entities. Robert Jackson (2004) has consistently argued that teachers need to present religious communities as they are and that children can be encouraged to appreciate the diversity and difference embedded in all religious communities. Similarly, Barnes (2006) has argued that the desire of many teachers to always present religions in a favourable light has resulted in a curriculum that misrep-resents religions as they really are so that pupil engagement is with ideas and practices that do not exist in the 'real world'.

If RE is to play a constructive role in a community cohesion agenda then it is clear that it must become less shy of dealing with the difficult questions in relation to reli-gions. Even young children do not enter the classroom without preconceptions or ideas about religion gleaned from the media, their parents or other sources. If we ignore the politicised environment in which many children gather their information and insist on teaching asocial, culturally neutral and apolitical versions of religion to children then not only will children fail to engage but the aims of the social cohesion agenda will be meaningless.

Reflection Points

1. To what extent is RE as it currently exists in primary schools able to support the aims of the community cohesion agenda?
2. Is the statutory requirement to privilege Christianity compatible with a social cohesion agenda in Britain?
3. Do schools based on a religious foundation contribute to social cohesion or encourage conflict and ethnic or religious segregation?

Assessment

> Not all aspects of religious education can be assessed. (Non-Statutory Framework for RE, QCA 2004: 35)

Teachers attempting to work out an approach to assessment must negotiate several tensions. RE teachers are encouraged to consider the same issues in assessment that apply to other subjects (Keast 2002) but at the same time they are also expected to integrate the fact that RE is organised differently and informed by different approaches to teaching and learning. Many of the factors that set RE apart from other curriculum subjects also apply to assessment. There are no national requirements for RE, there are no attainment targets nor a nationally agreed curriculum. Local Agreed Syllabi are advised by the Model Syllabus to use two attainment targets (AT1 and AT2), but as the Agreed Syllabi are not statutory, they can be interpreted differently (McCreery et al. 2008). This has now been developed, by the suggestion in the REC's NSFRE, in a direction away from an explicit use of the two attainment targets and towards a slightly more integrated approach based on three strands that focus on pupils developing subject knowledge alongside analytical, evaluative and articulation skills. The three strands are (a) 'Know and Understand', (b) 'Express and Communicate' and (c) 'Gain and Deploy Skills' (REC 2013: 27–30).

Guidance for assessing RE usually reminds teachers that assessment is an essential part of the process for teaching and learning that develops pupil learning and supports teachers' teaching. Although there are subjective elements to RE and assessment procedures generally, teachers do need to find common structures and standards so they can teach and support pupil development effectively. Many also believe that there are aspects of RE that are difficult, if not impossible, to assess. The NSFRE states that there are comments, discussions and experiences in RE that are integral to an RE lesson but not assessable.

The complexity of assessment in RE is arguably more challenging for primary teachers. At Key Stages 3 and 4, RE teachers may be using assessment geared towards GCSE or contextualising their teaching and assessment so that it leads towards GCSE standards.

The most recent Ofsted report, *Religious Education: Realising the Potential* (2013), identifies assessment as one of the weakest aspects of RE in primary schools and that it had declined since the last report, *Transforming Religious Education*, in 2010. The report noted that teachers were facing difficulties in using levels of attainment as set out in the Agreed Syllabi and that work rarely built on earlier learning (Ofsted 2010: 25).

While each SACRE has its own issues to deal with in terms of provision and declining attainment in their primary schools, some steps to address this seem to be under way. The REC has moved away from the AT1/2 approach to RE and towards a more nuanced blend of RE subject knowledge and skills, and the two biggest providers of faith school education, the Church of England and the Roman Catholic Church, have started to address the area of planning for assessment.

The Church of England now encourages academy schools under its leadership to create their own curriculum that reflects the spirit and culture of the Anglican community. Alongside this, and somewhat confusingly, they encourage Church of England schools that do not have academy status to adopt the Agreed Syllabus of their local area (Church of England 2014).

The Roman Catholic Department for Education and Formation has held on to the AT1/2 model but developed it further, recognising the impossibility of 'assessing' children's spirituality within AT2. Out of this it has introduced a new strand, *Reflection and Contemplation*, which allows teachers to assess pupils using the AT1/2 approach but also provides pupils and teachers with the opportunity to approach RE in an individual and context-specific way, appropriate to the child, class and school (Catholic Bishops' Conference of England and Wales 2012).

In a sense, the current poor record of assessment in RE and the fact that the quality of assessment has declined is not surprising. Considering the confusion many teachers experience in relation to the Agreed Syllabi and the differences between AT1 and AT2, it is no wonder that many primary teachers do not perform well in this area.

More positively, *Transforming Religious Education* identifies qualities that are associated with good practice in assessment in RE. These include:

- where planning clearly identifies the criteria used in assessing progress
- where planning identifies specific points when assessment would take place
- where pupils were helped to understand how they were being assessed and to apply the criteria in evaluating their own or each other's work.

In relation to the best practice for coordinators in RE, it says assessment was most useful:

- where assessment gave pupils an idea of what progress means in RE
- where assessment helped them to evaluate whether the teaching and the curriculum were effective
- where assessment helped to inform the next stage of planning.

The striking thing about these observations is that they should be common to the assessment of all subjects. Ofsted is making no recommendations about assessment in RE that are not made of other subjects. The poor practices associated with assessment in RE are more likely to be linked with the poor status of RE in many schools, the lack of specialist training and the ambiguities embedded in the current organisation of RE at local and national levels. Teachers committed to providing excellent lessons in RE will not find the solution to the many challenges facing the subject in assessment (Watson and Thompson 2007), but attempting to provide the same basic quality of assessment that they provide for all other subjects is a good first step.

Conclusion

The aim of this chapter has been to illustrate the many ways in which RE is in a state of transition and how these changes have implications for the way RE is taught and assessed. The local and national organisation of RE is changing, as is the understanding of what actually constitutes the content of the subject, and the nature of religion itself. Some of the pedagogical assumptions that have informed RE for the last 50 years, including the relationship of RE to the curriculum and the way pupils are expected to relate to religion, are no longer as certain as they once were. More importantly, the political and social environment in which we teach RE has become more sensitive to the role of religion in society.

Reflection Points

1. What are the advantages and disadvantages of RE as a subject were it to be integrated into the national curriculum?
2. In modern Britain is it still appropriate or justifiable to privilege the teaching of Christianity in RE?
3. What role, if any, does primary RE have in developing tolerance and social cohesion?

Further Reading

Chater, M. and Erricker, C. (2013) *Does Religious Education Have a Future? Pedagogical and Policy Prospects*. Abingdon: Routledge.
Jackson, R., Wiesse, S.M.W. and Williame, J.P. (eds) (2007) *Religion and Education in Europe*. Munster u a: Waxmann.

Kay, W. (2005) 'A Non-Statutory Framework for Religious Education: issues and opportunities', *British Journal of Religious Education*, 27 (1): 41–52.

McCreery, E., Palmer, S. and Voiels, V. (2008) *Teaching Religious Education: Primary and Early Years*. Exeter: Learning Matters.

Panjawani, F. (2004) 'Agreed Syllabi and un-agreed values: Religious Education and missed opportunities for fostering social cohesion', *British Journal of Educational Studies*, 53 (3): 375–93.

Stern, J. (2006) *Teaching Religious Education*. London: Continuum.

References

APPGRE (All Party Parliamentary Group for Religious Education) (2013) *RE: The Truth Unmasked. The Supply of and Support for Religious Education Teachers*. London. APPGRE.

Barnes, P. (2006) 'The misrepresentation of religion in modern British (Religious) Education', *British Journal of Educational Studies*, 54 (4): 395–411.

Blaylock, L. (2004) 'Six schools of thought in RE', *Resource*, 27 (1): 13–116.

Brown, A. (2002) 'The nature of RE within the school curriculum', in A. Brown and L. Broadbent (eds) *Issues in RE*. London: Routledge. pp. 3–15.

Catholic Bishops' Conference of England and Wales (2012) *Religious Education Curriculum Directory for Catholic Schools and Colleges in England and Wales*. London: Department of Catholic Education and Formation.

Chater, M. and Erricker, C. (2013) *Does Religious Education Have a Future? Pedagogical and Policy Prospects*. Abingdon: Routledge.

Church of England (2014) Making a Difference? London: Church of England Archbishops' Council.

Conroy, J., Lundie, D., Davies, R., Baumfield, V., Barnes, P., Gallagher, T., et al. (2013) *Does Religious Education Work?* London: Bloomsbury.

Cox, E. (1983) *Problems and Possibilities for Religious Education*. London: Hodder & Stoughton.

DfE (Department for Education) (1994) *Circular 1/94 Religious Education and Collective Worship*. London: DfE.

Erricker, C. and Erricker, J. (2000) *Reconstructing Religious, Spiritual and Moral Education*. London: RoutledgeFalmer.

Feldorf, M.C. (2004) 'The new National Framework for Religious Education in England and Wales: a critique', *Journal of Belief and Values*, 25: 241–8.

Grimmitt, M. (ed.) (2000) *Pedagogies of Religious Education: Case Studies in the Development of Good Pedagogic Practice*. Great Wakering, Essex: McCrimmon.

Hinnells, J.R. (2005) 'Why study religion?', in J. Hinnells (ed.), *The Routledge Companion to the Study of Religion*. London: Routledge.

Institute of Community Cohesion (2007) *Community Cohesion: Useful Links for Schools*. Coventry: Institute of Community Cohesion.

Jackson, R. (1997) *Religious Education: An Interpretative Approach*. London: Hodder & Stoughton.

Jackson, R. (2004) *Rethinking Religious Education and Plurality: Issues in Diversity and Pedagogy*. London: RoutledgeFalmer.

Keast, J. (2002) 'Assessing achievement in RE from Early Years to 'A' Level', in L. Broadbent and A. Brown (eds), *Issues in Religious Education*. London: RoutledgeFalmer.

McCreery, E., Palmer, S. and Voiels, V. (2008) *Teaching Religious Education: Primary and Early Years*. Exeter: Learning Matters.

NCFRE (2013) *A Review of Religious Education in England*. London: Religious Education Council. Available at: www.areiac.org.uk/public/downloads/NCFRE.pdf (accessed 4 February 2015).

Ofsted (Office for Standards in Education) (2007) *Making Sense of Religion*. London: Ofsted.

Ofsted (Office for Standards in Education) (2010) *Transforming Religious Education*. London: Ofsted.

Ofsted (Office for Standards in Education) (2013) *Religious Education: Realising the Potential*. London: Ofsted.

ONS (Office for National Statistics) (2012) 2011 Census. Religion in England and Wales 2011. Available at www.ons.gov.uk/ons/dcp171776_290510.pdf (accessed 21 September 2014).

QCA (Qualifications and Curriculum Authority) (2004) *The Non-Statutory Framework for Religious Education*. London: DfES.

REC (Religious Education Council for England and Wales) (2013) *A Curriculum Framework for Religious Education in England*. London: REC.

Rudge, L. (1998) '"I am nothing: does it matter?": A critique of current Religious Education policy and practice on behalf of the silent majority', *British Journal of Religious* Education, 20: 155–65.

Stern, J. (2006) *Teaching Religious Education*. London: Continuum.

Watson, B. and Thompson, P. (2007) *The Effective Teaching of Religious Education*. London: Pearson.

Wright, A. (2003) 'The contours of critical religious education: knowledge, wisdom, truth', *British Journal of Religious Education*, 25 (4): 279–91.

CHAPTER 12

AN INTRODUCTION TO FOREIGN LANGUAGES

Patricia Driscoll

Chapter Aims

This chapter will:

- introduce key debates about early foreign language learning and issues influencing provision in schools

- examine evidence about current practice in light of the requirements of the new statutory national curriculum

- outline some of the theoretical positions that underpin foreign language pedagogy

Introduction

The teaching of foreign languages at Key Stage 2 has finally achieved statutory status. The purpose of study and the aims are combined for Key Stages 2 and 3 in the new national curriculum, comprising the four skills of listening, speaking, reading and writing to enable pupils to 'express their ideas and thoughts in another language and to understand and respond to its speakers, both in speech and in writing' (DfE 2013: 212). Combining the aims and purposes of foreign languages across two key stages reinforces the need for teachers to strengthen links between primary and secondary schools in order to enable substantial progression across statutory provision from age 7 to 14. In Key Stage 2, the focus is on practical communication but no specific language is prescribed. Primary schools can choose to teach any modern foreign language (MFL) or an ancient language such as Latin or Greek where study will focus on reading comprehension and civilisation rather than practical communication. The aim of this chapter is to introduce readers to some of the most relevant issues surrounding foreign languages in primary schools, which may now share common aims and purposes with MFL at Key Stage 3, but which to date have been cultivated independently.

Early language learning is part of a recent world-wide phenomenon to increase the potential of learning languages while at school. Johnstone (2009: 33) suggests that it is 'the world's biggest policy development in education', which has undergone three waves of implementation. In 1964, primary foreign languages first attracted public attention in England with the launch of a 10-year feasibility study – French from the age of 8. The final evaluation (Burstall et al. 1974) reported some benefits from the additional years of learning, and children had developed positive attitudes and superior listening skills, but overall the early start had not yielded substantial gains in attainment in secondary school, so the project was abandoned. Critics of the evaluation (Bennett 1975; Buckby 1976; Gamble and Smalley 1975; Hoy 1977) pointed to flaws in the research design and raised questions about the appropriateness of the teaching methods for young learners, the training and the dubious practice of teaching all children together at the age of 11 irrespective of their primary learning, but, despite these criticisms, policy support and public funding were withdrawn and early foreign language practice disappeared rapidly. Whether early foreign language learning is worth it in the long run in terms of increased proficiency at secondary school and beyond has been the subject of much debate ever since. Other primary subjects, such as science, art, music and history, are not justified through such an instrumental lens; they are valued as part of a good education overall and generally considered of benefit for young children's development.

Interest rekindled in English schools in the late 1990s. Teachers experimented with different approaches, although the great majority focused on developing listening and speaking skills with an emphasis on teaching vocabulary and phrases in different topic areas. Some programmes focused on teaching one foreign language whereas others offered a taster of two, three or more languages. A few schools chose to concentrate on broader educational aims, such as the development of language awareness. Hawkins (1987), a key figure in developing the language awareness approach, argues that it provides an excellent foundation for learning any language, including the mother tongue or a foreign language at a later stage, as it introduces children to etymology, provides a forum for analysing the structure of language and offers an 'education of the ear'.

Schools rarely focused centrally on developing cultural awareness and recent evidence suggests that culture associated with foreign language learning remains on the fringes of most language lessons (Driscoll et al. 2013). Other approaches, although not widespread in the UK, were Content and Language Integrated Learning (CLIL), where the foreign language was used as the medium of instruction for teaching another curriculum subject, such as teaching aspects of geography in French. This rich variety of approaches can still be found in certain schools but in general there is a greater homogeneity of foreign language practice in England (Cable et al. 2010), though immersion programmes and bilingual schools are attracting attention with a handful established in England in recent years.

In 2000, the Nuffield Foundation stimulated real political interest and a subsequent policy drive when it recommended that beginning languages in state schools from the age of 7 would improve the language capability of the workforce (Nuffield Foundation 2000). Provision grew rapidly: in 2001, approximately 44% of schools offered languages at Key Stage 2 (Driscoll et al. 2004), but within 10 years 92% of schools were teaching foreign languages, with 69% teaching all year groups (Wade and Marshall 2009). In 2002, the government published the National Languages Strategy for England, *Languages for All: Languages for Life* (DfES 2002), which set out a strategy for lifelong language learning, starting with an early start. The strategy announced an entitlement for all learners by 2010: 'Every child should have the opportunity throughout Key Stage 2 to study a foreign language and develop their interest in the culture of other nations' (DfES 2002: 15).

A range of resources followed to help teachers deliver the entitlement, such as the *Schemes of Work for Key Stage 2* (QCDA 2000, 2007, 2009) and the Key Stage 2 Framework (DfES 2005a). The professional development of teachers became a priority as there were few primary teachers who had the confidence to teach the subject (Driscoll et al. 2004). The Training and Development Agency (TDA) funded primary language programmes in initial teacher education (ITE) with a placement abroad, which ran for 10 years from 2001 (Driscoll and Rowe 2012; Driscoll et al. 2014), and professional development for teachers. Ofsted (2010) noted that government-funded training and resources were key factors in the development of primary provision but with over 17,000 primary schools in England, staffing languages remains the major challenge for schools both in the UK and across the world (Enever 2011).

Over the last 10 years, there have been a number of research studies funded by policy makers (Cable et al. 2010; Driscoll et al. 2004; Lines et al. 2007; Muijs et al. 2005; Wade and Marshall 2009). Cable et al. (2010) investigated practice over three years through observations and interviews with headteachers, teachers and children in 40 case study schools and assessed children's attainment in eight schools. At the same time, the NFER (Wade and Marshall 2009) also conducted a three-year longitudinal study to investigate the nature and extent of language learning at Key Stage 2 through questionnaires to schools and local authorities.

The evidence suggests that, in general, schools in England are teaching one language, predominantly French, although some do introduce a second language for a short time. Classical languages are most frequently taught in independent schools. Findings consistently show that teachers report a keen interest in including language and cultural awareness within language lessons, but the main focus is to develop children's language competence and their confidence to handle the basics in a range of topic areas. Teachers and headteachers across the country also emphasise the importance of developing children's positive attitudes and sustaining their high levels of motivation through enjoyable, interactive and kinaesthetic learning.

Justifying a Place for Languages

Two major justifications are consistently revisited for early language learning: increased learning time and the predisposition of young children to learn languages based on the assumption of a critical age. Evidence regarding the increase in overall learning time lies with the assumption that more time dedicated to learning yields greater achievement. With competing subject demands on the secondary curriculum, it is difficult for curriculum planners to allocate more hours to MFL in secondary schools, even if it were a priority, therefore by extending provision downwards into primary schools further learning time can be added. The extended learning time argument, although reasonable, assumes that all learners are equal. Both Singleton (1989) and Johnstone (1994) argue that older learners are more efficient learners as they have better learning skills and greater experience in how to learn, which makes them faster. Learning time, they suggest, is therefore not equal.

In contrast to the learner efficacy argument, there is a growing body of evidence which indicates that young learners have positive attitudes towards learning foreign languages and that they are keen and motivated to learn (Burstall et al. 1974; Cable et al. 2010; Driscoll et al. 2004; Edelenbos et al. 2006; Muijs et al. 2005; Wade and Marshall 2009), so that learning time is more useful as learners are engaged and willing to learn. Whether motivation tips the balance of skill development and age-specific learner efficacy will no doubt continue to be the focus of future investigations. Krashen (1982) suggests that learner anxiety plays a role in effective language learning. He argues that learners have an *affective filter* which is lowered if they feel comfortable and are enjoying the experience, and raised, inhibiting learning, if they are anxious. If this is the case, then primary children's positive attitudes have a direct influence on the acquisition of knowledge and skills.

The critical age proposition draws from studies in first-language development which suggest that children's brains are more adaptable to acquiring language (Lenneberg 1967; Penfield and Roberts 1959). Whether this research can be transferred to second or foreign language learning is a matter of some debate (Birdsong 2005). Findings are inconclusive and contradictory; some studies provide evidence in support of critical age theory and other findings challenge the theory (Marinova-Todd et al. 2000). The evidence in support of a critical age for foreign language learning suggests that children are more able to acquire native-like pronunciation and are more efficient in oral and aural development (Blondin et al. 1998; Edelenbos et al. 2006; Singleton 1989; Vilke 1988), and that after puberty learning will be potentially less successful (Nikolov and Djigunovic 2006).

In terms of overall educational rather than linguistic advantages, Hawkins (1996) argues that 'language learning is both a valuable experience and a vital part of children's general education' (p. 169). Amongst the educational benefits, he includes improved listening skills, developing a greater awareness of language per se, enhanced self-confidence and general social skills as well as a heightening sense of empathy towards foreign people and cultures. He stresses that children's capabilities and enthusiasm for languages have been seriously underestimated, and that children do not see learning a new language as 'hard' – rather, they absorb it and use it creatively. Both Singleton (1989) and Johnstone (1994) point out that each age brings its own advantages and disadvantages but that if the benefits of early learning are to be realised languages need to be taught in an appropriate way in a supportive learning environment. Factors such as the teacher's subject knowledge, the position or role of the teacher in the school and whether they are a member of the school staff or an outsider (Driscoll 2000) will influence outcome and learner engagement. Learner variables are also significant and the importance of the learning context should not be underestimated when predicting levels of attainment (Donato et al. 2000).

Theories and Teaching Methods

Teaching methods have changed radically over the last 50 years as have the theoretical principles that underpin them. Traditionally taught in independent schools and universities in preparation for the world tour or as part of a 'good education', the subject was included in grammar schools after the Second World War, where students were taught reading, writing and analysis of texts through the *Grammar Translation Method*.

In the 1960s and 1970s the technological advances of tape recorders and film reels transformed teaching approaches and the audio-lingual method was designed. The new method still focused on form, but was based on behaviourist theory (Skinner 1957), which focuses on learner behaviour, where learners were drilled in 'typical' phrases, which they imitated and repeated until responses were automatic. The behaviourist theory was challenged by Chomsky (1965), who argues that learners recognise new sentences, not because of drilling and matching language against learnt items but because they have an innate cognitive ability to develop grammatical structures. He claims that all languages have common features and that humans inherit a universal set of principles and parameters that control the shape of language.

He calls this innate language mechanism, Universal Grammar. With the help, he argues, of a Language Acquisition Device (LAD), individuals are able to construct language consistent with Universal Grammar.

Chomsky's theory influenced a number of studies that focus on the cognitive processes of second or foreign language learning. Amongst the most influential are Krashen's theories (1982, 1985). He argues that all learners can access their LAD and that acquisition is at the heart of language development, with conscious learning acting as a *monitor* to modify or change what learners say. Grammar, according to Krashen, does not need to be taught as it develops following a substantial level of input of language. He argues that the greater the level of *comprehensible input* available to the learner, the more language will be acquired. In other words, teachers should provide learners with language that is a little beyond their current level of competence.

Long (1981, 1985) challenged the idea that comprehensible input is sufficient. He suggests an *Interaction Hypothesis* where more attention should be given to interaction in meaningful contexts as language development is a two-way process, so input alone is not enough. Swain (1985, 1995) further developed the discourse with her work on *Output Hypothesis*; she argues that learner production drives forward second-language learning of grammar, sentence structure and language rules. See Mitchell and Myles (1998) for a comprehensive introduction to second-language learning theories.

Further challenge to the behaviourist theory and the subconscious and conscious processes in cognitive theory are theories that highlight the influence of contexts and the socio-cultural processes of learning (Lantolf 1994). Socio-cultural theory puts forward the view that language learning is a public activity which lies in scaffolded and guided social interaction within a community. Drawing on Vygotsky's concept of the *Zone of Proximal Development* (ZPD), the socio-cultural theory posits that engaging and participating in activities with a more skilled individual, in this case a language teacher, the learner is inducted into a 'shared understanding of how to do things through collaborative talk until eventually they take over (or appropriate) new knowledge and skills into their own individual consciousness' (Mitchell and Myles 1998: 145). *Task Based Instruction* (Ellis 2003; Skehan 1989) draws upon socio-cultural theory and focuses on meaning-based activities or tasks related to natural or real situations, such as storytelling. Learners are not drilled in vocabulary and functions; rather they are given a framework for tasks to complete. For example, teachers may initiate a healthy eating discussion and a range of scenarios related to food and then set tasks for learners to complete through exploring authentic resources such as reading on the internet, writing emails, and so on.

From the 1970s the *Communicative Competence Approach* dominated language teaching in England and in many countries across the world. Rather than a defined method, the pedagogy focuses on the development of communicative strategies and activities to enable learners to speak appropriately in different authentic contexts. Johnstone (2014) argues that the emphasis on personalisation where learners were encouraged to talk about themselves sought to develop a more learner-centred approach; however, the teacher-led approach to pedagogy hindered learner agency. The aim of maximising target language input (Krashen 1982) and facilitating learner practice and production within meaningful contexts resulted in a '3P' approach to lesson structure. Hood (2014: 233) suggests that the 3Ps '(presentation, often characterised by the use of flash cards; practice, characterised by the use of 'paired drills'; and production, characterised ... by learners reading self-created dialogues from a script rather than speaking spontaneously with understanding)' resulted in restricted practice. However, the shift from written comprehension and explicit grammar teaching to communicative skills was more appropriate for teaching across the ability range in secondary and comprehensive schools..

Johnstone (2014) questions whether history is repeating itself as policy moves towards a more traditional analytical approach to language teaching, which proved successful for academically able learners in grammar schools, with its focus on facts, literacy and grammatical understanding. It is difficult to predict the impact of the new curriculum and the attainment targets on primary learners. On the one hand, reinforcing grammar and the emphasis on literacy could result in disenfranchising a corpus of learners who are currently highly motivated and have positive attitudes towards learning the subject (Cable et al. 2010). On the other hand, primary teachers spend a major part of their professional lives teaching literacy skills creatively to mixed-ability classes. Therefore, rather than repeating history, provision may improve, as learners have greater access to the creative cross-curricular potential of the written word and the wealth of opportunity offered by storybooks and the internet. The two case studies later in this chapter offer some insight into how two very experienced specialist teachers who are both linguists are approaching the teaching of grammar and literacy skills in foreign language lessons.

Staffing Languages

Wade and Marshall (2009) found that specialist teachers were involved in teaching in less than 20% of schools. Linguists can be internal members of the school staff and work as class teachers or subject leaders (who teach their own class and/or teach languages in other classes), as in Case Study 12.2, or they can be external to the school, employed to teach foreign languages peripatetically, as in Case Study 12.1. At the time of study, 2007–2009, approximately 11% of the specialists were external to the school, but overall Wade and Marshall reported a decline in the number of peripatetic teachers with an increase in the number of trained primary class teachers teaching languages.

In general terms, four main categories of teachers teach foreign languages at Key Stage 2 (Driscoll 2000; Driscoll et al. 2004; Muijs et al. 2005; Wade and Marshall 2009):

- generalist class teachers
- trained generalist class teachers (who have undergone subject knowledge or teaching methods CPD)
- primary specialist teachers (trained primary linguists)
- visiting specialist teachers (either from secondary schools, the local authority or commercial organisations, which can include non-qualified teachers, teaching assistants, foreign language assistants and other native speakers from the community).

This range of practitioners brings different types of professional knowledge and understanding to their role. In subjects such as foreign languages, there is a fundamental distinction between *competence* (the knowledge of language including grammatical understanding, gender accord and depth of relevant vocabulary and functions) and *performance* (the actual use of the language which requires reasonable pronunciation and a degree of fluency within the context of what is being said). Specialist teachers, whether external to the school or not, have a deep level of competence and the ability to perform – communicating in the target language consistently and spontaneously. They have a greater capacity to use strategies to help children develop a broader understanding of the language (Driscoll 2000), however if they are external to the school they may not know the learners well or understand what is taught in other curriculum areas, so they are unable to make connections unless they spend time sharing planning with class teachers and subject leaders.

Primary teachers working in primary schools, whether specialists or not, are part of the child's world and culture as they spend every day together. Generalist-trained primary teachers who have engaged in professional development for languages may have limited language levels, but through language pedagogy courses have gained insight into how to use commercial resources to support their limited levels of language. Recent innovations in teaching materials and resources, such as interactive whiteboards and the use of the internet in the classroom, enable teachers to provide access to native voices in the classroom, irrespective of their own language level. However, teachers who have limited linguistic skills may over-rely on the limited commercial resources available in schools and use a limited range of strategies for teaching foreign languages recommended by short training courses and commercial products. Evidence suggests that primary teachers who are committed to teaching foreign languages, supported by their senior management, draw upon their professional expertise, general teaching strategies and understanding of learners in their class to integrate foreign languages into their portfolio of subjects (Driscoll 2000). As Bruner (1986) argues, learning is a communal activity within a shared culture:

> It is not just that the child must make the knowledge his own but that he must make it his own in a community of those who share his sense of culture. It is this that leads me to emphasise … the importance of negotiation and sharing. (Bruner 1986: 127)

State of the Art in Pedagogy

The new curriculum (DfE 2013) specifies the subject content and the essential skills required to be taught. Provision should enable pupils to convey facts and communicate their ideas and feelings in spoken and written language. An increased focus on grammatical structures to teach reading and writing has implications for professional development as many generalist primary teachers currently lack the confidence to teach these skills (Wade and Marshall 2009).

A longitudinal study conducted by Cable et al. (2010) between 2007 and 2010, offers an in-depth analysis of foreign language provision in 40 case study schools in England. The findings indicate that lessons are mainly topic-based, with a maximum of 19 topics observed over the three years of the study including: greetings, days of the week, colours, animals, food, clothing, weather and time. Where schools offered more than one language, the same topics were generally recycled in the different languages. Many schools offered a combination of dedicated language lessons and additional opportunities for learning or communicating, for example, in the daily routines. Commonly between 30 and 40 minutes were dedicated to the language lesson. The great majority of lessons focused substantively on speaking and listening, although an increase in reading was noted over the three years of the project. Writing remained an underdeveloped skill. Ofsted also found that in most primary schools visited, writing was the least developed skill, although in around one in 10 schools 'writing was impressive because of the complex sentences pupils could form in Years 5 and 6' (Ofsted 2010: 10).

The Four Skills

Listening

The national curriculum (DfE 2013) states that pupils in Key Stage 2 should be taught to listen attentively to spoken language and show understanding by joining in and responding. Hurrell (1999: 70) suggests that listening in a language lesson 'requires a readiness and active co-operation on the part of the listener'. Cable et al.'s findings (2010) indicate that teachers tend to offer opportunities for children to actively listen for sound patterns, pronunciation, rhyme, intonation and rhythm, and to identify key words and phrases in more complex listening activities such as storybooks and poems. Vanderplank (2014) also notes that recently, for older learners, there has been a greater emphasis on teaching basic phonological skills and raising awareness of metacognitive strategies, such as predicting and evaluating for when providing listening activities.

Children in mainland Europe and in many other countries across the world have opportunities in their daily lives to hear English as a global language (Graddol 2006) in pop songs or on the television, and films are frequently subtitled rather than dubbed. Children, therefore, become familiar with the sounds and rhythm of English and accustomed to hearing extended conversations and presentations in the language they are learning at school. Children do not have such chances in England to 'educate their ears' (Hawkins 1984, 1987, 1996) and are generally reliant on teachers to provide them with high-quality listening resources including multi-media materials.

Speaking

The curriculum states that children should 'communicate ideas, facts and feelings in speech', 'engage in conversations ... speak in sentences using familiar vocabulary, phrases and basic language structures, describe people, places, things [and] develop accurate pronunciation and intonation' (DfE 2013). The emphasis is on progression of learning, so that after four years of study, in Year 6 children should be able to engage in short dialogues, descriptive presentations and role plays. This level of proficiency is currently achieved in some schools but practice is not widespread. The longitudinal study (Cable et al. 2010) assessed children's learning in each year group in eight of the 40 case study schools. The findings show that all pupils in Year 6 could produce more than 50 words, with the majority of children in Years 3–5 producing between 20 and 50 words, although some younger groups of children could also produce more than 50 words. Overall, learners produced a limited range of adjectives apart from colours and very few verbs (Cable et al. 2010).

The majority of language lessons were teacher-led with the repetition of words, phrases and chunks of language at the beginning of lessons, followed by fast-paced, interactive and kinaesthetic activities. A diet of 'fun', game-like team activities can become monotonous if not balanced with individual or quieter work and learners also need to be offered ways to respond that can demonstrate their understanding without speaking; as Hurrell (1999: 71) suggests, learners have the 'right to silence'.

Creating appropriate cognitive challenge is crucial to sustain children's interest and motivation. Storytelling activities can enhance children's oral proficiency and give children the opportunity of hearing longer texts slightly above their own language competence (Donato et al. 2000). Edelenbos et al. (2006) also highlight the value of stories, as they appeal to children's imagination and help children acquire a narrative discourse structure. Practice investigated in one of the case study schools in the longitudinal study is a case in point. The school used 'The Three Little Pigs' as the framework for a whole-school production and role plays in each year group. Year 6 worked on their characters, adapted the script and wrote the dialogue for each part using drawing and speech bubbles. The following extract from a researcher's field notes describes the work for Years 3 and 4 (Cable et al. 2010: 136):

> All children in Key Stage 2 worked on the story of '*Les Trois Petits Cochons*' ... Years 3 and 4 learnt through songs and games ... repeating individual phrases so they could join in with the Year 6 production, e.g. '*Non, non, non, crient les petits cochons: Attention, au grand loup mechant!*'

(Lesson observation 2007/08)

Reading

The introduction of the written word allows for more creative and diverse lessons as teachers can introduce rhymes, poems and storybooks as well as non-fiction texts that help to reinforce learning of the other three skills. Many children are also motivated by books, instructions and leaflets. The written word allows children to access what they are learning outside of the language lessons, should they be interested in taking their work home. Reading can also enhance language learning overall, as seeing the shape of words can help children to remember them as they make connections between the spoken and written word (Scarbeck 1998).

The national curriculum states that pupils should be taught to read carefully words, phrases and simple writing, use a dictionary and develop their ability to decode new words in familiar written material. These objectives appear straight-forward; however, as Woore (2014: 82) reminds us, reading is much more than a 'simple flow of information from text to reader'; he also highlights the importance of responding to learners individually as they engage in the complexity of reading in a foreign language. Hurrell (1999: 81) recommends drawing from teaching basic literacy skills in English, for example designing phonic-cloud mobiles used in many classrooms for helping children understand the links between sounds and spelling when decoding, such as 'Eu' with a list of words that incorporate the sound – *il pleut*, *deux*. Children may begin by linking simple phonemes and spellings and reading familiar words and phrases aloud that have been encountered orally. For more complex reading tasks beyond learners' competence level, Macaro and Erler (2008) recommend encouraging readers to deploy a combination of 'top-down' strategies, where they infer or predict from the context, and 'bottom-up' or decoding strategies.

Writing

As discussed above, writing is the least developed skill in primary language practice. Children frequently begin by writing words they have practised orally and then exper-iment with familiar longer phrases, and in some schools children progress to writing simple sentences from memory. The stated emphasis in the national curriculum (DfE 2013) on reading and writing includes descriptions, which calls for adjectives and adverbs as well as nouns and verbs. Hurrell (1999: 85) recommends that children be given dynamic writing tasks outside of their repertoire of language with the creation of word banks. She gives the example of a word bank, with cards categorised under five different headings: prepositions (for example, *devant*); objects and places (*la maison*); verbal phrases (*il y a*); nouns (*un parc*); and adjectives (*grand*, *grande*). Children learn to build up sentences by placing the cards in the correct order and with the support of a model they have more ownership and freedom over the text produced.

The curriculum also states that pupils should be taught to 'write phrases from memory and adapt these to create new sentences' (DfE 2013). Macaro (2007) suggests offering learners the challenge of 'free writing' their own texts. The level of inaccuracies in free writing may cause concern, but supported free writing allows children to test out for themselves their understanding of phoneme–grapheme correspondence and spellings as well as extend their vocabulary as they search for words they want to use. Creating opportunities for children to write letters or emails to their penpals, scripts for dramatic performances and their own stories can also offer a sense of purpose to the writing activities in contrast to doing gap-fill exercises or labelling images of familiar nouns.

Case Studies

The case studies below present examples of two lessons taught by specialist teachers which focus on grammatical structure, reading and writing skills rather than listening and speaking. The case studies are constructed from one lesson observation in each school and an interview with the specialist teacher. At the time of writing, in Case Study 12.1, the specialist worked as a part-time peripatetic teacher, teaching French across a number of schools. In Case Study 12.2, the specialist worked as a class teacher, teaching across the curriculum, and as a subject leader, supporting the development of languages across the school. She also worked as an Advanced Skills Teacher, supporting neighbouring schools to develop their foreign language curriculum.

 Case Study 12.1

Creativity

The case study offers an example of a creative approach to crafting complex sentences through the use of conjunctions. This lesson is part of a sequence of work that integrates French into the school's curriculum and, more specifically, into the topic of rainforests of Madagascar. The school has adopted a cross-curricular thematic approach to teaching the entire curriculum. The lesson observed focused on rainforests; subsequent topics include deserts and rivers.

'Content and Language Integrated Learning (CLIL)' offers a continuum of practice, with full immersion at one end, where a subject(s) is taught through the medium of a foreign language and at the other end where an aspect of a curriculum subject or theme is taught through the medium of a foreign language as in Case Study 1. The approach is already established in many schools across

(Continued)

(Continued)

Europe (Eurydice 2005), however integrating foreign languages into other subjects is still relatively rare in English primary schools (Hood 2014; Hood and

Aims/Learning Intentions:	*Context/Rationale/Link to Long Term Planning and Previous Learning:*	*Key Vocabulary:*
• I can identify the linguistic background of countries where there are rainforests • I can write questions in French about the things I would like to find out about Madagascar, using correct punctuation • I can understand that English rainforest vocab is translated from a wide range of language backgrounds • I can discover the French words for rainforest vocab in Madagascar, using a dictionary • I can form sentences in French to describe the rainforest in Madagascar, using a range of French conjunctions • I can compare and contrast aspects of culture in Madagascar	Building an IU work on Mali for current Yr 6s, and introducing Francophone Africa to Yr 5s. International Schools project developing IU and global awareness	• Rainforest vocab • Conjunctions
	Primary Languages Curriculum Map Term: 1 Yrs: 5/6 Theme: Madagascar	*Creative Curriculum Link:* • Exploring rainforests of Madagascar • French vocab of rainforests • Awareness of linguistic background of geographical feature
Language Ladder 'Can Do' Statements/Assessment: I can understand the main points from a short written text in clear printed script I can write a few short sentences with support, using expressions which I have already learnt	*Intercultural Understanding/International Schools Link:* **IU 5.3** Compare symbols, objects or products which represent their own culture with those of another country **IU 6.3** Present information about an aspect of culture International Schools – an in-depth look at a Francophone African country	*Grammar Emphasis/ SPAG Focus:* 5. Use a wide range of conjunctions to create compound and complex sentences 5. I can use full stops, commas, exclamation marks and question marks to punctuate sentences correctly

Figure 12.1   Curriculum map for term 1

Tobutt 2009). The national CLIL guidelines, circulated in 2009 in England, give the following definition for primary CLIL:

> a pedagogic approach in which language and subject area content are learnt in combination. The generic term CLIL describes any learning activity where language is used as a tool to develop new learning from a subject area or from a theme.

According to Mehisto et al. (2008), this approach offers 'just-in-time' rather than 'just-in-case' language. In other words, rather than teaching 'survival' language that potentially can be used when the learner travels or meets people from the country, the learner recycles language to access information that they need to use at the time.

The case study school is a small school in a large alliance which is confederated with another primary school. The specialist teacher teaches French to each class in Key Stage 2 for one hour a week in a timetabled lesson. The class teacher and teaching assistants leave the class during the French lesson for other duties. The specialist French teacher has adapted the medium-term plans for French in order to make direct links, wherever possible, with the school's creative curriculum. (See below the curriculum map and plan for the lesson.) The teacher explained the tension between the importance of mapping French onto the school's topic curriculum to develop a coherent learning experience and the importance of ensuring progression in languages. She explained that sometimes she prioritises the needs of 'French' in order for children to know basic vocabulary. For example, she said: 'With Year 4, my work is on the French school system – school vocabulary and classroom commands, which has nothing to do with the topics taught across the curriculum.'

Plan for the Lesson

The ecology of Madagascar created a context for exploring conjunctions in the lesson observed (see plan below). Children worked for an hour reading, translating, writing and using dictionaries. The teacher reported that one out of five lessons taught focuses specifically on grammatical skills, although information about the structure of the language is reinforced in some way in every French lesson. She explained that she regularly makes explicit links between French grammar and the spelling, punctuation and grammar (SPAG) objectives taught in English in order to reinforce grammatical understanding overall.

(Continued)

(Continued)

Yr Group: 4	Area of Work:	Week Beginning: 29/04/13
LI: I can use a conjunction to make complex sentences with accurate punctuation	**Success Criteria:** • I can build on previous knowledge of French conjunctions • I can understand what punctuation needs to change • I can use different conjunctions to change the meaning of the sentence	**G and T provision:** The 'hira gisy' text **SEN provision:** Flashcard conjunctions/study pack/sheet with clearly differentiated sentences
Cross-curricular link: Madagascar **International link: looking at Madagascan culture – text for conjunctions looks at Madagascan traditions**		
Starter: **Music from Madagascar** **Pairs: Word-tennis**	**Language Development:** • What did we find out about conjunctions last session? • How do we need to adapt punctuation – what needs to change? • How do we find the verb? • How do we build two sentences together? • Does it make a difference which conjunction we use? • Are there words that we don't want to repeat? • Have a go at the text – what skills are we going to need to use?	**Plenary, Assessment Activity:** Peer assessment re SC Peer assessment – look at whiteboards – use of conjunction? Use of punctuation? Group Plenary Evidence assessment – write out sentence on a speech bubble
Key vocabulary: et/puis/alors/donc/parce que/mais/pendant que		

Figure 12.2   Lesson plan

Foreign Language Lesson for Years 5 and 6

The lesson started with a quick 'warm-up' game of word-tennis in French: children in turn say a word or phrase they know, as they 'serve' to another pupil in the class. The teacher then wrote the learning intentions on the flip chart: *'I can manipulate conjunctions to make more complex sentences; I can swap around conjunctions; I can use my knowledge of conjunctions and previous knowledge'.* The children had already translated the texts about Madagascar's rainforests in previous lessons. Information, drawn from the United Nations, Educational, Scientific and Cultural Organisation (UNESCO) website, was printed in large letters onto a piece of A4 paper. The texts communicated 'real' information about global issues, sustainability and ecology. The authentic texts also formed part of the classroom display about rainforests.

The lesson was broadly divided into four tasks:

Task 1: Learners were asked to write down three conjunctions on mini white-boards in English and translate them into French with the help of their bilingual dictionaries. Once these were written, the teacher distributed a large printed sheet with seven conjunctions written in French (*et, alors, pendant que, donc, mais, puis, parce que*). Children were asked to check the conjunctions they had written against the printed list and translate the remaining words from French to English using dictionaries. A small group of children with special educational needs were given the printed sheet from the outset. The specialist teacher circulated each table, working with learners in turn. All learners then transferred the conjunctions onto Post-its.

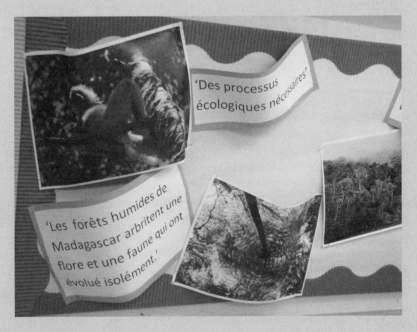

Figure 12.3   Classroom display

(Continued)

(Continued)

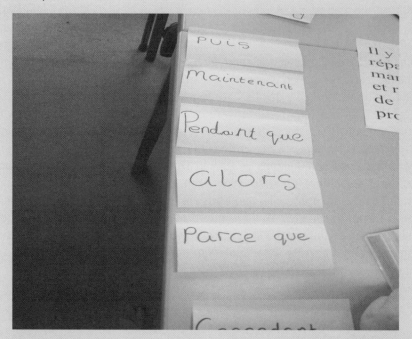

Figure 12.4   Post-its

Task 2: The teacher gave out four short typed texts about the ecology of Madagascar. Children were asked to decode and read aloud the texts to each other. The teacher circulated the room to offer help with pronunciation, intonation and meaning. Children worked in pairs and groups, identifying the proper nouns from the capital letters, guessing the meaning of the text from cognates and using dictionaries.

Task 3: Children created compound sentences joining together the short texts using the conjunctions written on the Post-its. The photograph below depicts one of the compound sentences joined by *parce que*. Some children eliminated the beginning of the second text as they read aloud and copy-wrote the sentences into their books. One child explained: '*I had two sentences that started with – les fôrets humides – once you put two sentences together you can get rid of part of the sentence which makes the writing shorter.*'

Task 4: The list of seven conjunctions was used again: in pairs, children discussed how they could change the meaning of the sentences by using a different conjunction. Children continued to copy the sentences into their books until the end of the lesson.

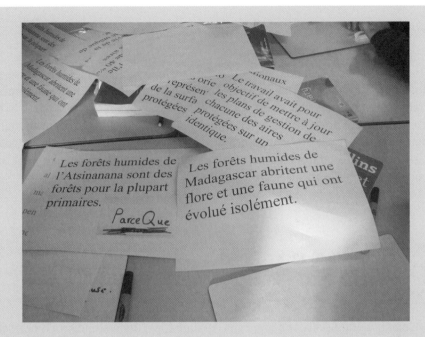

Figure 12.5   Creating compound sentences

Children appeared to work quietly for an hour, accessing linguistically challenging material by analysing and translating texts supported by a dictionary. Their skills were monitored through discussion as the teacher spoke to individuals and groups about the development of their dictionary skills, their use of conjunctions and their strategies for analysing texts. She encouraged peer feedback and self-assessment and took photographs as a record of children's work. At the end of the lesson she collected in the children's exercise books for marking.

Children encountered both new vocabulary and structures in French and new subject content about the rainforests through reading and writing in French. The teacher spoke about the potential of cross-curricular teaching for creative learning but emphasized that integrating languages across the curriculum takes substantially more time than lessons that are purely focused on language, as learners need to understand the concepts and content taught as well as the vocabulary and structures. In the absence of national recommendations about how much time should be allocated to languages, the length and frequency of lessons are in the hands of teachers and head teachers and depend to an extent upon their

(Continued)

(Continued)

commitment to the subject. By 2009, Cable et al. (2010) reported that about half of the language coordinators in the 40 schools reported creating links between languages and the rest of the curriculum although practice was not widespread, as most class teachers indicated that they did not always feel they were able to make links easily. Some teachers felt that the complexity of the content in many other subjects was too advanced for the children's level of language skills; teachers also reported a lack of confidence and linguistic competence and none of the schools had undertaken specific CLIL training.

 Case Study 12.2

Innovation

Developing writing skills and improving grammatical understanding do not necessarily sound innovative, but primary teachers are finding appropriate and age-friendly tasks for fast-paced lessons that promote critical thinking. This case study is one example. The teacher draws upon Victorian inventions that children are learning about in history.

At the time of writing, the specialist teacher had been teaching for over seven years in a medium-size urban school. Language lessons in the school are 45 minutes long and, where possible, foreign languages are used as a medium of communication for classroom instructions and registration. At least two foreign languages are taught at any given time in the school. Children in Key Stage 2 are encouraged to act as language ambassadors to promote languages in their family and community and the school offers a family French and Italian programme where families learn a foreign language together.

The teacher explained that she plans creative opportunities for oral engagement and interaction as well as regular opportunities for analysing a variety of text. She stressed the importance of children learning the rules in languages from the beginning and how to spell words rather than guessing from the pronunciation. She explained that she teaches sets of words with similar patterns alongside spelling exceptions to the rule, ensuring that high-frequency words as well as words that children find more challenging are practised regularly in different contexts. When asked about teaching grammar and writing, she indicated that she draws upon strategies for teaching English spelling, punctuation and grammar when teaching Spanish and children have become accustomed to comparing languages. She said:

> Children are able to refer to the article, singular, plural, verb, noun etc. in both languages ... their writing has become more creative as they know exactly what they have to change to make it better.

> I did a lesson on (not) using the double negative in English. We did this one game where they were only allowed to hold one cross up in a sentence. We did various activities working in groups. At some stage in the group session, I said that we never use a double negative in English. A child who was a lower ability said to me .... 'but we do use the double negative in Spanish though don't we ... !'. I was delighted! We were not talking about Spanish at all at that point! One of the highlights of the year!

A Spanish Literacy Lesson – Year 5

The children are drawn to the front of the class with their mini whiteboards and asked to sit on the mat. Many of the instructions are given in Spanish. The teacher writes two sentences on the interactive whiteboard – one in English, *The red telephones*, and the other in Spanish, *Los teléfonos rojos*. Children are asked to compare, identify and discuss the similarities and differences. After several minutes, children share their perceptions with the whole class. Below are a few of the comments made:

Pupil 1: Easy to guess, translate

Pupil 2: The word order is different– the adjective is after the noun

Pupil 3: The adjective is placed before the noun in English

Pupil 4: The accent is on the second 'e'

Pupil 5: We use 'ph' in telephone and they use 'f'

Pupil 6: The adjective changes

The teacher points out that the article also changes to a plural *los*. She asks children to look at the shape of words and identify the different sounds. She sits low on the carpet so that children can focus on the shape of her mouth as they listen to the pronunciation of each word. The children repeat.

(Continued)

(Continued)

The teacher asks the children to identify the learning intention of the lesson from the two sentences written on the whiteboard. One child volunteers: *'To compare how adjectives are used in different languages.'* She draws children's attention to the five steps to success that they need to think about when writing their sentences: *'noun, adjective, singular, plural, article'*. The teacher writes the learning intention on the board and asks the children to write it down in their topic books. Children sit in their 'English-ability' groups for learning. The teacher distributes separate activities for different groups.

One group is given a matching activity with phrases relating to Victorian inventions written in Spanish on one side of the page and English phrases on the other. Children are asked to match up the Spanish/English sentences and write notes analysing the differences in word order and agreements of the nouns, adjectives and articles. Once the matching is complete, with the aid of a diction-ary, children are asked to write their own phrases related to Victorian inventions in Spanish and English at the back of the topic books. Children write a variety of sentences using dictionaries. The teacher prompts them with questions as they create their own sentences, reminding them of the grammatical rules.

In another group, the teaching assistant supports a few children as they engage in an English and Spanish matching activity which requires identifying cognates and translating from Spanish phrases to English.

The higher ability group is given an image of the opening of Crystal Palace in London in 1862, depicting the crowds dressed in Victorian clothes. Children write descriptive sentences in English and then translate them into Spanish with the aid of dictionaries. The teacher reminds the group to identify gender agreements and prompts the children to remember the gender rules they have learnt as they describe the red curtains, yellow dresses and green trees. Children discuss in an animated way between themselves the various aspects of agreement – singular, plural, masculine and feminine – and consult their dictionaries. Occasionally voices are raised as children disagree about which descriptive words to use and the article/noun/adjective agreements. All children appear highly motivated and engaged in completing the tasks. The activity ends with self-assessment, the teacher reminding the children of the learning objective.

The teacher asks the children to return to the carpet with their mini white-boards. On the large whiteboard there are four nouns related to the Victorian inventions they had learnt about in their history lesson. The teacher also places a variety of colours on flash cards posted on one side of the board (see Figure 12.6). The children are invited to create their own sentences in Spanish. Some of the children work in pairs, others in groups. When asked for feedback, individual children volunteer a variety of singular and plural sentences. The teacher draws attention to the pronunciation of the article and corrects where necessary if errors are made. Children applaud each other's performance.

The activity changes into a written task. The teacher says a phrase in English, drawing from the four cards on the board, for example 'the red bicycles'.

Figure 12.6   Translation and justification of choice

Children discuss and write the translation in Spanish on their whiteboards. They are then asked to justify the grammatical structure of their sentences with other children, using the correct terminology. Children circulate the classroom and compare, justify and defend their sentences in an animated and excited way. As they discuss, they refer to the cards on the board as a point of reference. The task ends as a few children are asked to read aloud their sentences and share their justifications with the whole class. The activity is repeated but this time the teacher gives a Spanish sentence and children have to translate it into English on their whiteboards.

One of the main changes in the Key Stage 2 languages curriculum is the heightened focus on grammatical structure for an increased level of writing. This case study offers an insight into one teacher's approach to teaching grammar in a fast-paced lesson that required children to read, write, translate, compare and analyse sentence construction in a series of individual, pair and group activities.

Assessment

Despite the three main types of assessment criteria available until 2011 (DfEE 1999; DfES 2005b; McLagan 2006), evidence suggests that the assessment of foreign languages has been limited in most primary schools (Cable et al. 2010; Wade and Marshall 2009). The National Curriculum Attainment Targets (DfEE 1999), comprising eight level descriptors in each of the four skills with the first three targets recommended for use by primary schools, have now been replaced by the new curriculum. The national curriculum implemented in September 2014 (DfE 2013) states that by the end of Key Stage 2, pupils are expected to know, apply and understand the matters, skills and processes set out in the subject content section of the programme of study. The purpose of study highlights the importance of cultural awareness but no content is specified to be assessed. At present, schools find a range of creative ways of embedding cultural first-hand experiences into the wider curriculum (Driscoll et al. 2013), but these are not subject to an assessment regime.

There are 12 specified points in the subject content section of the new curriculum that overlap. They encompass the four skills and the development of basic grammatical understanding such as 'speak in sentences' or 'write phrases from memory, and adapt these to create new sentences' (DfE 2013: 2). Certain components are excluded from the subject content for pupils studying ancient languages, such as, 'present ideas and information orally', but, essentially, the curricula designed for Key Stages 2 and 3 are connected to ensure progression. Without effective assessment and appropriate information transferred about pupil learning, receiving teachers are unable to adapt their plans. We need much more research on how, what and when to assess for the full achievements of primary languages to be realised.

Conclusion

This chapter has explored some of the important issues in teaching and learning foreign languages. It is a relatively new subject in most primary schools, but through the commitment and inspiration of head teachers and teachers, foreign languages has become well established, with a high level of good practice and pupil engagement (Cable et al. 2010; Ofsted 2010; Wade and Marshall 2009). Certain challenges remain however. These include the shortage of well-qualified teachers with the appropriate language skills and confidence to teach (Wade and Marshall 2009), the lack of national funding designated for pre- and in-service training and a lack of appropriate resources for creative teaching and learning. If policy-makers are seriously committed to the importance of languages in education then support and training should be forthcoming, to help all teachers but specifically non-specialists to meet the new demands of the statutory national curriculum.

The requirements for reading and writing and grammar will undoubtedly change the pedagogy, which is predominantly one of 'fun', fast-paced kinaesthetic activities to promote listening and speaking (Cable et al. 2010). The case studies above give a snapshot of how two teachers are teaching grammatical structures and 'building foundations' (DfE 2013) for reading and writing. Finding positive, inclusive and effective ways of developing and sharing good literacy practice in foreign languages, without losing the essence of enjoyment and pupil engagement that have characterised the subject to date, will be, I suspect, our greatest challenge as we move into the new statutory era.

Reflection Points

1. In light of what you have read, what do you think is the best way of teaching foreign languages and why?
2. What sort of language and cultural activities and events could you organise in your school to broaden children's view of the world?
3. Could you draw upon strategies for teaching English when teaching foreign languages? If so, which strategies would you choose? For which skills and why?

Further Reading

Driscoll, P., Macaro, E. and Swarbrick A. (eds) (2014) *Debates in Modern Language Teaching.* London: Routledge.

Hasselgreen, A., Drew, I. and Sorheim, B. (2012) *The Young Language Learner: Research-Based Insights into Teaching and Learning.* Bergen, Norway: Fagnokforlaget.

Kirsch, C. (2008) *Teaching Foreign Languages in the Primary School.* London: Continuum.

Murphy, V. (2014) *Second Language Learning in the Early School Years: Trends and Contexts.* London: Oxford University Press.

References

Bennett, S.N. (1975) 'Weighing the evidence: a review of primary French in the balance', *British Journal of Educational Psychology*, 45: 337–40.

Birdsong, D. (2005) 'Interpreting age effects in second language acquisition', in J.F. Kroll and A.M.B. de Groot (eds), *Handbook of Bilingualism: Psycholinguistic Approaches.* New York: Oxford University Press. pp. 109–27.

Blondin, C., Candelier, M., Edelenbos, P., Johnstone, R., Kubanek-German, A. and Taeschner, T. (1998) *Foreign Languages in Primary and Pre-School Education: A Review of Recent Research Within the European Union.* London: CILT.

Bruner, J. (1986) *Actual Minds Possible Worlds*. London: Harvard University Press.

Buckby, M. (1976) 'Is primary French in the balance?', *Modern Language Journal*, 60: 340–6.

Burstall, C., Jamieson, M., Cohen, S. and Hargreaves, M. (1974) *Primary French in the Balance*. Slough: National Foundation for Educational Research.

Cable, C., Driscoll, P., Mitchell, R., Sing, S., Cremin, T., Earl, J., et al.(2010) *Language Learning at Key Stage 2: A Longitudinal Study, Final Report*. London: DCSF.

Chomsky, N. (1965) *Aspects of the Theory of Syntax*. Cambridge, MA: MIT Press.

DfE (Department for Education) (2013) *National Curriculum in England: Primary Curriculum*. www.gov.uk/government/collections/national-curriculum (accessed 22 September 2014).

DfEE (Department for Education and Employment) (1999) *Modern Foreign Languages: The National Curriculum for England*. London: DfEE.

DfES (Department for Education and Skills) (2002) *Languages for All: Languages for Life – A Strategy for England*. Nottingham: DfES.

DfES (Department for Education and Skills) (2005a) *Key Stage 2 Framework for Languages*. Nottingham: DfES.

DfES (Department for Education and Skills) (2005b) *The Languages Ladder*. Available at: http://janetlloyd.net/JLN2/user/image/languages-ladder.pdf (accessed 29 October 2014).

Donato, R., Tucker, G.R., Wudthayagorn, J. and Igarashi, K. (2000) 'Converging evidence: attitudes, achievements, and instruction in the later years of FLES', *Foreign Language Annals*, 33 (4): 377–93.

Driscoll, P. (2000) 'Modern foreign languages in English primary schools: an investigation of two contrasting approaches'. Unpublished PhD thesis, University of Kent.

Driscoll, P. and Rowe, J. (2012) 'The impact of the placement abroad on trainee teachers' identity and professional practice', *Education 3–13,* 40 (4): 1–16.

Driscoll, P., Earl, J. and Cable, C. (2013) 'The role and nature of the cultural dimension in primary modern languages', *Language Culture and Curriculum*, 26 (2): 146–60.

Driscoll, P., Jones, J. and Macrory, G. (2004) *The Provision of Foreign Language Learning for Pupils at Key Stage 2*. DfES Research Report RR572. Nottingham: DfES Publications.

Driscoll, P., Rowe, J. and Thomae, M. (2014) 'The sustainable impact of a short comparative teaching placement abroad on primary school language teachers' professional, linguistic and cultural skills', *The Language Learning Journal*, 42 (3): 307–20.

Edelenbos, P., Johnstone, R. and Kubanek-German, A. (2006) *Languages for the Children of Europe: Published Research, Good Practice and Main Principles*. Brussels: European Commission.

Ellis, R. (2003) *Task-based Language Learning and Teaching*. Oxford: Oxford University Press.

Enever, J. (ed.) (2011) *Early Language Learning in Europe*. London: British Council.

Eurydice (2005) *Key Data on Teaching Languages at School in Europe*. Eurydice European Unit/European Commission. Available at: www.eurydice.org.

Gamble, C.J. and Smalley, A. (1975) 'Primary French in the balance: "Were the scales accurate?"', *Journal of Modern Languages*, 94 (7): 94–7.

Graddol, D. (2006) *English Next*. London: British Council.

Hawkins, E. (1984) *Awareness of Language*. Cambridge: Cambridge University Press.

Hawkins, E. (1987) *Modern Languages in the Curriculum*. Cambridge: Cambridge University Press.

Hawkins, E. (1996) 'Languages teaching in perspective', in E. Hawkins (ed.), *30 Years of Language Teaching*. London: CILT.

Hood, P. (2014) 'Content and language integrated learning: has its time come?', in P. Driscoll, E. Macaro and A. Swarbrick (eds), *Debates in Modern Languages Education*. London: Routledge. pp. 232–44.

Hood, P. and Tobutt, K. (2009) *Modern Languages in the Primary School*. London: SAGE.

Hoy, P.H. (1977) *The Early Teaching of Modern Languages: A Report on the Place of Language Teaching in Primary Schools by a Nuffield Foundation Committee*. London: Nuffield Foundation.

Hurrell, A. (1999) 'The four language skills: the whole works!', in P. Driscoll and D. Frost (eds), *The Teaching of Modern Foreign Languages in the Primary School*. London: Routledge.

Johnstone, R. (1994) *Teaching Modern Languages at Primary School*. Edinburgh: Scottish Council for Research in Education.

Johnstone, R. (2009) 'An early start: what are the key conditions for generalized success?', in J. Enever, J. Moon and U. Raman (eds), *Young Learner English Language Policy and Implementation: International Perspectives*. Reading: Garnet Education. pp. 31–41.

Johnstone, R. (2014) 'Languages over the past 40 years: does history repeat itself?', in P. Driscoll, E. Macaro and A. Swarbrick (eds), *Debates in Modern Languages Education*. London: Routledge. pp. 9–21.

Krashen, S. (1982) *Principles and Practice in Second Language Acquisition*. Oxford: Pergamon.

Krashen, S. (1985) *The Input Hypothesis: Issues and Implications*. Harlow: Longman.

Lantolf, J.P. (1994) 'Sociocultural theory and second language learning: Special issue', *Modern Language Journal*, 78 (4).

Lenneberg, E. (1967) *Biological Foundations of Language*. New York: Wiley and Sons.

Lines, A., Easton, C., Pullen, C. and Schagen, S. (2007) *Language Learning Provision at Key Stage 2: Findings from the 2006 Survey*. Research brief RBX02-07. London: DfES.

Long, M.H. (1981) 'Input, interaction and second language acquisition', in H. Winitz (ed.), *Native Language and Foreign Language Acquisition: Annals of the New York Academy of Sciences*, 379: 259–78.

Long, M.H. (1985) 'Input and second language acquisition theory', in S.M. Gass and C.G. Madden (eds), *Input in Second Language Acquisition*. Rowley, MA: Newbury House. pp. 377–93.

Macaro, E. (2007) 'Do near-beginner learners of French have any writing strategies?', *Language Learning Journal*, 35 (1): 23–35.

Macaro, E. and Erler, L. (2008) 'Raising the achievement of young-beginner readers of French through strategy instruction', *Applied Linguistics*, 29 (1): 90–119.

McLagan, P. (2006) *My Languages Portfolio: European Languages Portfolio – Junior Version*. London: CILT.

Marinova-Todd, S.H., Marshall, B. and Snow, C.E. (2000) 'Three misconceptions about age and L2 learning', *TESOL Quarterly*, 34 (1): 9–34.

Mehisto, P., Marsh, D. and Frigols, M.J. (2008) *Uncovering CLIL: Content and Language Integrated Learning in Bilingual and Multilingual Education*. London: Macmillan Education.

Mitchell, R. and Myles, F. (1998) *Second Language Learning Theories*. London: Arnold Publishers.

Muijs, D., Barnes, A., Hunt, M., Powell, B., Arweck, E., Lindsay, G. and Martin, C. (2005) *Evaluation of the Key Stage 2 Language Learning Pathfinders*. London: DfES.

Nikolov, M. and Djigunovic, J.M. (2006) 'Recent research on age, second language acquisition, and early foreign language learning', *Annual Review of Applied Linguistics*, 26: 234–60.

Nuffield Foundation (2000) *Languages: The Next Generation, Final Report of the Nuffield Languages Inquiry*. London: Nuffield Foundation.

Ofsted (Office for Standards in Education) (2010) *Modern Languages: Achievement and Challenge 2007–2010, Age 5–19*. No. 100042. www.ofsted.gov.uk/resources/modern-languages-achievement-and-challenge-2007-2010 (accessed 22 September 2014).

Penfield, W. and Roberts, J. (1959) *Speech and Brain Mechanisms*. Princeton, NJ: Princeton University Press.

QCDA (Qualifications and Curriculum Development Agency) (2000, 2007, 2009) *Schemes of Work for Key Stage 2 Languages*. Available at: http://webarchive.nationalarchives.gov.uk/20100612050234/ and at: www.standards.dfes.gov.uk/schemes3/subjects/?version=5 (accessed 22 September 2014).

Scarbeck, C. (1998) *The First Steps to Reading and Writing*. London: CILT.

Singleton, D. (1989) *Language Acquisition and the Age Factor*. Clevedon, OH: Multilingual Matters.

Skehan, P. (1989) *Individual Differences in Second-Language Learning*. London: Edward Arnold.

Skinner, B.F. (1957) *Verbal Behaviour*. Englewood Cliffs, NJ: Prentice Hall.

Swain, M. (1985) 'Communicative competence: some roles of comprehensive input and comprehensible output in its development', in S.M. Gass and C. Madden (eds), *Input in Second Language Acquisition*. Cambridge, MA: Newbury House.

Swain, M. (1995) 'Three functions of output in second language learning', in G. Cook and B. Seidlhofer (eds), *Principles and Practice in Applied Linguistics: Studies in Honour of H.G. Widdowson*. Oxford: Oxford University Press. pp. 125–44.

Vanderplank, R. (2014) 'Listening and understanding', in P. Driscoll, E. Macaro and A. Swarbrick (eds), *Debates in Modern Languages Education*. London: Routledge. pp. 53–65.

Vilke, M. (1988) 'Some psychological aspects of early second-language acquisition', *Journal of Multilingual and Multicultural Development*, 9 (1–2): 115–28.

Wade, P. and Marshall, H., with O'Donnell, S. (2009) *Primary Modern Foreign Languages: Longitudinal Survey of Implementation of National Entitlement to Language Learning at Key Stage 2*. London: DCSF.

Woore, R. (2014) 'Developing reading and decoding in the modern foreign languages classroom', in P. Driscoll, E. Macaro and A. Swarbrick (eds), *Debates in Modern Languages Education*. London: Routledge. pp. 81–95.

CHAPTER 13

AN INTRODUCTION TO CROSS-CURRICULAR LEARNING

Jonathan Barnes

Chapter Aims

This chapter will:

- demonstrate the links between creative thinking and cross-curricular activity

- draw attention to different approaches to cross-curricular teaching and learning

- establish a range of methods through which cross-curricular activity can be used to raise standards in children's subject learning

Introduction

The world beyond the classroom is cross-curricular. Through my window I see walls, trees, people walking by, cars, birds, clouds and the occasional aeroplane – I understand none of them fully from the perspective of just one curriculum subject. I describe and appreciate the cherry tree outside using a combination of geographical, artistic, poetic, philosophical and historical vocabularies. Others might perceive the same scene by linking thoughts from mathematics, science, design, music, movement or religious education. We each look on the world, its objects, patterns and experiences, with different eyes. Cross-curricular learning recognises these multiple viewpoints and seeks to build more knowledgeable, lasting and transferable understandings of the world around us.

Cross-curricular teaching and learning has a long history. Plato referred to the importance of linking emotional, practical and intellectual skills, combining music and movement, drama and literature, philosophy and politics. The educational luminaries of the Enlightenment, like Comenius, Rousseau, Froebel, Pestalozzi, each in their way championed cross-curricular approaches. These ideas were developed in the late nineteenth and twentieth centuries by progressives like Steiner, Dewey, Montessori and Isaacs. Like Hadow (1931), Plowden (1967) and the Education Reform Act of 1988 before them, the latest primary education reports recognise that the combined skills and disciplines of a number of subjects are used in solving real-life problems. Today many teachers continue to see cross-curricular approaches as motivating, enjoyable and capable of building relevance and meaning into a curriculum sometimes seen as narrowed (see NFER 2011; Robinson and Aronica 2010; Wrigley et al. 2012).

Links between curriculum subjects have also been closely associated with engendering creative thinking (see Ofsted 2010; Roberts 2006; Thomas Tallis School 2013). Influential psychologists Csikszentmihalyi (1997) and Sternberg (2003) established such links, arguing that creative ideas frequently stem from interactions between subjects or cultures. Making connections between subjects has, however, become controversial. The new National Curriculum in England (DfE 2013) omits reference to cross-curricular links while the National College for School Leadership (NCSL) lists:

- focus on alternative curriculum days and themed weeks, with suspended timetable opportunities for specialist off-site activities facilitated by parents and community volunteers
- focus on adapting a published topic approach, modified according to context and applied across schools to enable the sharing of resources and good practice
- focus on a play-centred approach to learning

among its recommendations for school leaders (NCSL 2012). Educationalists, such as Gardner (1999, 2004, 2006) and Hirsch (2006), unusually agree on the importance of learning the distinctive knowledge, language and skills of each subject discipline, but Gardner sees their frequent integration as essential for profound and transferable learning while Hirsch argues for a pure 'knowledge curriculum' of continued subject separation. The Cambridge Primary Review (Alexander 2010) stressed the dual importance of progression in subject knowledge *and* thematic curricula, though ex-Secretary of State for Education Estelle Morris could not imagine the words 'cross-curricular theme' passing the lips of Michael Gove, Secretary of State between 2010 and 2014 (*Guardian* 2011). Ofsted, in its rigorous appraisal of successful primary and secondary schools, makes clear that there is no necessary conflict between single-subject learning and cross-curricular learning; both can exist profitably side by side (Ofsted 2010).

The Scottish and Northern Irish primary curricula are explicit on the value of cross-curricular approaches. The Scottish Curriculum for Excellence, for instance, mentions interdisciplinary work 28 times in its introductory documentation (Scottish Government 2008). The Scottish curriculum groups some subjects together under: expressive arts, health and well-being, social sciences and 'technologies'. It also takes a single-subject approach to mathematics, science, language and RE. In its introduction, the Scottish Government says:

> Interdisciplinary studies, based upon groupings of experiences and outcomes from within and across curriculum areas, can provide relevant, challenging and enjoyable learning experiences and stimulating contexts to meet the varied needs of children and young people. Revisiting a concept or skill from different perspectives deepens understanding and can also make the curriculum more coherent and meaningful from the learner's point of view. Interdisciplinary studies can also take advantage of opportunities to work with partners who are able to offer and support enriched learning experiences and opportunities for young people's wider involvement in society. (Scottish Government 2008)

This chapter highlights evidence suggesting that cross-curricular approaches at their best are highly motivating, inclusive and able to raise standards in all subjects.

State of the Art in Cross-Curricular Pedagogy

Much learning is informal. Many of the most meaningful experiences for children happen outside the classroom. Casual, unplanned, social and multi-sensory modes of learning are often as influential as any brilliantly planned and well-taught lesson. Educationalists have begun to recognize the mass of connections children make to life beyond curriculum and classroom (see Austin 2007; Barnes 2015; Fumoto et al. 2012; Scoffham 2013; Wrigley et al. 2012). We are reminded of the often overriding significance of the inner priorities of children in their attitude to learning (for example, Abbs 2003; Hicks 2006). Others ask us to listen to 'pupil voice' (Cheminais 2008; Desailly 2012; Ruddock and McIntyre 2007) or consider education's role in the intellectual, social and psychological health of young people (Clift and Camic 2015; DH 2005; UNICEF 2007; WHO 2008). Research such as the Children's Society's *Good Childhood* Report (Layard and Dunn 2009) and UNICEF's Innocenti Report Cards (UNICEF 2013) share many commonalities. Each report stresses comparatively high rates of unhappiness, stress, dissatisfaction and poor relationships in young people in the UK. From them we learn that many children are preoccupied by:

- their family and peer relationships
- their own changing selves
- their personal futures.

Other researchers, for example Hicks (2006), find that young people are frequently worried about global issues like sustainability, poverty, pandemics, global warming, war, terrorism and natural disasters. They tend also to be very interested in new technologies, in particular communications technologies like mobile telephones, social networking sites and computer games.

Despite the unsurprising nature of the above preoccupations, few feature centrally in the curricula of our schools. Indeed, in the new primary national curriculum for England (DfE 2013) 'issues' like sustainability, global warming and poverty are omitted. In the world beyond the contrived settings of school, effective and deep thinking and learning (see Marton and Booth 1997) take place on personal and emotional as well as intellectual levels. It is to the sensory and personal inner world of learning that neuroscience has recently turned its attention.

Neuroscience increasingly offers hard evidence that the insights and observations of past psychologists and pedagogues may be valid. As neuroscientist and psychologist Gardner has observed:

> the brain learns best and retains most when the organism is actively involved in exploring physical sites and materials and asking questions *to which it actually craves the answers*. Merely passive experiences tend to attenuate and have little lasting impact. (Gardner 1999: 82, my italics)

Building on such observations and in the context of all learning, Alexander (2010) reports:

> Neuroscientific research ... has shown ... that learning is strengthened not only in relation to how many neurons fire in a neural network, but also how they are distributed across different domains, such as the motor and sensory cortices ... multisensory approaches (Visual, Auditory and Kinaesthetic rather than Visual, Auditory or Kinaesthetic) are to be encouraged. (Alexander 2010: 96–7)

Translating neuroscientific insights into pedagogy is not a straightforward affair, but neuroscience and education overlap in their belief in the importance of the sensory, physical and exploratory impulses in human learning (Howard-Jones 2012). While such findings do not point directly at the cross curriculum, they do suggest the need for a multiplicity of approaches and contexts for effective learning.

Emotional engagement is also essential for meaningful learning. Neuroscientists have for the past 20 years been pointing to research that shows that the human brain processes stimuli (often unconsciously) at an *emotional* level well before it processes them intellectually (Damasio 1994; Goleman 1996; LeDoux 2002; McGilchrist 2010). If the human mind is to perceive something as important, it must first be aware of its emotional significance. The message that 'we feel therefore we learn' (Immordino-Yang and Damasio 2007) suggests that to activate neural systems across the brains of learners, the teacher must construct emotionally relevant situations to help them learn:

When we educators fail to appreciate the importance of students' emotions, we fail to appreciate a critical force in students' learning. One could argue, in fact, we fail to appreciate the very reason that students learn at all. (Immordino-Yang and Damasio 2007: 9)

Bringing together evidence from across what Greenfield (2003) calls the 'new science of learning', Alexander also suggests that children's learning should be tied to:

existing experience of the world

multisensory activity

social settings in which language is used

metacognition (including pretend play)

ample opportunity to follow 'what naturally interests them' (Alexander 2010: 98)

I have argued (Barnes 2015; Barnes and Shirley 2007; Scoffham and Barnes 2009) that cross-curricular pedagogies are better placed to motivate, sustain, be meaningful and socially satisfying than a curriculum purely devoted to separated subject teaching. Each item in Alexander's list above also implies a degree of cross-curricularity. Indeed, the curriculum recommendations of the Cambridge Primary Review include cross-curricular themes like 'ethics and citizenship', 'the arts' and 'the social sciences'.

Retained, transferable and useful learning is more likely to result from experience or exposure that has been genuinely entered into by the child. Abbs (2003) reminds us that learning cannot be conferred on the child; it has to be accepted by them. Learning has to be made an existential experience; it has to have personal meaning to be deeply rooted. Meaningful or 'powerful' experiences are possible in and out of the classroom and are significant starting points for learning, as are opportunities to put learning into practice (Perkins 2010).

The Importance of Powerful Experiences

Any activity that 'lights us up' or makes our eyes sparkle is a powerful motivator. Engaging experiences are not necessarily showy, complex or time-consuming, they are simply activities that capture children's senses, emotions, enquiring minds and their desire to be active. Discovery, invention, physical involvement and creative activity often enthuse us and have probably always generated deep, committed and transferable learning (Panksepp 2004). The quest for deeply involving, ecstatic (literally out-of-body) experience drives many of us. The psychologist Csikszentmihalyi (2002) calls such timeless moments 'flow' experiences. Flow, he says, describes an optimal learning situation in which ideas and solutions stream from the unconscious mind; self-consciousness, personal worries and self diminish and time seems to stand still.

We feel such sensations when we are doing the things we most love, perhaps reading, drawing, mountain climbing, jogging, singing, knitting. In such times both body and mind work at their best and we feel fulfilled. We look back on such times as happy times. Csikszentmihalyi suggests that a teacher who maximises flow-inducing activity in their classroom also maximises the learning of children.

A curriculum built around the concept of flow would require the planning of a series of experiences likely to be so powerful and emotionally significant that most, if not all, children in a class feel involved in them. An emotionally powerful experience need not be spectacular – it may be a well-read story, a visit to the playground pond or reminiscences by the school 'lollypop lady'. It might equally be a trip to the swimming pool, museum or the local wood. Powerful, personally involving experiences do not have to be placed at the beginning of a course of study; they can come in the middle or at the summation of the work done in a unit of work. Such experiences *should*, however, make real contact with the lives and feelings of both children and their teacher, and require the application of knowledge and skills from several curriculum subjects. Again, many of the most powerful of these experiences occur outside the classroom (Austin 2007; Knight 2013).

Social scientists since Vygotsky claim that learning is primarily a social and cultural activity (see Noddings 2003; Rogoff 2002; Wenger 1998). Problems and challenges too are more easily faced and learned from when tackled in teams and creative advances are usually made in collaborations (John-Steiner 2001). Neuroscientific and social scientific insights come together in suggesting that lasting, transferable learning in both pure subject and cross-curricular contexts is generated by:

- emotional relevance
- engagement in fulfilling activity
- working on shared challenges with others.

These three features are likely to become a reality if learning is planned around shared and engaging experiences. The scientific evidence (as well as the professional experience of many teachers) suggests that powerful, personally involving and shared experiences, planned as part of a lesson or for a series of lessons, provide the best chances of including and improving all learners.

Innovation

Creativity and cross-curricularity are linked. The publication of the *All Our Futures* report by the National Advisory Committee on Creative and Cultural Education (NACCCE 1999), resulted in a renewed interest in creativity, creative thinking, creative teaching and creative learning. It recommended the setting up of partnerships between innovative workers in the community and schools. Such partnerships were not to be based on one-off arts projects but on using creative approaches to transform the whole school. Creativity was not seen as only connected to the arts; innovative practice was to include work in all subjects and across subjects. When the Creative Partnerships programme was set up in a range of economically deprived areas of England, the positive results of creative collaboration soon became apparent in a wide range of studies (for example, Brice Heath and Wolf 2004; Cremin et al. 2009; Parker 2013; Roberts 2006). Most Creative Partnerships links with schools lasted for a year, some for three years, and in that time cross-curricular approaches naturally dominated in the combined work generated by creative practitioners, school staff and children.

The range of publications supporting teachers in developing creative approaches to learning also multiplied in this period. Led by Beetlestone (1998), Craft (2000, 2005), Fisher (2005) and Jeffrey and Woods (2003), creativity was brought into the core language of pedagogy. Many examples of creative approaches to teaching and learning rested on cross-curricular projects. Government advice via the now defunct Qualifications and Curriculum Authority (QCA) also stressed cross-curricular approaches to creativity (QCA 2005). Usually involving two, or at the most three, subject areas, these projects used the connections between different subject mindsets to promote creative thinking. Cross-curricular practice can be defined as: when the skills, knowledge and attitudes of two or more subjects are applied to a problem, theme or idea. The limitation to two subjects (English is developed in any cross-curricular pairing) arises from research into the effectiveness of interdisciplinary methods (for example, Roth 2000).

The year 2011 marked a change in government rhetoric. Creative Partnerships, the biggest creative education project in the world (Thomson 2014), was disbanded and the subsequent 2014 National Curriculum for England (DfE 2013) hardly mentioned the word 'creative'. Links between subjects are not specifically recommended, but the rationale behind the new 'slimmed down' national curriculum left it to teachers to devise the most suitable teaching approaches. Many schools continue to plan for cross-curricular and creative experiences because they appreciate their motivational and inclusive qualities.

Innovation does not automatically engage all children. Well-planned, creative and shared cross-curricular experience alone will not capture every child's interest. The wise pedagogue will devise a range of easily accessible and practical entry points to maximise the chances of mental, sensory and social involvement. I have collected a number of easily resourced and flexible entry points called 'focus exercises' to help children concentrate on their physical and emotional interaction with place, idea, story, object or person (Barnes 2015). Focus exercises are seen as the initial contact with an experience; they are not tied to specific-subject disciplines – indeed, subject labels ought to be avoided when using them. Neither should they be too focused.

Too sharp a focus can have the effect of directing the child to only one class of experience; the focus exercise should lead to multiple interpretations. The aim is simply for the learner to 'get to grips' with the experience in a personal, sensory way. Drawing, for example, is not used as an art activity but as a means of focusing the mind and brain and increasing the use of language (Brice Heath and Wolf 2004, 2005). Collections are not seen as a science, art or design and technology activity but simply a means of involving children in their own choices or sharpening the use of their senses. Sight, sound, smell or emotional trails may use maps but they are not initially intended to extend understanding of geography, neither do reflections necessarily link to religious education. The focus exercises use touch, taste, smell, sight and feeling to motivate. They give a sense of control within clear, structured activities. Individual or group motivation arising from the focus exercises can then be used to develop and progress thoughts, connections, skills and knowledge within chosen subject disciplines. The essence is that each of these exercises is designed to help the learner engage in a 'present tense' way with a subject, place, person or object. Each focus exercise is also open-ended; the data collected could be used in many different ways.

In addition to pointing to the importance of powerful experiences, I have developed a series of focus exercises aimed at provoking creative and cross-curricular thinking at all levels. These I outline below.

Focus Exercises to Launch Creative and Cross-Curricular Thinking

Mapping

Make your own map of a short journey you have taken. Show significant landmarks (buildings, plants, shadows, street furniture, any unexpected things which strike you as important). Use your map in one of the following ways:

(a) emotional maps: How do you feel in each place? Mark on your map with words or colours the emotions you feel in different places. For example: which place makes you feel small, lonely, excited, frightened, cold, happy or sad?

(b) sound maps: What are the dominant sounds in different areas of your map? Draw symbols or write words that capture the locations of different sounds in the environment.

(c) smell maps: What smells can you identify in this place? Mark on the boundaries between different dominating smells. For example: Where does the food smell strike you? Where is there a more natural smell? How are the smells different?

Figure 13.1   Student teachers making a sound map

Big picture

On a large sheet of paper (A1 or A2) each of four people draw a big impression of the skyline in front of them. One person should draw the skyline looking north, one east, one south and one west. Use bold, colourful felt-tip pens. The four should then join their drawings to make a continuous collaborative image of 360⁰ of the skyline.

Figure 13.2   A child and his teacher drawing a big picture

Emotional frames

Everyone is given a viewfinder with a different *key word* written on it (for example, red, sad, lonely, awesome, dangerous, circle). Using your viewfinder to frame it, look around for details (small ones are usually best) that visually illustrate or summarise that key word. Capture your decision in a photo and also include the key word on your viewfinder in the photo. This will remind you of the theme. Take five different photographs using the same word.

Figure 13.3　A child's emotional frame photo

Repeating patterns and measurements

Using a marked piece of string as a measure, measure and draw one of the repeated modules that make up a building, floor or design. Label the drawing with the measurements made with your measuring string. Make a drawing to show how the shapes fit together.

Story and journey sticks

Individually use a story stick (a piece of card or a real stick with double-sided tape on it) to collect five small items from your walk. Do not collect any living creature. Theme your collection (such as life, decay, colour) or relate it (same colour, same noun but different examples, such as leaves) or make it a random collection of things that catch your eye. Map your journey when you get back to class, showing where you found your objects. Discuss your choices with your team.

Figure 13.4   A child's journey stick

Colour match

Collect coloured paint samples showing a range of shades of a single colour (available from DIY shops). Stick double-sided tape to each card and ask children to collect natural and made colour matches from the environment. Attach as many examples of each colour as possible to its corresponding paint colour.

Questions

In your group discuss answers to the following questions:

- What would you like to leave here as a gift?
- What would you like to take back with you if you could?
- How many people high do you think that building or tree is?
- How do you feel in this place?

- How many different shades of [colour] can you find?
- What natural life can you see?
- What soft things can you see/What hard things are there here?
- If you worked here what would you have to wear?
- If you owned this what would you wear?

Fridge magnet poems

Fold a piece of A4 paper in half, four times to make 16 folded rectangles. Make a short journey around the school (or playground, forest or street) collecting 16 random words that strike you. Come back to class. Tear out the 16 rectangles and arrange on the desk and try to make a sentence or poem out of at least nine of the words. You can add in any extra small words like *the, and, of, under, above,* and so on.

Creativity

Creativity differs from innovation. Creative ideas often appear completely new to the child, group or class. Innovations are usually novel improvements to existing ideas. The open-ended nature of the focus exercises listed above often generates surprising and highly creative connections. Connections between the exercises and the previous experience of the child are common and frequently lead to original, valuable and imaginative ideas. With support children can turn these ideas into products or performances: posters, talks, tables, collections, art exhibitions, dances, dramas, debates or compositions. The transferable nature of the skills developed through the focus exercises shows in a wide variety of outcomes recorded in a number of studies (for example, Barnes and Shirley 2005; Dismore et al. 2008; Scoffham 2013).

Focus exercises can be used as a sensor and personally controlled starting point for learning in subject-led directions too. The 'emotional frames' exercise, for instance, has been used at the beginning of a modern languages project in French, where children tested the meaning of words like *tranquille, claire, laide, belle*. Frames were also used for a history project where groups took mutiple photos of 'eighteenth-century', 'Victorian', 'late medieval' houses in a single street. In mathematics one teacher wrote short number sentences on each frame and children had to collect photos of the correct answer from aspects of the environment. These examples point to a form of cross-curricular practice where subject learning in a number of different subjects can arise from analysis of the same experience. However, there are other ways of being cross-curricular.

A Taxonomy of Cross-Curricular Approaches

My own research into cross-curricular pedagogies has identified six common and contrasting ways of using more than one subject to respond to a problem, theme or issue. These styles of cross-curricular teaching and learning have different aims, depend upon a range of planning strategies and result in different learning opportunities:

- *tokenistic*
- *hierarchical*
- *multidisciplinary*
- *interdisciplinary*
- *opportunistic*
- *double focus*

Each suggested category places a different emphasis on combining subjects; each has a different aim.

Having used focus exercises like those above to maximise interaction with an experience, the teacher should choose the cross-curricular approach best suited to the learning they wish to promote in their children. Each approach has a different aim. All can be used with all subject disciplines. There are at least six different ways in which they manifest themselves.

Tokenistic cross-curricular approaches

Token cross-curricular approaches are only cross-curricular in name. They do not make real connections between subjects or develop learning in more than one subject. Perhaps a song might introduce a history topic but nothing is made of the song and little done to enhance learning in music; the only aim is to bring some extra interest to a history theme.

Hierarchical cross-curricular learning

Hierarchical cross-curricular learning occurs when ideas from one subject are used to enhance learning in another. The aim is for learning in a dominant subject, perhaps English, mathematics or science, to be enhanced by the introduction of a subsidiary subject, perhaps art, music or dance. If the linkage is genuinely cross-curricular there will be measurable learning in both subjects. Songs, chants, rhythms and timbres, for example, might serve as aids to mathematical or language learning but the teacher must establish clear, new learning aims within music even if the main intention is to enhance learning in the dominant subject.

Multidisciplinary cross-curricular learning

Multidisciplinary cross-curricular learning, on the other hand, gives parity of importance to two subjects. Two sets of disciplines taken from the curriculum subjects may
be used to throw light on a single experience. The aim of multidisciplinary cross-
curricular learning is to use a single stimulus for two distinct purposes. Despite arising
from the same experience, the subject disciplines do not necessarily meet or affect
thinking in each other; learning within the subjects is kept separate. The teacher plans
progression, vocabulary, specific skill acquisition in two subject disciplines that are
most relevant to the experience. It is important for the teacher to name the subjects
chosen and to make the children aware of the new learning that has occurred. English
is likely always to be present in cross-curricular learning because speaking and listening are always generated, and often writing and reading are necessary for extending
the thinking generated by an engaging experience.

Interdisciplinary cross-curricular learning

In interdisciplinary cross-curricular learning the intention is to *connect* or *combine*,
often creatively. New learning in two subject disciplines is put together to generate an
original and valued product, presentation or idea. In this kind of cross-curricular
approach the intertwining of the disciplines deepens the response to a single experience and adds an important element of unpredictability and imagination to the results.
To assess learning the teacher often uses some kind of 'performance of understanding'
(see Blythe 1998) where learning in each subject is some kind of presentation.
Teachers should plan appropriate means of integration of the two subjects and be
clear about the objectives for each discipline, therefore this approach is more complex, and perhaps more risky, than multidisciplinary.

Opportunistic cross-curricular learning

In opportunistic cross-curricular learning the child leads. Planning is done in response
to children's responses to a shared experience; the teacher may have only a vague
subject expectation. Typically children and teacher share a powerful personal experience, such as a visit, visitor or other powerfully presented stimulus. The teacher, or
teaching assistant, listens carefully to children's reactions, observing changes in behaviour. Children may be asked what they would like to do to understand or express the
experience better. Opportunistic methods are generally the preserve of the most confident and experienced teachers because they involve a degree of risk and uncertainty.
The aim of opportunistic cross-curricular methods is to use children's natural curiosity

and enthusiasm to motivate learning. The adult role is to add challenge, new skills and new knowledge to existing interest. In Csikszentmihalyi's terms, the added challenge or newly taught skill is more likely to ease the child from attention and interest towards a state of flow.

Double-focus cross-curricular learning

Double-focus cross-curricular learning attempts to establish a balance. Research has shown (for example, Roth, in Wineburg and Grossman 2000) that cross-curricular approaches can sometimes sacrifice progression and deep subject understanding in favour of simple enjoyment. Cross-curricular learning is generally effective in securing progression only when the teacher's subject knowledge is secure and children are aware of their growing subject understanding. The 'double focus' suggests two different modes of learning operating simultaneously, one subject-specific and the other cross-curricular. The separate subject curriculum continues throughout the year, *however* the year is punctuated with frequent opportunities to put newly learned skills and knowledge into action in cross-curricular contexts. In double-focus approaches teachers should plan a string of powerful experiences for every year group in and out of school. Separate subject studies will use imaginative and engaging pedagogies to extend the disciplinary vocabulary, skills and knowledge; the greater the pure subject or discipline input, the more value each subject will have in a cross-curricular setting.

Pure subject skills and knowledge are quickly put into action in 'real world' and relevant contexts. Ideally these powerful personal experiences should be every six weeks or so and consist of field trips, special visitors, visits to galleries, theatres and museums, themed weeks, science fairs, investigative maths days, and so on. Each context can become the subject of a two-subject analysis, and again English will inevitably be extended in all responses. Through the school year each curriculum subject should have its turn in helping make sense of and extending the experience. Curriculum planning for double-focus cross-curricular learning starts with planning powerful personal experiences and matching particular experiences to two different curriculum viewpoints (see Barnes 2015). Additionally, a range of subjects may be applied to a single theme or the skills of one subject, like English or art, and can throw light on a number of themes.

Additional Perspectives on Cross-Curricular Teaching and Learning

Planning, progression and assessment are central to ensuring challenge and progress in school learning. Successive governments have been right to emphasise the seamless links between assessment and good quality learning. Cross-curricular learning is more effective when these aspects of teaching are given attention. But teachers' attitude and approach, the classroom atmosphere and learning environment they construct, their particular pedagogical style, also strongly affect the learning dispositions of children. Cross-curricular approaches can provide an engaging new perspective for children and equally for their teachers.

A Community of Learners

Cross-curricular learning promotes authenticity in teaching and learning. Using the powerful personal experiences described, teacher and class can quickly enter the world of 'real world learning' (Lucas et al. 2013). Authentic learning experiences involve adult and child learners together. Full teacher participation in the learning process does more than motivate children. Through the mirror neurons, the quizzical looks on teachers' faces provoke deeper enquiry in children as they mirror their teachers' curiosity. The process of learning alongside children also generates high degrees of sustained job satisfaction and increased awareness of personal creativity amongst teachers (Barnes 2013a; Barnes and Shirley 2007; Cremin et al. 2009). A pedagogy and teacher development programme that works towards genuine co-learning contributes significantly to the resilience of teachers and their capacity to give more to their roles (Barnes 2013b).

Planning

Cross-curricular learning is not without its dangers. In past manifestations spurious links were often made between too many subjects, and little sense of progression or subject record keeping was possible (see Alexander et al. 1992). The current focus on progression and rigour has served to remind all teachers of the importance of challenge and a sense of personal growth in learning. Subject progression will perhaps be more difficult to assess as attainment levels have been taken from the foundation subjects in the new national curriculum for England, but establishing learning targets remains vital to the sense of personal development. Progress towards particular subject objectives is not easy to manage, even when only two subjects are involved and detailed planning towards clear and achievable objectives is central. Teachers can map out the direction of planning by asking, 'What new learning, new vocabulary or new skill do I want each child to understand by the end of this lesson?'

New words hold new concepts. Well-chosen vocabulary can often provide the 'backbone' of the well-planned lesson. After deciding upon the experience children will share teachers should identify words in each chosen subject that hold the new ideas, skills or processes they want their children to understand. These new words, highlighted, used frequently and pointedly throughout the session, can provide the framework.

New vocabulary also holds new knowledge and gives children a sense of their own progress towards a goal.

Progression

If we want to avoid the 'bland broth' (Roth 2000) that results from some cross-curricular approaches, detailed forethought is essential. Planning progressive objectives in knowledge and skills requires the teacher to have a secure understanding of the unique skills and core knowledge of the discipline. Children equally need to be aware of progress in themselves. The Cambridge Primary Review (Alexander 2010) uses international and strong evidence to remind us that cross-curricular learning mirrors the way children's minds work, but teachers also need to be aware of how the learning brain thrives on challenge and difficulty and how the sense of genuinely seeking an answer stimulates the capacity to find one. Knowledge of the ways in which the new science of learning can help us plan new challenges and lasting learning is essential to every teacher (see Claxton et al. 2010). While joy and engagement are vital motivators and sustainers they cannot alone generate secure subject development (see House of Commons 2007). The levelled statements in the pre-2014 curriculum in England, and those in Wales, Northern Ireland and Scotland, remain valuable sources of guidance on the detail of subject progress in addition to the new progression frameworks devised by the national curriculum subject expert panels.

Staff Development

Effective pedagogy demands teachers who see themselves as flourishing people. Successful cross-curricular activities need enthusiasm and commitment on the part of the teacher. Teachers might start by considering how they may become enthusiastic learners in their own right. They may share staff development that frequently exposes them to real, relevant, positive and life-changing experiences themselves. Staff who share creative and cultural experiences and who feel they are developing their own creativity are more capable of sustaining a fulfilling life in education (Barnes 2013b). As a result of meaningful professional development, teachers may be better able to plan a series of powerful experiences to span the year for each class, and those experiences must also be potentially life-changing.

Child-Led Learning

The pedagogy of cross-curricular teaching and learning might include a readiness to allow children to choose the experiences they deem important or it may mean planning a series of events with children's preoccupations in mind. The United Nations Convention on the Rights of the Child (UNICEF 1989) expects children to have a say in what and how they are taught. The outcomes from powerful experiences, focus exercises and different forms of cross-curricular thinking in many case studies have been greatly enriched because pupil-led responses were encouraged (Barnes and Shirley 2005, 2007; Cremin et al. 2009; Engaging Places website). Teachers in these contexts have been far from redundant. Their role was primarily to teach the skills and knowledge demanded by the children as projects developed but simultaneously they supported and co-reflected as well as provided the security and safety elements that adults should.

Assessment

Harvard's Project Zero has offered an adaptable format for planning and assessing such experiences (Harvard website). I have adapted the Harvard format for cross-curricular purposes and included an example three-session plan in Figure 13.5. The 'teaching for understanding' approach is founded upon providing plentiful opportunities for children to put their learning into practice in authentic situations. In asking children to apply their new knowledge and skills to real and engaging challenges, the successful pedagogue helps ensure the existential, meaningful and satisfying conditions required for deep learning. In planning both feedback and a yardstick for progression, the teacher uses their experience and knowledge to make assessment part of a pleasurable and enriching learning journey.

Assessment Definitions

Overarching Understanding Goal (OUG): the essential understanding you wish to develop as a result of the teaching. This is usually values or 'big-picture' based: for example, that the children understand the importance of examining several different types of evidence before arriving at a conclusion (a history OUG); that the children understand that specific combinations of sound and silence can express emotions as well as words (a music OUG).

Understanding Goal (UG): what specific skills or knowledge you want children to learn as a result of this unit (tied to attainment levels in the national curriculum).

Performance of Understanding: opportunities throughout the unit of work for children to demonstrate the level and depth of their understanding and whether they have reached the OUG or UGs. The teacher will teach the required skills or knowledge and then give children a chance (independently or in groups) to use their new learning to solve a problem or create a product, presentation, collection, exhibition, performance or composition. This is both an assessment opportunity for teachers and children and a chance to understand the usefulness of the new learning.

Sequence of events	Performances of understanding (opportunities for children to show the current level of their understanding)	Assessment (How will you know that children have engaged, sustained interest and achieved new and transferable learning?)
Day 1: A powerful personal experience – a visit, visitation, story, event or surprise designed to fully engage the whole class. Followed up by focused questioning and direct teaching that arises from the experience	'Introductory performance(s)' (showing the knowledge children have already) What did we see/hear/taste/smell/feel? What do we already know about these things? Use brainstorms, mind maps, diagrams, lists, searches, drawings, discussions e.g. Visiting a castle: In groups of 4/5 look around you: what can you see/ photograph/record/draw, beginning with the letter: 'a', 'b', 'c', etc.	**Formative feedback:** Instant, informal and oral, given by peers and teacher, on spoken, written or drawn reflections by children **Criteria:** Developed collaboratively by children and teachers
Day 2: Developing a theme – teaching new knowledge, skills and attitudes related to two curriculum subjects and directly connected to the powerful personal experience	'Supported performances' (demonstrating in groups and with help from teacher/others, the new skills and knowledge acquired during the module) e.g. Back at school after the castle visit: After history teaching and learning, each table of 6 pupils makes a brief presentation about a given aspect of: castle life – domestic, defensive, attacking, building, modern-day function After science teaching and learning, each table gives a brief presentation on: forces, decay, strong structures, materials, mural ecology	**Formative feedback:** Instant, informal and oral, given by peers, teacher, visitors including parent helpers whilst children are working AND from self during and after the supported performances **Criteria:** Negotiated, children complete a summary sheet about their learning
Day 3: Applying new knowledge – more teaching in the chosen curriculum subjects, culminating in the setting of a real problem or challenge that requires the new knowledge to be used	'Culminating performances' (showing how combined knowledge and skills can be applied to a new problem) e.g. End of module event: Each group of 6 is set a task: (a) plan a history/science field trip to the local church/shopping centre/street etc. What would you want the children to learn? How would you make sure they learned it? How could they share their learning with a younger class? (b) plan and shoot a video that shows the science and history to be found in the school building/street near the school, local church etc.	**Formative feedback:** From the groups themselves during and after performance, then formalised written evaluations (two items of focused praise and one question) **Criteria:** Matched against the prescribed knowledge in the national curriculum and the progression suggested by the subject associations

Figure 13.5   Sample planning sheet for cross-curricular three-day module, adapted from Blythe (1998)

Conclusion

This chapter ends with a series of provocative questions. Both Plowden (1967) and Alexander (2010) recognised that in the hands of teachers who did not have good subject knowledge and good knowledge of how children learn, cross-curricular methods can be counter-productive. Enjoyment is not the only aim of education; we aim at excellence too, but many children do not discover what they will be excellent at unless they first feel a sense of pleasure in school. Cross-curricular learning as described in this chapter will generate enjoyment, but it is for the best teachers to use that enjoyment to build motivations towards new and deep learning.

Reflection Points

1. How do we as teachers gain the levels of subject knowledge that will give us confidence to approach subject learning in a cross-curricular way?
2. Is cross-curricular learning motivating for all children?
3. Is it true that cross-curricular methods stimulate creative thinking and learning? What evidence do you have?
4. Why do you think that not all children respond well to a purely separate subject-based curriculum?

Further Reading

Austin, R. (2007) *Letting the Outside In*. Stoke-on-Trent: Trentham Books.

Barnes, J. (2015) *Cross-Curricular Learning 3-14*, 3rd edn. London: SAGE.

Cremin, T. and Arthur, J. (2014) *Learning to Teach in the Primary School*, 3rd edn. London: Routledge.

Fisher, R. (2005) *Unlocking Creativity: A Teacher's Guide to Creativity across the Curriculum*. London: Fulton.

Robinson, K. and Aronica, L. (2009) *The Element: How Finding Your Passion Changes Everything*. London: Allen Lane.

Rowley, A. and Cooper, H. (eds) (2009) *Cross-Curricular Approaches to Teaching and Learning*. London: SAGE.

Wineburg, S. and Grossman, P. (2000) *Interdisciplinary Curriculum Challenges to Implementation*. New York: Teachers College Press.

References

Abbs, P. (2003) *Against the Flow*. London: Routledge.

Alexander, R. (ed.) (2010) *Children, Their World, Their Education: Final Report and Recommendations of the Cambridge Primary Review*. Abingdon: Routledge.

Alexander, R., Rose, J. and Woodhead, C. (1992) *Curriculum Organisation and Classroom Practice in Primary Schools*. London: DES.

Austin, R. (2007) *Letting the Outside In*. Stoke-on-Trent: Trentham Books.

Barnes, J. (2013a) 'What sustains a fulfilling life in education?', *Journal of Education and Training Studies*, 1 (2): 74–88.

Barnes, J. (2013b) 'What Sustains a Life in Education?' Unpublished PhD thesis, Canterbury Christ Church University.

Barnes, J. (2015) *Cross-Curricular Learning 3–14*, 3rd edn. London: SAGE.

Barnes, J. and Shirley, I. (2005) 'Strangely familiar: promoting creativity in Initial Teacher Education'. Paper presented at the British Educational Research Association (BERA) conference, Cardiff, 16 September.

Barnes, J. and Shirley, I. (2007) 'Strangely familiar: cross curricular and creative thinking in teacher education', *Improving Schools*, 10 (2): 162–79.

Beetlestone, F. (1998) *Creative Development: Learning in the Early Years*. London: Scholastic.

Blythe, T. (1998) *The Teaching for Understanding Guide*. San Francisco, CA: Jossey Bass.

Brice Heath, S. and Wolf, S. (2004) *Visual Learning in the Community School*. London: Creative Partnerships.

Brice Heath, S. and Wolf, S. (2005) 'Focus in creative learning: drawing on art for language development', *Literacy*, 39 (1): 38–45.

Cheminais, R. (2008) *Engaging Pupil Voice to Ensure That Every Child Matters: A Practical Guide*. London: Fulton.

Claxton, G., Lucas, B. and Webster, R. (2010) *Bodies of Knowledge: How the Learning Sciences Could Transform Practical and Vocational Education*. Winchester: The Centre for Real World Learning.

Clift, S. and Camic, P. (eds) (2015) *Oxford Textbook of Creative Arts, Health and Wellbeing: International Perspectives in Practice, Policy and Research*. Oxford: Oxford University Press.

Craft, A. (2000) *Creativity Across the Primary Curriculum*. London: Routledge.

Craft, A. (2005) *Creativity in Schools: Tensions and Dilemmas*. London: Routledge.

Creative Partnerships website: www.creative-partnerships.com (accessed 23 September 2014).

Cremin, T., Barnes, J. and Scoffham, S. (2009) *Creative Teaching for Tomorrow*. Deal: Future Creative.

Csikszentmihalyi, M. (1997) *Creativity: Flow and the Psychology of Discovery and Invention*. New York: HarperCollins.

Csikszentmihalyi, M. (2002) *Flow: The Classic Work on How to Achieve Happiness*. London: Rider.

Damasio, A. (1994) *Descartes' Error*. London: HarperCollins.

Desailly, J. (2012) *Creativity in the Primary Classroom*. London: SAGE.

DfE (Department for Education) (2013) *The National Curriculum in England: Primary Curriculum*. London: DfE.

DH (Department of Health) (2005) *The Healthy Schools Standard Guide for Schools*. London: Crown.

Dismore, H., Barnes, J. and Scoffham, S. (2008) *Space to Reflect*. London: Creative Partnerships.

Engaging Places website: www.engagingplaces.org.uk/teaching+and+learning (accessed September 2014).

Fisher, R. (2005) *Unlocking Creativity: A Teacher's Guide to Creativity Across the Curriculum*. London: David Fulton.

Fumoto, H., Robson, S., Greenfield, S. and Hargreaves, D. (2012) *Young Children's Creative Thinking*. London: SAGE.

Gardner, H. (1999) *The Disciplined Mind*. New York: Simon & Schuster.

Gardner, H. (2004) *Changing Minds: The Art and Science of Changing Our Own and Other People's Minds*. Boston, MA: Harvard Business School.

Gardner, H. (2006) *Five Minds for the Future*. Boston: Harvard Business Press.

Goleman, D. (1996) *Emotional Intelligence*. London: Bloomsbury.

Greenfield, S. (2003) *Tomorrow's People*. Harmondsworth: Penguin.

Guardian (2011) 'Michael Gove loves his traditional curriculum but it won't do for today', available at: www.theguardian.com/education/2011/mar/22/michael-gove-traditional-curriculum (accessed 28 February 2014).

Hadow Report (1931) *The Primary School. Report of the Consultative Committee*. London: HMSO.

Harvard Teaching for Understanding website: http://learnweb.harvard.edu/alps/tfu/info3e.cfm (accessed 23 September 2014).

Hicks, D. (2006) *Lessons for the Future: The Missing Dimension in Education*. London: Routledge.

Hirsch, E. (2006) *The Knowledge Deficit*. New York: Houghton Mifflin.

House of Commons Education and Skills Standing Committee (2007) *Creative Partnerships and the Curriculum*. Eleventh Report of the Session 2006–2007. London: TSO.

Howard-Jones, P. (2012) *Education and Neuroscience: Evidence, Theory and Practical Application*. London: Routledge.

Immordino-Yang, M. and Damasio, A. (2007) 'We feel therefore we learn: the relevance of affective and social neuroscience to education', *Brain, Mind and Education*, 1 (1): 3–10.

Jeffrey, B. and Woods, P. (2003) *The Creative School*. London: Routledge.

John-Steiner, V. (2001) *Creative Collaboration*. Oxford: Oxford University Press.

Knight, S. (2013) *Forest Schools and Outdoor Learning in the Early Years*, 2nd edn. London: SAGE.

Layard, R. and Dunn, J. (2009) *A Good Childhood*. London: Penguin.

LeDoux, J. (2002) *The Synaptic Self.* New York: Viking.

Lucas, B., Claxton, G. and Spencer, E. (2013) *Expansive Education: Teaching Learners for the Real World*. Maidenhead: Open University Press.

Marton, F. and Booth, S. (1997) *Learning and Awareness*. Mahwah, NJ: Lawrence Erlbaum Associates.

McGilchrist, I. (2010) *The Master and His Emissary: The Divided Brain and the Making of the Western World*. New Haven, CT: Yale University Press.

NACCCE (1999) *All Our Futures: The Report of the National Advisory Committee on Creative and Cultural Education*. London: Crown.

NCSL (National College for School Leadership) (2012) *Designing a Creative, Contextualized Primary Curriculum*. Available at: file:///Users/jonathanbarnes/ Downloads/designing-a-creative-contextualised-primary-curriculum-summary.pdf.

NFER (2011) 'Was it right to abandon the creative curriculum?', www.nfer.ac.uk/nfer/ PRE_PDF_Files/11_44_06.pdf (accessed 23 September 2014).

Noddings, N. (2003) *Happiness and Education*. Cambridge: Cambridge University Press.

Ofsted (Office for Standards in Education) (2010) *Creative Approaches that Raise Standards*. Available at: www.creativitycultureeducation.org/wp-content/uploads/ learning-creative-approaches-that-raise-standards-250.pdf (accessed 28 February 2014).

Panksepp, J. (2004) *Affective Neuroscience: The Foundations of Human and Animal Emotions*. Oxford: Oxford University Press.

Parker, D. (2013) *Creative Partnerships in Practice: Developing Creative Learners*. London: Bloomsbury.

Perkins, D. (2010) *Making Learning Whole*. San Francisco: Jossey Bass.

Plowden Report (1967) *Children and their Primary Schools. Report of the Central Advisory Council for Education (England)*. London: HMSO.

QCA (Qualifications and Curriculum Authority) (2005) *Creativity: Find It, Promote It – Promoting Pupils' Creative Thinking and Behaviour across the Curriculum at Key Stages 1, 2 and 3 – Practical Materials for Schools*. London: QCA.

Roberts, P. (2006) *Nurturing Creativity in Young People*. London: DCMS.

Robinson, K. and Aronica, L. (2010) *The Element: How Finding Your Passion Changes Everything*. London: Allen Lane.

Rogoff, B. (2002) *The Cultural Nature of Human Development*. New York: Oxford University Press.

Roth, K. (2000) 'The photosynthesis of Columbus: exploring interdisciplinary curriculum from the students' perspective', in S. Wineburg and P. Grossman (eds), *Interdisciplinary Curriculum: Challenges to Implementation*. New York: Teachers College Press.

Ruddock, J. and McIntyre, D. (2007) *Improving Learning through Consulting Pupils.* London: Routledge.

Scoffham, S. (ed.) (2013) *Teaching Geography Creatively.* London: Routledge.

Scoffham, S. and Barnes, J. (2009) 'Transformational experiences and deep learning: the impact of an intercultural study visit to India on UK Initial Teacher Education students', *Journal of Education for Teaching*, 35 (3): 257–70.

Scottish Government (2008) *Curriculum for Excellence.* Available at: www.education-scotland.gov.uk/images/building_the_curriculum_3_jms3_tcm4-489454.pdf (accessed 28 February 2014).

Sternberg, R. (2003) *Wisdom, Intelligence and Creativity Synthesised.* Cambridge: Cambridge University Press.

Thomas Tallis School (2013) Creative Tallis: Cross-curricular Creativity website: www.creativetallis.com/cross-curricular-creativity.html (accessed 28 February 2014).

Thomson, P. (2014) A critical review of the Creative Partnerships archive. Available at: http://culturalvalueproject.wordpress.com/2014/02/20/pat-thomson-a-critical-review-of-the-creative-partnerships-archive-how-was-cultural-value-understood-researched-and-evidenced/ (accessed 28 February 2014).

UNICEF (1989) *The United Nations Convention on the Rights of the Child.* Available at: www.unicef.org.uk/Documents/Publication-pdfs/UNCRC_PRESS200910web.pdf (accessed 21 July 2014).

UNICEF (2007) 'Child poverty in perspective: an overview of child well-being in rich countries', Innocenti Report Card 7, 359 (1449): 1367–77.

UNICEF (2013) 'Child well-being in rich countries', Innocenti Report Card 11. Available at: www.unicef.org.uk/Latest/Publications/Report-Card-11-Child-well-being-in-rich-countries/ (accessed 21 July 2014).

Wenger, E. (1998) *Communities of Practice: Learning, Meaning and Identity.* Cambridge: Cambridge University Press.

WHO (World Health Organization) (2008) *Inequalities in Young People's Health.* Available at: www.euro.who.int/__data/assets/pdf_file/0005/53852/E91416.pdf (accessed 23 September 2014).

Wineburg, S. and Grossman, P. (eds) (2000) *Interdisciplinary Curriculum Challenges to Implementation.* New York: Teachers College Press.

Wrigley, T., Thomson, P. and Lingard, B. (2012) *Changing Schools: Alternative Ways to Make a World of Difference.* London: Routledge.

CONCLUSION: THE WAY FORWARD

Justine Earl

This book sets out to inspire a renewed interest in the primary curriculum, exploring good practice in individual subjects and considering creative, innovative approaches.

The author of each chapter writes about their subject in a way that is both passionate and informed. The chapters challenge the reader to consider new ways of planning and teaching. Above all, the reader is asked to consider what it is to have a professional approach to learning and teaching. No matter the stage you are at in your career (student teacher, novice or more experienced colleague) this book asks you to look again at what you know and how you might develop your knowledge, expertise and practice.

You will have understood from this book and from other sources that there have been a great number of changes in primary education in England over the last 20 years, with a relentless stream of new initiatives from central government. Throughout this time, schools responded to new requirements, continuously changing their provision. Schools worked hard to move towards implementing a coherent, creative and relevant curriculum that reflected their own principles and beliefs about primary education. They aimed to provide a broad, rich approach to learning and teaching, which responded to their locality and the needs and interests of their pupils and their community.

Reviews of the curriculum by Rose (2009) and compiled by Alexander (2010) offered ways forward for the National Curriculum in England which linked subjects together into areas. Other curriculum models have already moved to grouping subjects, such as the Early Years Foundation Stage Guidance and the National Curriculum for Scotland. The Rose Review suggested six areas of learning with Religious Education as a separate subject. These areas were linked to three broad aims. The Cambridge Review offered eight domains underpinned by 12 aims. The curriculum structure set out in the final report of the Cambridge Review noted that 70% of the curriculum should be nationally controlled and that 30% should be locally proposed and non-statutory. One key message from this review was that any curriculum should be implemented 'flexibly and creatively by each school' (Alexander 2010: 276).

We are now in the interesting position that the new National Curriculum for England (2014) is statutory for all state-funded schools except academies and free schools. In effect this means that if your school is not an academy or a free school, it will not be able to approach the new curriculum flexibly. Of course, statutory assessments in the form of SATs still apply to *all* schools and will be closely aligned to the new National Curriculum. This means that every school would be sensible to use the new documents as a starting point to ensure that they are not disadvantaging their pupils when it comes to national assessment points. However, it seems puzzling that a new curriculum will limit some schools more than others. There are still significant uncertainties around the development of the curriculum (how individual schools in individual contexts will respond) and around assessment arrangements. What we do know is that the demands on pupils in terms of progress will be greater and the required attainment of each pupil, and therefore each school, will be raised.

It could be argued that the new National Curriculum follows through on the central government commitment to hand more autonomy to schools and teachers, as set out in *The Importance of Teaching: The Schools White Paper 2010* (DfE 2010):

> We envisage schools and teachers taking greater control over what is taught in schools, innovating in how they teach and develop new approaches to learning. (p. 40)

It has been asserted that because the slimmed-down national curriculum requirements set out only the essential knowledge that children require, teachers are more able to focus on *how* to deliver this knowledge. This is indeed the message of the government. Yet, close examination of the new requirements tells a somewhat different story. While some subjects have been reduced in terms of content detail, others have increased, both in amount and level of challenge required of primary pupils. The overriding focus in all the subjects on knowledge rather than skills results in a shift of emphasis to learning more facts, rather than developing transferable skills and understanding.

If we take the new programmes of study for English as an example, we see that there is an increased emphasis on the technical aspects of language at the expense of the creative aspects. This means that there is more to list and for teachers to tick off. For example, content is prescribed for spelling, vocabulary and punctuation with very specific items set out for year groups.

Decoding is now to be taught by the use of phonics strategies only. There is no requirement for pupils to build up their sight vocabulary or to use a range of strategies when reading, such as semantic and syntactic cues. This is an example of teachers being told exactly *how* to teach in a key aspect of learning, regardless of huge controversy around research in this area.

The one area of English that has been slimmed down is speaking and listening, which is now called spoken language. The initial draft of the curriculum did not include a programme of study for speaking and listening at all. After widespread criticism during consultation, a single, brief programme of study has been included. This is for the whole of the primary phase, unlike reading and writing, which are split into year groups. If you think back to what you have read in each chapter of this book, you can decide for yourself how important the development of spoken language is for all learners, as a basic building block as well as a key aspect of creativity, deep learning and intellectual exploration.

In mathematics, more demanding content has been introduced earlier than before. There is the new subject of computing, which will make new demands on teachers' knowledge, as well as new topics in history and the statutory inclusion of languages in the curriculum. All of this makes demands on schools to address needs, aspects of curriculum design and time allocation.

The National Primary Teacher Education Council (2013) raised a number of concerns in response to the new national curriculum. These included the likelihood that many pupils are now less likely to experience a broad and balanced curriculum due to the increased demands of the English and mathematics programmes of study. The council also expressed disappointment at the lack of interrelationships between subject disciplines, noting the richness of learning that comes from the exploration of concepts across the boundaries of individual subjects.

In this new era of curriculum demands, it will be more important than ever that you draw on your professionalism to mediate what you are being asked to do, in your own particular setting, in order to be an effective teacher for *your* learners.

Being a Professional

Each chapter of this book contains words such as 'principles', 'beliefs' and 'values'. These words are part of what it is to be a professional. Being a professional means balancing autonomy and decision-making with regulation and accountability. If, as a teacher, you are aware of your own principles and beliefs (including where these come from) you are more able to respond to the changes in education in an informed, professional manner rather than in a reactive and compliant way.

I would argue that teachers with a professional approach are able to:

- demonstrate their knowledge of subjects, pedagogy and the children they teach, drawing on reading and research
- reflect on their own practice, including researching specific aspects in depth, in order to innovate

- be responsible for their own development
- respond critically to external demands.

By reading this book you have already demonstrated your commitment to develop-ment and enrichment of practice. In the face of a great deal of advice regarding what and how to teach, without deep understanding of good practice firmly based in research and theoretical concepts, a practitioner can be at the mercy of the latest educational fad.

It is not possible to be an expert in all areas of the primary curriculum. However, it is possible to be an informed and professional practitioner who knows the impor-tance of reflecting on and improving practice. All teachers have subjects that they would consider as their strengths and some subjects with which they feel less confi-dent. Whatever the level of confidence, each subject needs to be approached with enthusiasm and energy. Pupils respond to teachers who are positive about the subjects they teach and who communicate the purposeful and authentic nature of the activities they offer.

Subject knowledge goes beyond individual pieces of knowledge and must include knowing why it is important as well as how to teach it. For example, it is not enough to know what an adjective is; it is necessary to understand the relevance of that knowledge for children, as well as the best ways to teach it. Good teachers demon-strate their subject knowledge through the methods they choose as well as through their selection of appropriate resources and activities.

In the English chapter, Andrew Lambirth makes it clear that knowing about chil-dren's texts, particularly children's literature, is part of essential subject knowledge in English and literacy. Research by the United Kingdom Literacy Association reported on the development project 'Teachers as Readers: Building Communities of Readers' (Cremin et al. 2009). The teachers in the study began the project with a limited knowl-edge of children's literature on which to draw in order to plan meaningful interactions with text. Through a series of professional development sessions the teachers in the projects were supported to try out new practice with children's texts at its heart. By developing this aspect of subject knowledge, the study found that teachers developed confidence in selecting and using texts, which impacted on children's achievement and attainment. It is essential that subject knowledge is considered in its broadest sense, engaging with quality professional development whenever possible. Making time for professional discussion is a key approach to enriching practice for all parties.

In order to teach well, you need to understand the influences on a subject, the changing nature of that subject's pedagogy and the external pressures upon it. You need to be aware of the best approaches to that subject as explored in research stud-ies, which this book helps you to do. You also need to consider your own strengths that you bring to the teaching of each subject.

The chapters in this book refer to the Cambridge Primary Review led by Robin Alexander, with its final report published in 2010. As the most comprehensive inquiry into primary schooling in Britain since the Plowden Report 40 years ago, it is a rich source of support for those trying to improve their practice and to evaluate their curriculum provision with an aim to innovate. Not only are we offered the interim and final reports, but the review provides us with a range of research reports on which to draw. These detailed documents cover every conceivable aspect of primary education, from aims and values to the quality of learning, culture and diversity; cognitive development; children's lives outside school; learning from international contexts; and many more. As teachers, you will find all the reports invaluable. The final report, entitled *Children, Their World, Their Education* (Alexander 2010), presents the findings of the review organised around 10 themes. This report allows you to engage with the underpinning principles, the 78 formal conclusions and the 75 recommendations of the review. Consider engaging with the content of this research and finding out what it has to offer you as a practitioner.

Innovative and Creative Practice

Every chapter of this book calls for innovative practice in each subject. Consider what you now understand such practice to look like. The individual chapters have encouraged thinking about going beyond the predictable and the routine.

At the same time, it is made clear that all practice has to be carefully considered and informed by research. Innovation is not without careful planning, evaluation and review.

Interestingly, schools have historically been able to apply to make adaptations to the National Curriculum and there is evidence that curriculum innovation has been supported and encouraged centrally in the past. For example, the Ofsted report entitled *Curriculum Innovation in Schools* (2008) found that the changes that most of the schools in the small-scale study had made had improved pupils' achievement and personal development. It was noted that successful change was possible because of strong leadership, a shared understanding of the reasons and need for innovation, as well as committed staff who were supported through preparation and training.

The then National College of School Leadership (NCSL) reported on individual schools' attempts to increase creativity by curriculum change. It produced a summary report 'Lifting the lid on the creative curriculum: How leaders have released creativity in their schools'. The approaches that the schools in this study took are all very different, but what united them is of interest here. The report claimed that:

> They were all *child-centred*. Each school genuinely put the children right in the centre of their learning, developing community and care as well as curiosity and creativity.
>
> All put an *emphasis on skills* before content and had an explicit focus on learning to learn.
>
> There was a *slow and organic approach* to learning. Taking time to consolidate and celebrate were key features of each school.
>
> There was a *flexible and dynamic curriculum*. Creative initiatives were supported and encouraged. Children were often in cross-phase groups for special events to help make learning exciting and challenging.
>
> (Burgess 2007: 4)

The report also acknowledges that the work was only successful because of:

the confidence and professional autonomy of the headteacher;

the shared vision;

communication and open debate rather than imposed change;

the space and time provided for pupils and teachers to own the learning process.

(Burgess 2007: 4)

The NCSL became the National College for Teaching and Leadership (NCTL), with a main aim of helping schools help each other to improve through the work of outstanding headteachers. There is little explicit evidence of projects or support around developing creative practice. If you believe that enriched, creative practice can also contribute to the standards agenda, you will continue to aim to include innovative practice in your work.

The national initiative Creative Partnerships (2002–2011) was supported by the Arts Council and aimed to develop long-term and innovative partnerships between schools in England and creative professionals. Partnerships were offered under three categories: Schools of Creativity (those at the cutting edge of creative practice); Change Schools (those in challenging circumstances who wished to develop the whole school); and Enquiry Schools (those who wished to target creative learning at a particular group of pupils and teachers). The organisation also supported teachers through ongoing and intensive opportunities for professional learning.

Projects encompassed a huge range of subjects and other areas of primary and secondary education, such as building communities and pupil voice. One infant school wanted to use song to strengthen its relationships with children and parents. Staff worked with professional musicians, including a gospel choir, and drew on world music found in the cultures of the school community. A primary school worked on its whole-school teaching of mathematics, using visits to view public art in Newcastle and Gateshead. Year 4 children worked on developing their understanding of measurement together with sculptor Richard Broderick, civil engineer John Loader, who had been part of the team responsible for installing the Angel of the North, and author David Almond. Funding for Creative Partnerships was withdrawn by Arts Council England in September 2011. Some information is still available at www.creative-partnerships.com.

You may have noticed tensions that already exist in primary schools between the desire to innovate and the pressure to prepare children for their Statutory Assessment Tasks (SATs). Continued assessment of pupils through statutory tests, as well as lessons devised specifically to meet certain assessment focuses, may not always fit comfortably with a more innovative approach to the curriculum. It can sometimes be hard for a school with either highly successful SATs results or under pressure due to apparent underachievement to decide to innovate. The desire may be there to review practice and consider innovation, but this could be seen as too much of a risk.

In its conclusions, the aforementioned Cambridge Review (Alexander 2010) reports on the perceived tension between curriculum breadth and the achievement of standards. It claims that this has led to a loss of entitlement to a broad and balanced curriculum. The Review notes that there has been a policy-led belief that breadth must come second to the need to reach required standards, but that this is a mistake:

> evidence going back many decades, including reports form HMI and Ofsted, consistently shows this belief to be unfounded. Standards and breadth are often positively related, and high performing schools achieve both. (2010: 493)

It only takes a moment to consider the impact of creating a core of nationally controlled subjects (mathematics and English perhaps) and the related downgrading of the other subjects. Think about the opportunities you have, or have had, while training to observe and teach all subjects. You may well have found that you rarely experienced some subjects. What did this mean for you as a teacher and what does this mean for the children?

The Cambridge Review found that headteachers praised the quality and dedication of their teachers, but they also voiced their concerns about some staff members who were over-reliant on dictated, official prescription. The headteachers felt that younger teachers in particular 'were trained merely to implement national strategy requirements and lacked the skill, or will, to improvise' (2010: 411). Hopefully, readers of this book will not follow this trend.

Assessment

However the curriculum is organised, assessment needs to be an integral part of teaching. All assessment should aid learning. Every chapter of this book has looked at the assessment of each subject, mainly dealing with issues of formative assessment. This is because making continuous moment-to-moment judgements, and providing immediate feedback to pupils, is the most useful and powerful type of assessment in the primary classroom.

The UK Assessment Reform Group (1999) identified five key principles of Assessment for Learning (AfL):

- the provision of effective feedback to students
- the active involvement of students in their own learning
- adjusting teaching to take account of the results of assessment
- recognition of the profound influence assessment has on the motivation and self-esteem of pupils, both of which are critical influences on learning
- the need for students to be able to assess themselves and understand how to improve.

These principles can be applied to any subject across the curriculum. You might want to consider what they mean to you and the approaches to assessment that you have used so far in your teaching.

To date, much of the development of Assessment for Learning in English schools has been informed by the work of Black and Wiliam (1998). The organisation Learning and Teaching Scotland, funded by the Scottish Government, calls this approach to assessment 'Assessment is for Learning' (AifL). AifL works with three main uses of assessment:

Assessment for Learning – using assessment to support classroom learning and teaching

Assessment as Learning – using assessment to promote autonomy in learning

Assessment of Learning – using assessment evidence to make sound judgements about learning and school effectiveness

(www.ltscotland.org.uk/assess/about/aboutaifl.asp)

When using assessments to inform future teaching and learning, you will want to be talking the language of the subjects, not just the language of levels. For example, your pupils should be able to articulate their learning and their decisions about their work in a meaningful way. Children need a meta-language with which to talk about their progress.

Without this focus on talking about learning, a formulaic approach to success can develop. When children make choices about their work in order simply to fulfil the given criteria, for example to achieve a National Curriculum level, without deliberation and careful thought, these choices have nothing to do with real learning. This is most likely to happen in the complex area of writing – where children are often asked to add certain words, stylistic features or grammatical structures in order to achieve a particular level or standard. This is no more than writing by numbers and cannot allow the child's voice and choices to come across to the reader. This 'kit' approach is not a good way to teach children the skills necessary to be able to write in a range of contexts in the future. Feedback to children about their writing must take into account the purpose of the text, the intention of the writer and the desired impact on the reader. Talking about pupils' writing in terms of response and affect is more important for the learner than identifying criteria for a prescribed standard.

The Cambridge Review calls for a thorough reform of the assessment system in England, with formative assessment of all aspects of the curriculum throughout the primary stages. The final report recommends 'a broader, more innovative approach to summative assessment' in order to recognise the achievements and attainments of pupils across the curriculum (Alexander 2010: 498).

In England, the summative assessment approach that has most status is the external examination – in the case of primary school pupils, the Statutory Assessment Tasks (SATs). Historically, SATs in England have focused on mathematics, reading and writing and science. In Autumn 2010, the government commissioned Lord Bew to examine Key Stage 2 testing, assessment and accountability. In June 2011 he published his review. Recommendations included teacher assessment of extended writing, a new spelling, punctuation and grammar test, reviewing the use of national curriculum levels and ranking Key Stage 2 pupils on a vertical scale. The government has taken these recommendations forward in its response to consultation on primary school assessment and accountability (DfE 2014).

The government has decided that a reception baseline should be the starting point from which to measure a school's progress. There will not be centrally provided assessments, but criteria will be created for the baselines in order to guide schools, and a list of assessments that meet these criteria will be published. From September 2016 onwards, the reception baseline will be the only measure used to assess progress, and at this point the Early Years Foundation Stage Profile will no longer be compulsory.

At Key Stage 1, the most notable change is that there will be an externally set test in grammar, punctuation and spelling, which will help to inform the teacher assessment of writing. The new assessments will first take place in summer 2016. The government also intends to work closely with Ofsted in order to improve Key Stage 1 moderation, currently identified as a source of unreliable assessment by Her Majesty's Chief Inspector of Education in his 2013 Annual Report.

At the end of Key Stage 2, new performance descriptors will be introduced to inform the teacher assessments. Pupils will be assessed as meeting one of several performance descriptors for writing and there will be a single performance descriptor for science, reading and mathematics. The results of tests in reading, mathematics and grammar, punctuation and spelling will be reported to parents as scaled scores. Parents will receive their child's score as well as the average for their school, the local area and nationally.

The well-established system of levels to report children's attainments and progress will be removed from September 2014. This means that the levels will not be updated to link with the new curriculum, making it tricky for schools to continue to use the levels system with which they are familiar.

According to the DfE website:

> Schools will be expected to have in place approaches to formative assessment that support pupil attainment and progression. The assessment framework should be built into the school curriculum, so that schools can check what pupils have learned and whether they are on track to meet expectations at the end of the key stage ... Schools will have the flexibility to use approaches that work for their pupils and circumstances, without being constrained by a single national approach. (www.education.gov.uk/schools/toolsandinitiatives/cuttingburdens/b00197599/myths-and-facts/curriculum-assessment)

In an ideal world, schools would be able to develop their own particular assessment framework. Schools have the expertise and the knowledge to do so. They know their practices and they know their pupils. A school that was able to undertake a research-driven, action research study into effective practice in formative and summative assessment could create an approach that was rigorous, adaptable, easy to manage and highly relevant to that school. Any project like this would be enhanced by schools working together to identify, share and develop good practice, perhaps led by the NCTL.

In reality, it is hard to see how this would be possible in the given time frame. The most likely outcome is that schools will need to draw on external support, such as packages created by publishers.

So what effect does all this have on you as you begin to develop your teaching career? At first, you may feel that you do not have much of a voice in your school and that you are not well placed to influence change. If this is the case, you could not be more wrong. You are in an excellent position to make a worthwhile contribution to curriculum review and development. Now you need to think about what it is that equips you to make a real difference in your school.

The Way Forward

Chapter 15 of the final report of the Cambridge Review recommends renewed professional discussion about pedagogy and what knowledge is required to be a good teacher. The report encourages us to consider teaching 'in a principled rather than pragmatic way' (2010: 412). When you think about what teaching means for you and about your own aims for primary education, you are drawing on your beliefs, values and principles.

If you believe that essential knowledge for teachers includes knowing about the content of the curriculum, recognising how to teach it, understanding children as learners and having knowledge of the self, then you will be less concerned with the timetabling and organisation of the subjects and more preoccupied with the best way of teaching everything well. The Cambridge Review concludes that approaches to learning have been compromised, resulting in the valuing of memorisation and recall over understanding and enquiry. It advocates 'the pursuit of knowledge in its fullest sense' (p. 493). To be part of this pursuit, you need to be an informed practitioner committed to ongoing learning and development.

There are many ways to continue your learning journey once you have qualified. Search for Continuing Professional Development (CPD) courses that give you the opportunity to reflect on areas of your practice linked to taught sessions and readings. Masters courses run by universities allow you to understand your practice in a deeply informed manner, through a high level of critical reflection. Such CPD will support you as you develop your professional identity and find your voice as you begin to influence change in your setting. By joining subject associations as well as a teaching union, you will find places to share information, current developments and enriching experiences such as conferences, where you will be able to talk about your work in an informed and exciting way.

As you begin your career, you will need to approach new opportunities from a principled, professional and informed position. How can you go about doing this? One approach is to reflect purposefully on the practice and curriculum frameworks you encounter.

For a number of years many schools have been moving towards a curriculum that connects subject disciplines together. How these connections have been made varies from setting to setting, with some selecting themes and content, others underpinning their links with a clear sense of skills progression. However your school is making subject links, you will want to reflect on how successful this approach is for the pupils you teach. You can keep a note of the successes of each unit, considering all aspects of learning and engagement with the curriculum.

Use all the time you have on your programme (if you are still a student teacher), in your NQT year and beyond to reflect critically on your practice, your sessions, reading and developing understandings in order to establish *your* principles. You need to know what kind of teacher you want to be and how you will offer connected, relevant and interesting learning to your pupils. You will be able to think about the uniqueness and value of the separate subject disciplines and then consider how to link across them in a meaningful way. You will need to see the relevance of any discreet teaching that you do, then challenge yourself and your pupils to relate it to the rest of the learning occurring in and out of your classroom.

You can do this only if you question current approaches and how they impact on the pupils you teach. Deciding what to change and how can only work from an understanding of so many things: how children learn; what interests them; what is important in each subject; which subject links are relevant and useful and which are tenuous and distracting. You also need to find useful contexts in which learning makes sense for the pupils. Of course, you must understand what matters to you and why. Only by being aware of what it is that you passionately believe can you make good choices for your pupils. You need to be a principled practitioner who is ready to defend your position in professional discussions and to offer suggestions to colleagues in an informed way.

Above all, you need an enthusiasm for all aspects of the curriculum and a desire to constantly enrich the experiences of the children you teach. You could think of the way you mediate the curriculum for your pupils as creating memories. As Jonathan Barnes discusses in his chapter, it is important to offer 'powerful, emotionally engaging experiences'. It might seem to you that you are taking risks which may not work out. However, risk-taking teachers are often successful in bringing out the most useful, interesting and innovative learning in children. However, things rarely happen by chance and you will be engaging in careful planning, rigorous assessment and well-thought-out progression.

As you grow in experience and confidence, you will be able to maintain your principled and informed approach to learning and teaching, especially if you revisit your beliefs and values regularly. Strive to resist the implementation of any approaches that aim to simplify learning, however seductively manageable they might seem. Be suspicious of any resources or approaches promising to be the easy answer to your challenges. Use these selectively and constantly adapt them to your own context.

Continue to engage in professional dialogue and development, always checking that your understanding of issues of pedagogy is grounded in sound, evidence-based research. The Cambridge Review found that many submissions to the report expressed deep concerns that 'expertise for primary teaching is now more about compliance than the exercise of independent judgement' (2010: 411). Make sure that you are not part of a workforce that accepts prescription without thought; routine in learning without justification; curriculum change without rationale.

References

Alexander, R. (ed.) (2010) *Children, Their World, Their Education: Final Report and Recommendations of the Cambridge Primary Review.* Abingdon: Routledge.

Assessment Reform Group (1999) *Assessment for Learning: Beyond the Black Box.* Cambridge: University of Cambridge, School of Education.

Bew, P. (2011) *Independent Review of Key Stage 2 Testing, Assessment and Accountability: Final Report.* Available at: www.educationengland.org.uk/documents/pdfs/2011-bew-report-ks2tests.pdf (accessed 23 September 2014).

Black, P. and Wiliam, D. (1998) *Inside the Black Box: Raising Standards through Classroom Assessment.* London: King's College School of Education.

Burgess, T. (2007) *Lifting the Lid on the Creative Curriculum: How Leaders Have Released Creativity in Their Schools through Curriculum Ownership.* Nottingham: National Centre for School Leadership.

Cremin, T., Mottram, M., Collins, F., Powell, S. and Safford, K. (2009) 'Teachers as readers: building communities of readers', *Literacy,* 43 (1): 11–19.

DfE (Department for Education) (2010) *The Importance of Teaching: The Schools White Paper 2010.* London: TSO.

DfE (Department for Education) (2013) *The National Curriculum in England Framework Document.* London: DfE.

DfE (Department for Education) (2014) *Reforming Assessment and Accountability for Primary Schools: Government Response to Consultation on Primary School Assessment and Accountability.* London: DfE.

National Primary Teacher Education Council (2013) *Comments on Proposals for Revised National Curriculum 2014.* Available at: http://www.naptec.org.uk/docs/naptec-publications/NaPTEC-comments-revised-curriculum.pdf

Ofsted (Office for Standards in Education) (2008) *Curriculum Innovation in Schools.* London: Ofsted.

Ofsted (Office for Standards in Education) (2013) *The Annual Report of Her Majesty's Chief Inspector of Education, Children's Services and Skills.* London: Ofsted.

Rose, J. (2009) *Independent Review of the Primary Curriculum: Final Report.* London: DCSF. Available at: http://publications.education.gov.uk/default.aspx?PageFunction= productdetails&PageMode=publications&ProductId=DCSF-00499-2009 (accessed October 2010).

INDEX